EXPERIMENTS *with* ECONOMIC PRINCIPLES: MICROECONOMICS

Second Edition

THEODORE C. BERGSTROM

University of California, Santa Barbara

JOHN H. MILLER

Carnegie Mellon University

Irwin
McGraw-Hill

Boston   Burr Ridge, IL   Dubuque, IA   Madison, WI   New York   San Francisco   St. Louis
Bangkok   Bogotá   Caracas   Lisbon   London   Madrid
Mexico City   Milan   New Delhi   Seoul   Singapore   Sydney   Taipei   Toronto

McGraw-Hill Higher Education ✖

A Division of The McGraw-Hill Companies

Experiments with Economic Principles
Microeconomics

This book is printed on acid-free paper.

1 2 3 4 5 6 7 8 9 0 DOW DOW 9 0 9 8 7 6 5 4 3 2 1 0 9

ISBN 0-07-229518-X

Vice president and editor-in-chief: *Michael W. Junior*
Publisher: *Gary Burke*
Senior sponsoring editor: *Lucille Sutton*
Senior marketing manager: *Nelson Black*
Project manager: *David Sutton*
Senior production supervisor: *Richard DeVitto*
Designer: *Francis Owens*
Cover designer: *Deborah Chusid*
Editorial assistant: *Katharine Norwood*
Printer: *RR Donnelley & Sons Company*

The cover illustration is "The Alchemist," from a book called Memoirs of Extraordinary Popular Delusions and the Madness of Crowds, by Charles Mackay, LL.D., originally published in 1841. This book has amusing chapters on economic folly, including the South-Sea Bubble and "Tulipomania."

Mackay's chapter on alchemists begins with a statement that Adam Smith might have enjoyed:

"Dissatisfaction with his lot seems to be the characteristic of man in all ages and climates. So far, however, from being an evil, as at first might be supposed, it has been the great civiliser of our race; and has tended, more than anything else, to raise us above the condition of the brutes... (p. 98)"

Library of Congress Cataloging-in-Publication Data

Bergstrom, Theodore C.
    Experiments with economic principles / Theodore C. Bergstrom, John
H. Miller.
        p.   cm.
    Includes index.
    ISBN 0-07-229518-X (alk. paper)
    1. Economics Problems, exercises, etc. I. Miller, John H. (John
Howard), 1959- . II. Title.
HB171.B4815 1999
330'.076—dc21
                                        99-35213
                                               CIP

http://www.mhhe.com

A Note to Users

Theodore C. Bergstrom

Ted Bergstrom was an undergraduate mathematics major at Carleton College and received his Ph.D. from Stanford University. He has taught at Washington University in St. Louis and the University of Michigan, and currently is the Aaron Raznick Professor of Economics at the University of California, Santa Barbara. Professor Bergstrom is a coauthor, with Hal Varian, of *Workouts in Microeconomic Theory*. His research interests include microeconomic theory, public finance, welfare economics, game theory, international trade theory, demography, economic anthropology, and evolutionary biology. His most recent research interests have been the economics of the family and the evolution of human preferences.

Address: Department of Economics, UCSB
Santa Barbara, CA 93106
e-mail: tedb@econ.ucsb.edu

John H. Miller

John H. Miller earned his Ph.D. from the University of Michigan after receiving undergraduate degrees from the University of Colorado. He is currently an Associate Professor of Economics at Carnegie Mellon University, where he has taught since 1989, and an External Professor at the Santa Fe Institute. In 1995 he received the Elliot Dunlap Smith Award for Distinguished Teaching and Educational Service from Carnegie Mellon University. His research interests include microeconomic theory, experimental economics, computational economics, game theory, political economy, complex adaptive systems, and adaptive computation. His recent research has focused on experimental approaches to understanding cooperation and on the computational modeling of complex social systems.

Address: Social and Decision Sciences, Carnegie Mellon University
Pittsburgh, PA 15213-3890
e-mail: miller@zia.hss.cmu.edu

Preface

Taking a course in experimental economics is a little like being a guest at a cannibal's house. Maybe you will be a diner, maybe a part of dinner, maybe both.

If you take a laboratory course in the physical sciences, you get to mix smelly chemicals, or monkey with pulleys, or dissect a frog, but you are always the experimenter and never the subject of the experiment. In the experiments conducted in this class, you and your classmates will be the *participants* as well as the scientific *observers* who try to understand the results.

It is hard to imagine that a chemist can put herself in the place of a hydrogen molecule. A biologist who studies animal behavior is not likely to know what it feels like to be a duck. You are more fortunate. You will be studying the behavior and interactions of people in economic situations. And as one of these interacting economic agents, you will be able to experience first-hand the problems faced by such an agent. We suspect that you will learn nearly as much about economic principles from your experience as a participant as from your analysis as an observer.

Theodore C. Bergstrom
John H. Miller

Acknowledgments

Like everyone in the economics profession, we owe a great debt to Vernon Smith of the University of Arizona and Charles Plott of the California Institute of Technology for convincing us that economics can be a laboratory science. While working on this book, we were fortunate to receive advice and encouragement from Ken Binmore, Dan Friedman, Janet Gerson, Mark Isaac, John Kagel, Preston McAfee, John McMillan, Peter Morgan, Jack Ochs, Al Roth, and Shyam Sunder.

John Miller thanks his colleague Steve Spear, with whom he initially developed a course that taught principles of economics by means of classroom experiments, and Robert Dalton, Mark Kamlet, Steven Klepper, George Loewenstein, and Shyam Sunder, who were generous with their support and ideas. Many of the ideas in this book were first tested in Carnegie Mellon classrooms. Ted Bergstrom is grateful to the University of Michigan for supporting a new course in experiments with economics.

We are grateful to a series of skilled and helpful teaching assistants, including Josh Anderson, Bevin Ashenmiller, Chau Do, Alexander Elbittar, Scott Fay, Anita Gantner, Young Lee, Apollo Lupescu, Bob Montgomery, Elizabeth Newlon, Jongsur Park, David Rode, Patricia Silva, and Brian Zikmund-Fisher.

We had expert editorial assistance from Hilary Ryall and two talented undergraduates, Karen Bergstrom and Teddy Kang. Our editor, Lucille Sutton, at McGraw-Hill has been a pleasure to work with. This book is written in LaTeX, using graphics routines from Tim Van Zandt's delightful PSTricks package. We thank TeX wizards Oz Shy and Hal Varian for teaching us to cast a few of the powerful typesetting spells that lie at their command.

Instructors who used the first edition have given us much useful advice for preparation of the second. Among our many benefactors were Rob Gilles, John Kagel, Evelyn Korn, Dave Kovach, Mike Lucchesi, Preston McAfee, Jan-Eric Nilsson, Phil Prosseda, Greg Saltzman, Ray Sikorra, and Steve Trejo. Hal Varian provided a lot of good ideas and sound advice for our new chapter on Network Externalities.

Finally, we thank several classes of students at Carnegie Mellon, Michigan, and the University of California at Santa Barbara, who enthusiastically carried out their dual roles as scientists and lab rats. We hope that they learned as much from us as we did from them.

A Note to Users

We got tired of it. Lecturing to sleepy students who want to "go over" material that they have already highlighted in their textbooks so that they can remember the "key ideas" until the midterm. We wanted to engage our students in *active learning*, to exploit their natural curiosity about economic affairs, and to get them to ponder the questions before we try to give them answers. We found that conducting economic experiments in class, with discussions before, during, and after the experiments, was an effective way of getting students to use economics to think about the world around them. *Experiments with Economic Principles* is the result of these efforts.

This book was designed for students who have not previously taken any economics courses, but we have discovered that it also works very well for students who have taken traditional economics courses. Each chapter contains an *experimental section* with instructions for an experiment, a *discussion section* which presents economic theory related to the experiment, a lab notes section, and a homework assignment. The alternation between experiment and discussion sets the rhythm of the class. In the lab, students participate in a market or social interaction and record the results in their lab notes. At the next class meeting, the experimental results are discussed and a theoretical explanation of events in the lab is offered, along with a discussion of applications to the real world. Finally, there is a homework assignment that is designed to help students to solidify the ideas they have explored.

Each of us had long been tempted to try a course based on participatory experiments, but wondered whether it would really work. Would students actually take an interest and participate according to the rules? Will the students actually learn in this way?

We have tried it and it works. Students have no trouble grasping the rules for the experiments and, while they do not always play as cleverly as they might, they always play competently and seriously. Better yet, they are enthusiastic about what they are doing. They love getting involved with markets and then figuring out what happened rather than simply being lectured at. They have fun. As instructors, we feel the same way. This classroom experience is a lot more rewarding than trying to interest sleepy students in abstractions with which they have no experience. Evidence from their performance on homework and examinations suggests that students are learning well.

If you try it, we think you'll be convinced.

Instructor's Manual

Instructors who are considering this book for adoption can obtain a copy of the Instructor's Manual by request from the publisher. This manual has detailed instructions on how to conduct the experiments. For each experiment, there are copies of the information sheets and sales contracts that can be photocopied for distribution to the students. The Instructor's Manual also reports the outcomes of classroom experiments that we have conducted in our own classes.

On the Internet

We plan to maintain a dialog with users of our text by means of the World Wide Web. Our Website includes links to the class web pages of users of our text, a file of news items related to the topics covered in our text, and several other items that may be of interest to adopters or potential adopters. If you have suggestions, comments, or questions you can contact us through the Website or directly by e-mail or ordinary mail.

The address of our Website is:

`http://zia.hss.cmu.edu/miller/eep/eep.html`

The Literature of Experimental Economics

The experiments in this book are intended primarily for teaching purposes, rather than for gathering new scientific data. Many of these experiments, however, are similar to experiments that have been carried out in laboratories under carefully controlled conditions. Since in the classroom we are dealing not with paid subjects, but with tuition-paying students, we made some changes in design from that used in the scientifically-motivated experiments. These changes reflect our efforts to set a brisk pace of activity in the classroom, in order to maintain students' interest and enthusiasm, and to give them a good rate of return per unit of time that they invest in learning.

In most of the market experiments in this book, we use a "trading-pit" design that is quite similar to trading procedures used in commodities markets like the Chicago Board of Trade futures market. Market participants move around the classroom until they find someone with whom they can make a deal. When a deal has been made, the transactors deliver a slip of paper to the market manager, which identifies the buyer and seller and records the sales price, Buyer Value, and Seller Cost. As sales information is turned in, the market manager records prices (in the case of a large class this can be just a sampling of prices) on the blackboard for all to see. This procedure is essentially the same as that used almost 50 years ago in a series of experiments by Professor E. H. Chamberlin [2] in his classroom at Harvard. Chamberlin, who had developed a theory of imperfect competition, emphasized the *difference* between his experimental outcomes and that predicted by competitive theory.

Professor Vernon Smith [10], who as a student had participated in Chamberlin's classroom experiments, decided to try experimental markets in his classes at Purdue. Smith changed Chamberlin's procedures in two ways that he thought would be likely to lead to outcomes more in accord with competitive theory. Smith conducted transactions by means of a "double oral auction" in which bids and offers are made publicly and all transactions are cleared through a central auctioneer. In each trading session, Smith also ran multiple rounds, which repeated the same trading environment. This enabled participants to use their experience of market outcomes from previous rounds in deciding their actions in later rounds. Smith discovered that usually by the second or third round, prices and quantities were strikingly close to competitive equilibrium values. Smith's double oral auction experiments have been replicated hundreds of times throughout the world and with many variations in the shapes of demand and supply curves and in market institutions. Experimenters have almost uniformly found a close correspondence between the experimental results and the predictions of competitive equilibrium theory.

For classroom instructional purposes, we have followed Smith in running more than one round with the same trading environment, but we have deviated from Smith's procedure by using a "trading pit" rather than a double oral auction. We find that this trading-pit procedure is faster and is more easily administered in a classroom than a double oral auction. Like Smith, for most of the markets that we tried, we found that after two or three repetitions of trading with the same market conditions, most transactions occur at prices that are very close to the competitive equilibrium price. Because sales occur simultaneously in a trading-pit market, even large classes can conclude a round of trading in about 5 minutes.[1] For most of the experiments that we have run, we find that running two rounds of trading for each market environment is sufficient. This enables us to comfortably run three,

---

[1]In a very large class, recording all of the transactions on the blackboard would slow things down but, for a large class, it is sufficient to simply record a random sample of transaction prices as they are brought to the market manager.

or sometimes even four, different experimental sessions during a single class period, where each session tests a different market environment.

Chamberlin and Smith both emphasized that the informational conditions in the trading-pit are not the same as those posited in the standard competitive model. The standard (Walrasian) competitive model assumes very large numbers of market participants, all of whom have perfect information about the best price at which they can buy or sell. This information is not available in either Smith's or Chamberlin's experimental environment. Smith argues on this account that the results of his repeated double oral auction experiment are remarkable evidence that near-competitive outcomes are likely to be achieved under much more realistic informational conditions than those usually assumed. Accordingly, the theory of competitive supply and demand is likely to be a more powerful tool for approximate prediction of market outcomes in the real world than had been previously suspected.

There is interesting evidence from market simulations that the trading-pit environment is likely to lead to a close approximation of competitive outcomes, even with very unsophisticated traders. D. K. Gode and Shyam Sunder [5] ran simulations of a trading pit with random encounters between traders, who make *random* bids and offers, subject only to the constraint that no trader makes money-losing bids or offers. Trades occurred at either the buyer's or the seller's price whenever the buyer bid at least as much as the seller's offer price. They found that prices converged quite closely to competitive equilibrium prices. We have run similar simulations with the demand and supply curves for our experimental markets and have found results similar to those of Gode and Sunder.

Suggested Reading

If you want to read more about economics laboratory experiments, we recommend three recently published books. *Experimental Methods: A Primer for Economists* by Daniel Friedman and Shyam Sunder [4] is an engaging discussion of the methods and philosophy of experimental economics. *Experimental Economics* by Douglas Davis and Charles Holt [3] is a textbook on experimental economics, suitable for advanced undergraduate or graduate courses. *The Handbook of Experimental Economics* edited by John Kagel and Alvin Roth [6] contains authoritative and well-written surveys of several areas of experimental economics.

If, after completing these experiments, you want to find out more about topics such as demand and supply analysis, taxation, price floors and ceilings, monopoly, the theory of the firm, or comparative advantage, you will find more extended discussions in any of the standard intermediate micro-economics textbooks. Topics related to network externalities, auctions, and bargaining are less well covered in most of the standard texts. The Fifth edition of Hal Varian's *Intermediate Microeconomics* [11] has a good discussion of auctions and an excellent treatment of Network Externalities. For those who want to learn more about auctions and bargaining, we recommend *Games, Strategies, and Managers* by John McMillan [8], which has an entertaining mixture of real-world observations and theory and is readily accessible to undergraduate students. We also recommend *Auctions and Auctioneering* by Ralph Cassady [1] for a fascinating account of the many different kinds of auctions used in markets around the world. Most of the popular books about "the new information economy" are heavy on gossip and speculation, and light on economic thinking. But there is now a delightful exception. *Information Rules* by Carl Shapiro and Hal Varian [9] is a treat to read both for economic novices and professional economists. This book is full of gritty real-world examples related to the economics of information technology.

Bibliography

[1] Ralph Cassady. *Auctions and Auctioneering*. University of California Press, Berkeley, 1967.

[2] E. H. Chamberlin. An experimental imperfect market. *Journal of Political Economy*, 56(2):95–108, April 1948.

[3] Douglas Davis and Charles Holt. *Experimental Economics*. Princeton University Press, Princeton, N.J., 1993.

[4] Daniel Friedman and Shyam Sunder. *Experimental Methods: A Primer for Economists*. Cambridge University Press, Cambridge, 1994.

[5] D. K. Gode and Shyam Sunder. Allocative efficiency of markets with zero-intelligence traders: Market as a partial substitute for rationality. *Journal of Political Economy*, 101:119–137, 1993.

[6] John Kagel and Alvin Roth. *The Handbook of Experimental Economics*. Princeton University Press, Princeton, N.J., 1995.

[7] Tim Lang and Colin Hines. *The New Protectionism*. New Press, New York, 1993.

[8] John McMillan. *Games, Strategies, and Managers*. Oxford University Press, New York, 1992.

[9] Carl Shapiro and Hal Varian. *Information Rules*. Harvard Business School Press, Cambridge, Mass., 1999.

[10] Vernon Smith. An experimental study of competitive market behavior. *Journal of Political Economy*, 70(2):111–137, April 1962.

[11] Hal R. Varian. *Intermediate Microeconomics*. W.W. Norton, New York, fifth edition, 1999.

Contents

Part I

Competitive Markets

Experiment 1

Supply and Demand

An Apple Market

It is a sunny Saturday morning at the Farmers' Apple Market. You and your classmates have come to the market to buy and sell apples. Your objective is to make as much profit as possible.

Buying and Selling

At the beginning of today's class, you will be given a personal information sheet that indicates whether you are a **supplier** or a **demander** in the market.

If you are a supplier, you will find your **Seller Cost** for a bushel of apples listed on your personal information sheet. Your Seller Cost is the cost to you of producing a bushel of apples to sell. If you don't sell any apples, you don't have to produce any apples, and you will have zero costs. You are allowed to sell *at most one* bushel of apples in any round of this experiment. If your Seller Cost is C and you agree to sell a bushel of apples for a price P, then your **profit** (or **loss**) will be the difference, $P - C$, between the price and your seller cost. Sometimes you may not find any demanders who are willing to pay you as much as your Seller Cost. If this is the case, you are better off not selling any apples and taking zero profits.

Example:

> A supplier has a Seller Cost of $10 and she can sell one bushel of apples. If she sells a bushel of apples for a price of $16, she will make a profit of $16 − $10 = $6. If she sells a bushel for $30, she will make a profit of $30 − $10 = $20. If she sells a bushel for $7, she will make a *loss* of $3. If she does not sell, her profit is zero.

If you are a demander, your **Buyer Value** for a bushel of apples will be listed on your personal information sheet. Your Buyer Value is the amount of money that it is worth to you to have a bushel of apples. You are not allowed to buy *more than one* bushel in any round of this experiment. If your Buyer Value is V and you agree to buy a bushel of apples for a price P, then your profit (or loss) will be the difference, $V − P$, between your Buyer Value and the price you pay. If you don't buy any apples, your profit is zero. If you cannot find a supplier who is willing to sell you a bushel of apples for your Buyer Value or less, then you are better off not buying any apples and taking zero profits.

Example:

> A demander has a Buyer Value of $40. If he buys a bushel of apples for $16, he will make a profit of $40 − $16 = $24. If he buys a bushel of apples for $30, he will make a profit of $40 − $30 = $10. If he buys a bushel of apples for $45, he will make a *loss* of $5. If he doesn't buy any apples, his profit is zero.

To make a purchase or sale, first find somebody who might be willing to make a deal with you. Suppliers can make deals only with demanders and demanders can make deals only with suppliers. When a supplier meets a demander, they can negotiate about the price in any way they wish. You don't have to reveal your Seller Cost or Buyer Value to your bargaining partner, but you can if you want.

When a supplier (seller) and demander (buyer) agree on a price, they should fill out a *sales contract* and bring it to the market manager. **Only one sales contract should be turned in for each sale.** The sales contract records the seller's and buyer's names or identification numbers, the price, and a few other details about the sale. As sales contracts are turned in, the sales prices will be written on the blackboard where everyone can see them.

When you have completed your transaction and turned in your sales contract, please return to your seat. **In any single round of trading you are not allowed to buy or sell more than one bushel of apples, but you can always choose not to trade if no profitable trades are available.**

Transactions, Rounds, and Sessions

A **transaction** is a single deal between a buyer and a seller and is completed when the buyer and seller give a filled-in sales contract to the market manager. A **round** of trading begins when the market manager declares trading to be open and ends when there are no more transactions to be made between willing buyers and sellers. A market **session** can include two or more *rounds* of trading.

After the first round of trading is completed, your instructor may conduct one or more additional rounds within the same session. In later rounds of a session, everyone has the same Buyer Value or Seller Cost as in the first round. The reason for having more than one round of trading in a session is that in later rounds, buyers and sellers know what happened in earlier rounds and may use this information to decide what prices to ask or offer. After a round of play is completed, you should look at the record of transactions on the blackboard to see whether you can expect to get a better price in the next round by seeking a new trading partner and/or by holding out for a more favorable price.

Your role as a supplier or demander and your Seller Cost or Buyer Value do not change as you move from one round to another within the same session. When you start a new session, you will have a new role, as described on your Personal Information Sheet.

Some Advice to Traders

Even if you are normally a shy person, let your "trading personality" be more flamboyant. Shrinking violets, though charming in many situations, are likely to miss profitable trading opportunities. To maximize your profits, you should approach trading aggressively. Don't be afraid to shout or gesture for attention. Let people know how much you are willing to pay or the price at which you are willing to sell. When you think that you could get a better price than someone offers you, do not hesitate to propose a price that you like better.

Remember that you don't have to deal with the first person you encounter. Different people have different Buyer Values and Seller Costs. If someone can't, or won't, offer you a favorable price, be ready to shop around for a better deal with someone else.

If you haven't yet made a trade, keep an eye on the prices of previous transactions that are posted on the blackboard. This may give you some idea of what price to demand or what price to offer in your own negotiations.

Keep in mind that you want to "buy low, sell high." Demanders make greater profits, the lower the price they have to pay. Suppliers make greater profits, the higher the price they can get.

Remember that it is better to make no trade at all than to trade at a loss.

Warm-up Exercise

After reading the instructions for this experiment, please check your understanding by answering the following questions.[1]

Suppose that a supplier with a Seller Cost of $20 meets a demander with a Buyer Value of $40.

W 1.1 If the supplier sells a bushel of apples to the demander for a price

of $35, how much profit will the supplier make? $ _____ And how much

profit will the demander make? $ _____ How much is the total profit made by the two traders? (Find this by adding the buyer's profits to the seller's

profits.) $ _____

W 1.2 What is the *highest* price of apples that would permit both the

seller and the buyer to make a profit of $1 or more? $ _____ If this price is charged, how much is the sum of buyer's profits plus seller's profits?

$ _____

W 1.3 What is the *lowest* price of apples that would permit both the seller

and the buyer to make a profit of $1 or more? $ _____ At this price, how

much is the sum of buyer's profits plus seller's profits? $ _____

---

[1]Answers to these warm-up exercises can be found on page 24.

Discussion of Experiment 1

In Search of a Theory

We have a mystery on our hands. In the Apple Market experiment, the prices at which apples were traded seemed to be closing in on certain values. But what determines the values to which prices converged?

It would be nice to have a *theory* that predicts outcomes, not only for the specific market that we observed experimentally, but for a variety of markets under widely varying conditions. We would like a theory that allows us to answer questions like:

- If every supplier's Seller Cost increases by $10, will the market price increase by exactly $10, by less than $10, or by more than $10?

- Suppose that the government decides to pay $10 to every person who buys a bushel of apples. Such a payment is called a **subsidy** to apple consumption. Will suppliers absorb some or all of the subsidy by increasing their prices, or will demanders get all of the benefits from the $10 subsidy?

- If bad weather reduces the quantity of apples that each producer could supply, what will be the effect on the price of apples and what will happen to the total revenue of suppliers?

Economists have just such a theory. It is known as **supply and demand theory** or, more formally, as **competitive equilibrium theory**. This theory offers answers to the above questions and to many others. These answers are often quite surprising and interesting. Of course, a theory that predicts market outcomes will not be much good if these predictions are badly wrong. Therefore it is important to see whether supply and demand theory does a good job of predicting the outcomes of our experiments. If the theory does well in these experimental environments and continues to do well as we add more elements of realism, then we can put some credence in its predictions for actual markets. If this simple theory does not perform well, then we must look for a better theory.

A Model of Competitive Markets

In our classroom experiment, particularly in the early rounds, some sellers were able to get higher prices for their apples than others. Similarly, some buyers were able to find a seller who would sell cheaply and others could only find sellers who insisted on a high price. Every participant in the market would like to get the best deal possible, but different participants will have different ideas about what is possible. To describe all market participants' beliefs about the prices at which they can trade and their luck about whom they meet would be an overwhelmingly complicated task, even for this simple market.

Instead of trying to describe this complex reality in full detail, let's try to make a simplified *model* of competitive markets. The art of good modeling in economics, as in all of science, is to find the "right" simplifications. The model should remove enough complication from the actual situation to allow us to analyze and predict outcomes, without removing so much reality that it seriously distorts our predictions about the way the market will behave. We are looking for a manageable model of markets that makes good predictions of the outcomes that we observe in experimental markets and in actual markets of the commercial world. Specifically, we would like a model that uses the information that we have about the distribution of Buyer Values and Seller Costs to predict the average price and number of transactions that are likely to take place in the market.

An effective way to simplify this problem is to assume that all buyers pay the same price for apples and that all sellers sell at this same price. As you found in your classroom experiment, this assumption is not very accurate, especially in the first rounds of trading, but in later rounds, as traders become better informed about the prices they can hope to find, the differences between prices paid for apples by different people tend to disappear.

If there were just one price for apples, those suppliers who could make a profit at this price would sell apples and those who would take a loss would not sell any. Similarly, those demanders who could profit by buying apples at the prevailing price would buy and those who would lose money would not buy. At this price, it would be possible to satisfy everybody's wishes only if the quantity of apples that demanders wanted to buy were *the same* as the quantity that suppliers wanted to sell. At an arbitrarily chosen price, there is no reason to expect that demanders would want to buy the same amount that suppliers would want to sell. But as we will see, there will be *some* price at which the total quantity of apples that demanders are willing to buy is equal to the total quantity of apples that suppliers are willing to sell. This price, at which "supply equals demand," is known as the **competitive equilibrium price**. The number of units bought and sold at this price is known as the **competitive equilibrium quantity**.

Graphing Supply and Demand

Supply curves and **demand curves** are the main tools that we use to study competitive equilibrium. The supply curve tells us the total amount of a good that suppliers would want to sell at each possible price. We can draw a supply curve if we know each supplier's Seller Cost. In this experiment, since each supplier supplies at most one unit, the number of units that suppliers are willing to supply at any price P is equal to the number of suppliers whose Seller Costs are less than or equal to P.

The demand curve tells us the total amount of a good that buyers would want to buy at each possible price. We can draw this curve if we know each demander's Buyer Value. In this experiment, each demander buys either one bushel of apples or no apples, and thus the total number of bushels that demanders are willing to buy at any price P is equal to the number of demanders whose Buyer Values are greater than or equal to P.

We can show the way that the interaction of suppliers and demanders determines the outcome in a market by drawing the supply and demand curves on the same graph. Competitive equilibrium prices and quantities are found where the supply curve crosses the demand curve.

An Example

We will use a specific example to show how to draw supply and demand curves and find equilibrium prices and quantities. In this example:

- There are 10 high-cost suppliers who have Seller Costs of $25 a bushel.

- There are 20 low-cost suppliers who have Seller Costs of $5 a bushel.

- There are 15 high-value demanders who have Buyer Values of $30 for a bushel of apples.

- There are 15 low-value demanders who have Buyer Values of $10 for a bushel of apples.

This information is summarized in Table 1.1

Table 1.1: Distribution of Types–Example Market

Type of Agent	Number of Agents	Cost	Value
Low-Cost Supplier	20	5	▓▓▓
High-Cost Supplier	10	25	▓▓▓
High-Value Demander	15	▓▓▓	30
Low-Value Demander	15	▓▓▓	10

Making a Supply Table

A **Supply Table** shows the number of bushels of apples that suppliers would offer at each possible price. We can construct a Supply Table for the example market using the information in Table 1.1.

Table 1.2: Supply Table–Example Market

Price Range	Amount Supplied
$P < \$5$	0
$\$5 < P < \$25$	20
$P > \$25$	30

In the example market, low-cost suppliers have a Seller Cost of $5 a bushel and high-cost suppliers have a Seller Cost of $25 a bushel. At any price below $5 a bushel, a supplier who sold a bushel of apples would lose money because it costs every supplier at least $5 to produce a bushel of apples. Thus at prices below $5, nobody would want to supply any apples, so the total number of bushels supplied to the market would be zero. We therefore enter 0 as the amount supplied in the first line of Table 1.2.

If the price, P, is between $5 and $25, the 20 low-cost suppliers can each make money by selling a bushel of apples, since their costs are only $5. But the high-cost suppliers would lose money if they sold apples for any price that is below $25, since it costs them $25 to produce a bushel of apples. Therefore at prices between $5 and $25, the 20 low-cost suppliers will each sell a bushel of apples, but the high-cost suppliers won't sell any apples. The total quantity of apples supplied at prices between $5 and $25 will be 20 bushels, and so we enter 20 as the amount supplied in the second line of the Supply Table.

At prices above $25, all of the high-cost suppliers *and* all of the low-cost suppliers can make money by selling apples. Since there are 10 high-cost

suppliers and 20 low-cost suppliers, the total amount supplied at prices above
$25 is 30 bushels. Therefore we enter 30 as the amount supplied in the last
line of the Supply Table.

Making a Demand Table

We can construct a **Demand Table** for this market in much the same way.
The Demand Table shows the number of bushels of apples that demanders
want to buy at all possible prices.

    The highest Buyer Value for a bushel of apples is $30. If the price is
above $30, no buyer will want to buy any apples. So for all prices above
$30, the number of bushels demanded is 0. We record this fact in the first
line of Table 1.3.

Table 1.3: Demand Table–Example Market

Price Range	Amount Demanded
$P > \$30$	0
$\$10 < P < \$30$	15
$P < \$10$	30

    If the price of apples is between $10 and $30, all 15 of the high-value
demanders can make profits by buying a bushel of apples, but low-value
demanders will lose money if they buy apples. So at prices between $10
and $30, the total demand for apples is 15 bushels, and we write 15 as the
amount demanded in the second line of Table 1.3.

    If the price of apples is below $10, then all of the high-value demanders
and all of the low-value demanders can make a profit by buying apples.
There are 15 high-value and 15 low-value demanders, so that total demand
for apples at any price below $10 is 30 bushels. Therefore we enter 30 as
the amount demanded in the bottom line of Table 1.3.

Drawing Supply and Demand Curves

The supply and demand tables will help you to graph the supply curve and
the demand curve. The first step is to draw a pair of axes, with *price of
apples* measured on the vertical axis and *quantity of apples* measured on the
horizontal axis. This has been done in Figure 1.1.

Figure 1.1: Supply and Demand for Apples

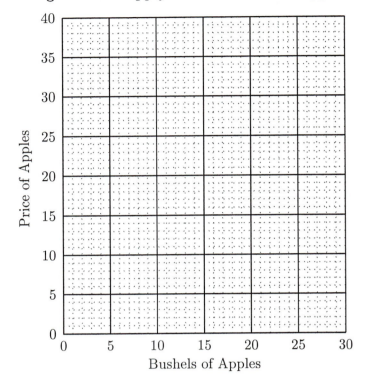

Drawing the Supply Curve

A **supply curve** shows the total number of apples that sellers would be willing to sell at each possible price. You can use the information in the Supply Table 1.2 to draw a supply curve. We suggest that as you read this discussion, you follow through by drawing the lines and points requested in the text. Your graphs will be easier to read if you draw the supply and demand curves in two different colors.

As we see from the Supply Table (Table 1.2), at prices below $5, the amount of apples supplied is 0. Thus the supply curve must show that at these prices no apples will be supplied. This means that the supply curve includes a vertical line that follows the vertical axis from the origin $(0,0)$ up to the point $(0,5)$ where price is $5 and quantity is 0.[2] Draw this line segment.

---

[2]The notation (X, Y) stands for the point on the graph that is located at a horizontal distance of X from the left side of the graph and at a vertical distance of Y from the bottom of the graph.

From the Supply Table, we see that at any price between $5 and $25, the total quantity supplied is 20 bushels. Therefore the supply curve includes a vertical line segment drawn from the point $(20, 5)$ up to the point $(20, 25)$. Add this line segment to your graph.

At prices above $25, we see from the Supply Table that the quantity supplied is 30 bushels. Therefore the supply curve includes a vertical line starting at the point $(30, 25)$ and going straight up to the point $(30, \text{one zillion})$. We don't want you to run out of ink drawing one line, so just draw a line segment from the point $(30, 25)$ to the top of the box.

Your supply curve so far contains three vertical line segments. But we haven't yet answered the question of what happens at a price of exactly $5 or of exactly $25. At a price of $5, all of the high-cost suppliers would lose money if they sold any apples. At this price, the low-cost suppliers won't *make* any money by selling apples, but they won't *lose* any money either. They will be *indifferent* between selling and not selling. Since at a price of $5, each of the 20 low-cost suppliers would be satisfied with supplying any quantity between 0 and 1 bushel, we can say that at a price of $5, suppliers in total would be willing to supply any quantity of apples between 0 and 20 units. We show this fact by adding a horizontal segment at a price of $5 on our supply curve. On the graph, this segment is a line from the point $(0, 5)$ to the point $(20, 5)$.

At a price of $25, all 20 of the low-cost suppliers will want to supply apples, and the 10 high-cost suppliers would just break even. At this price, each of the 10 high-cost suppliers is willing to supply any amount between zero and one unit. So at a price of $25, the total quantity supplied can be any amount between 20 and 30 bushels. This implies that the supply curve includes a horizontal segment at a price of $25. This segment runs from the point $(20, 25)$ to the point $(30, 25)$.

Drawing the Demand Curve

Now that you have drawn a supply curve, it is time to draw a **demand curve.** The demand curve shows the total quantity of apples that demanders would like to buy at each possible price. Like the supply curve, the demand curve consists of vertical and horizontal line segments. You can use the Demand Table (Table 1.3) to draw the demand curve, much as you used the Supply Table to draw the supply curve. You can probably do this without reading more details, but in case you get stuck, you will find detailed hints on how to draw the demand curve on the "Lookup Page," which is found on page 23.

We suggest that you try to draw the supply and demand curves for this example before you peek at the Lookup Page. After you have tried, you can check to see if you got it right.

Finding Equilibrium Price and Quantity

The **competitive equilibrium price** for a good is the price at which the total amount that suppliers want to sell is equal to the total amount that demanders want to buy. The quantity that is supplied and demanded at the competitive equilibrium price is the **competitive equilibrium quantity**. If you have drawn the supply and demand curves on a graph, how can you find the competitive equilibrium price? Before reading the answer that appears below, see if you can figure it out for yourself.

> **Answer:** Remember that the quantity demanded or supplied at any price is found by locating the price on the vertical axis and reading across until you reach the supply or demand curve. If at some price, supply equals demand, it must be that at this price, the supply curve and the demand curve are touching each other. Thus to find the competitive equilibrium price, simply draw the supply and demand curves and find where they cross. If the two curves intersect at a single point, then you can read across to the vertical axis to find the competitive equilibrium price and down to the horizontal axis to find the competitive equilibrium quantity. (Sometimes the supply and demand curves may overlap at more than one point. In this case, there will be more than one competitive equilibrium price and/or quantity.)

If you look at the supply and demand curves that you drew, you can see that at any price higher than the competitive equilibrium price, suppliers want to sell more apples than demanders want to buy. At any price lower than the equilibrium price, demanders want to buy more apples than suppliers are willing to sell. But at the competitive equilibrium price, suppliers want to sell exactly as many apples as demanders want to buy.

Exercise: Reading Supply and Demand Curves[3]

You have drawn supply and demand curves using the numerical information in a Supply Table and a Demand Table. Now it is time to practice working the other way around—reading numerical information from supply and demand curves.

Figure 1.2 shows supply and demand curves on which you can practice. To make things a little more exciting, let's suppose that there are not two, but *three* different kinds of demanders and also *three* kinds of suppliers.[4]

Figure 1.2: More Supply and Demand

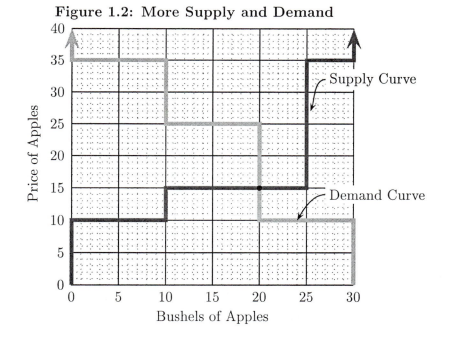

Exercise 1.1 How many bushels of apples will suppliers want to

supply at a price of \$40?_____ At a price of \$30?_____ At a price

of \$12?_____ At a price of \$5?_____

Exercise 1.2 How many bushels of apples will demanders want to

---

[3]Answers to these questions can be found on page 24.

[4]If the excitement is too overwhelming, you might want to take a break and read a few pages of a text in accounting or political science to calm yourself down.

buy at a price of $30?_____ At a price of $20? _____ At a price

of $5? _____ At a price of $40? _____

Exercise 1.3 At a price of $15, suppliers are willing to supply any

amount of apples between _____ bushels and _____ bushels.

Exercise 1.4 At a price of $25, demanders are willing to buy any

amount of apples between _____ bushels and _____ bushels.

You can also use supply and demand curves to determine the *inverse* relation, namely, the price at which a given quantity would be demanded or supplied. For example, we see from the supply curve that the only price at which suppliers would be willing to supply 5 bushels of apples is $10. If the price were lower, suppliers would not want to supply any apples. If the price were higher than $10, they would want to supply more than 5 bushels. (Of course, at a price of $10, they would also be willing to supply any other number of bushels between 0 and 10.)

Exercise 1.5 Suppliers would be willing to supply exactly 15 bushels

of apples at a price of $ _____ and exactly 5 bushels of apples at a

price of $ _____ .

Exercise 1.6 Suppliers would be willing to supply exactly 10 bushels

of apples at any price between $ _____ and $ _____ .

Exercise 1.7 Demanders would be willing to buy exactly 15 bushels

of apples at a price of $ _____ and exactly 5 bushels of apples at a

price of $ _____ .

Exercise 1.8 Demanders would be willing to buy exactly 10 bushels

of apples at any price between $ _____ and $ _____ .

If, at the current price, the quantity of apples that demanders want to buy is greater than the quantity that suppliers want to sell, we say that there is **excess demand**. If, at the current price, the quantity of apples that suppliers want to sell is greater than the quantity that demanders want to buy, we say that there is **excess supply**.

Exercise 1.9 For each of the following prices, write "S" if there is excess supply and "D" if there is excess demand. $40 _____ $30 _____ $20 _____ $12 _____ $5 _____

Exercise 1.10 There is excess supply at prices higher than $ _____ and there is excess demand at prices lower than $ _____ .

Exercise 1.11 At a competitive equilibrium price, there is no excess demand and no excess supply. For the supply and demand curves in Figure 1.2, the competitive equilibrium price is $ _____, and the competitive equilibrium quantity is _____ bushels.

Profits of Buyers and Sellers

Reservation Prices and Consumers' Surplus

In our classroom experiment, if a supplier sells a bushel of apples for a price higher than her Seller Cost she will make a profit, and if she sells for a price lower than her Seller Cost she will lose money. We define a **supplier's reservation price** for a unit of a good to be the lowest price at which she is willing to sell this unit. In this experiment, every supplier's reservation price for a bushel of apples is equal to her Seller Cost.

In this experiment, a demander will make a profit if he buys a bushel of apples for a price lower than his Buyer Value and he will take a loss if he pays more than his Buyer Value. We define a **demander's reservation price** to be the highest price that he would be willing to pay for a unit of the good rather than do without. In this experiment, the most that a demander would be willing to pay for a bushel of apples is his Buyer Value and thus his reservation price is equal to his Buyer Value.[5] We sometimes refer to a supplier's reservation price as her **minimum willingness-to-accept** and to a demander's reservation price as his **maximum willingness-to-pay**.

---

[5]As we will see in later experiments, suppliers' reservation prices are not always the same as their Seller Costs, and demanders' reservation prices are not always the same as their Buyer Values.

In real-world markets, some goods are used by people who intend to re-sell them or use them in manufacturing, while other goods are purchased by people who buy them for their own use and enjoyment. Those who demand goods for their own consumption are known as **consumers**. In experimental markets, we motivate demanders to act like real-world consumers by assigning Buyer Values that will be paid to them by the market manager if they buy a unit of the goods. In real-world markets, there is of course no market manager to make such payments. Instead, consumers receive benefits directly from consuming the goods that they buy.

A demander's **consumer's surplus** from purchasing a unit of some good is defined to be the difference between his reservation price and the price he actually has to pay. In this experimental market, where demanders' reservation prices equal their Buyer Values, a buyer gets a consumer's surplus equal to the difference between his Buyer Value and the price that he pays. Another name for this difference is demander's profit. In this book, we use the terms *consumer's surplus* and *demander's profit* interchangeably.

Calculating Profits and Consumers' Surplus

Let us calculate total profits made by suppliers and demanders for a market with the supply and demand curves shown in Figure 1.3. First we calculate the total profit of all *suppliers*. In this example, low-cost suppliers each have costs of $5 per bushel and high-cost suppliers each have costs of $25 per bushel. At the equilibrium price of $10 per bushel, while the low-cost suppliers can make a profit by selling a bushel of apples, the high-cost suppliers would make losses if they produced. So each of the 20 low-cost suppliers will want to supply one bushel, and none of the high-cost suppliers will want to supply any apples.

The only sellers at $10 are the 20 low-cost suppliers. Each of the 20 low-cost suppliers receives $10 for her apples and has to pay her Seller Cost of $5. Thus, her profit from selling apples is $10 − $5 = $5. The total profits made by the 20 low-cost suppliers is therefore $20 \times \$5 = \$100$. Since at a price of $10, the high-cost suppliers do not supply any apples at all, they have zero revenue, zero costs, and zero profits. Total profit of all suppliers equals the total profit of low-cost suppliers plus total profit of high-cost suppliers. This is $100 + $0 = $100.

Now we calculate total consumers' surplus of all the *demanders* in the market. At the competitive equilibrium price of $10, the high-value demanders, who have Buyer Values of $30, will make a profit by buying apples. The consumer's surplus of each high-value demander is $30 − $10 = $20.

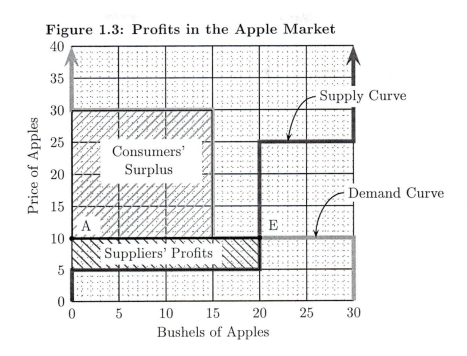

Figure 1.3: Profits in the Apple Market

Since there are 15 high-value demanders, the total consumers' surplus of all high-value demanders is $15 \times \$20 = \$300$. Each of the low-value demanders has a Buyer Value of $10 for a bushel of apples. Since the price of apples is also $10, the low-value demanders who buy apples will each have a consumer's surplus of $10 − $10 = 0. (They are neither better off nor worse off than the low-value demanders who don't buy any apples.) Since all low-value demanders receive zero profits, whether or not they buy apples, the total amount of consumers' surplus received by low-value demanders is 0. Therefore, the total amount of consumers' surplus made by all demanders is $300 + 0 = $300.

We also want to measure the *total profit of all market participants*. This is obtained by adding the total profit of suppliers to the total consumers' surplus of demanders. In the example considered here, total profit of all market participants is $100 + $300 = $400.

Figure 1.3 shows a useful geometric way to find total profits in competitive equilibrium from the graph of the supply and demand curves. First draw a horizontal line from the point E, where the supply and demand curves cross, to the point A, where this horizontal line meets the vertical axis. The area that is *below* the line AE and *above* the supply curve represents the total profits made by suppliers. The area *above* this line and *below* the demand curve represents the total consumers' surplus. This geometric trick works because for each unit sold, the vertical distance from the line AE to the supply curve equals the profit made by the seller of that unit. If we add these profits over all units sold, we have the total profits made by suppliers, which is the area of the region labeled "Suppliers' Profits." Similarly, for each unit sold, the vertical distance between the demand curve and the line AE is the Consumer's Surplus (Demander's Profit) made by the buyer of that unit. Adding these surpluses over all units sold, we have the total consumers' surplus, which is the area of the region labeled "Consumers' Surplus."

Other Implications of Competitive Theory

So far, we have been interested in how well competitive equilibrium works at predicting the outcome in trading environments like our classroom market. If competitive equilibrium turns out to be a good predictor of what happens, then it will be interesting to know more about other implications of the competitive equilibrium theory.

Who Trades in Competitive Equilibrium?

Competitive equilibrium theory makes interesting predictions about which suppliers will sell and which demanders will buy. In competitive equilibrium, it must be that if a supplier can make a profit by selling at the competitive price she will do so, and if she would make a loss, she will not sell. This implies that every supplier whose Seller Cost is lower than the competitive equilibrium price will sell a bushel of apples, and no supplier whose Seller Cost is higher than the competitive equilibrium price will sell any apples. Similarly, in competitive equilibrium, every demander will buy if he can make a profit by buying at the competitive equilibrium price and will not buy if he makes a loss from doing so. Therefore the theory predicts that every demander whose Buyer Value is higher than the competitive equilibrium price will buy a bushel of apples, and every demander whose Buyer Value is lower than the competitive equilibrium price will buy no apples.

Predicting the actions of suppliers or demanders when their Seller Costs or Buyer Values are exactly equal to the competitive price is slightly more complicated. If a supplier's Seller cost equals the price, she is indifferent between selling and not selling. Similarly, if a demander's Buyer Value equals the price, he is indifferent between buying and not buying. In equilibrium, however, we know that the total number of apples sold has to equal the total number of apples bought. This fact gives us enough information to calculate the total number of bushels of apples traded by sellers or buyers who make exactly zero profits by trading. The best way to see how to do this is to look at an example.

Example:

>Let us consider a market in which the demand and supply curves are as described by Figure 1.3 on page 19. Let us suppose that each supplier can supply at most one bushel and that each demander can use at most one bushel of apples. There are 20 suppliers with Seller Costs of $5 and 10 suppliers with Seller Costs of $25, and there are 15 demanders with Buyer Values of $30 and 15 demanders with Buyer Values of $10 for a bushel of apples. We see from Figure 1.3 that the competitive equilibrium price is $10. Since the 20 suppliers with Seller Costs of $5 will all make a profit at this price, they will each supply one bushel in competitive equilibrium. Since the 10 suppliers with Seller Costs of $25 would all lose money if they sold, none of them will supply any apples. The 15 demanders with Buyer Values of $30 will all make a profit by buying apples for $10, so we know that in equilibrium they must all be buying apples. But what about the demanders with Buyer Values of $10? Since the competitive equilibrium price of apples is $10, they are just indifferent between buying and not buying. Looking at the demand and supply curves in Figure 1.3, we see that the total number of bushels of apples that are sold in competitive equilibrium must be 20. We know that the 15 high-value demanders will each demand one bushel. This leaves 5 bushels to be consumed in equilibrium by the low-value demanders. This can happen only if 5 of the demanders with Buyer Values of $10 buy apples (and the other 10 do not).

Efficiency and Competitive Equilibrium

Economists are interested in the efficiency of market outcomes. A market outcome is said to be **efficient** if the sum of the profits made by all individuals in the market is as large as possible. A market outcome is said to be **inefficient** if some other possible arrangement of trades will result in higher total profits for all participants. If one set of market institutions leads to an inefficient outcome, then it may be possible to find alternative institutions that result in higher total profits. Higher total profits could, in principle, be redistributed in such a way that *everyone* is better off after the redistribution than they were before the reform.[6]

---

[6]It might be that although *total* profits with alternative institutions are higher than they were with the original institutions, the direct effect of the change makes some participants worse off than they were before the change. Even if there is enough total gain for the "winners" to compensate the "losers," it is not always possible to determine who the winners and losers will be.

Experimental economists define the **market efficiency** of an experimental market outcome to be the actual total profits of market participants expressed as a percentage of the highest possible amount of profits that could be achieved in the market. If the total profits actually made by market participants are equal to the maximum possible amount, then market efficiency is said to be 100%. If the total profits actually made are only 80 percent of the maximum possible amount, then market efficiency is said to be 80 percent, and so on.

Among all possible arrangements of traders, it turns out that if the profits of buyers and sellers depend only on the trades that they make themselves, the market efficiency of competitive equilibrium is 100%. We state this important result as follows:

Proposition 1.1 *In markets where the profits of buyers and sellers depend only on the trades that they themselves make, competitive equilibrium is efficient. That is, the sum of the profits of buyers and sellers in competitive equilibrium is at least as large as it would be with any other arrangement of trades.*

You already know nearly enough to complete a proof of this proposition. A rigorous, general proof requires a slightly more intricate argument than is appropriate for this course, and is probably best left for an intermediate economic theory course. But the following sketch of an argument can be expanded to provide a rigorous proof.

The total amount of profits made by buyers and sellers is equal to the sum of the Buyer Values of those who buy a unit of the good *minus* the sum of the Seller Costs of those who sell a unit of the good. Recall from the warm-up exercises that (regardless of the price) the total profit made by the buyer and seller in any trade is equal to the buyer's Buyer Value minus the seller's Seller Cost. Therefore total profits made by any arrangement of trades is completely determined by who makes trades and who does not. In competitive equilibrium, every demander who buys a unit of the good has a Buyer Value that is at least as high as the competitive equilibrium price, which in turn is at least as high as the Seller Cost of every supplier who sells. Moreover every demander who does not trade has a Buyer Value that is no larger than the competitive equilibrium price, and every supplier who does not trade has a Seller Cost that is no smaller than the competitive equilibrium price. Using these facts one can show that you cannot increase total profits above the competitive equilibrium level either by having more or by having fewer people trading, nor by exchanging some of the individuals trading for some of those who are not trading.

Lookup Page for Supply and Demand Curves

Here are the hints that we promised on how to draw a demand curve.

The highest Buyer Value for apples is 30, so we know that at prices above 30, nobody will want to buy apples. Therefore the demand curve includes a vertical line extending from the point $(0, 30)$ to the top of the box. At prices greater than 10 but less than 30, the demanders with Buyer Values of 30 will want to buy apples, and the demanders with Buyer Values of 10 will not want to buy. There are 15 demanders with Buyer Values of 30, so that 15 units will be demanded at any price between 10 and 30. This means that the demand curve includes a vertical segment running from $(15, 10)$ to $(15, 30)$. At prices below 10, every demander wants to buy one bushel. There are 30 demanders in all, so total demand will be 30 bushels. The demand curve, therefore, includes a vertical segment running from $(30, 0)$ to $(30, 10)$.

Figure 1.4: Supply and Demand–Example 1

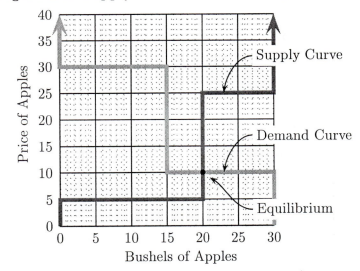

At a price of exactly 30, the 15 high-value demanders are indifferent between buying or not. Total demand could be any amount between 0 and 15. Therefore the demand curve includes a horizontal segment running from $(0, 30)$ to $(15, 30)$. At a price of exactly 10, the 15 high-value demanders will all want to buy one unit. The 15 low-value demanders will be indifferent between buying and not buying, so at a price of 10, demand can be any amount between 15 and 30. Therefore the demand curve includes a horizontal segment running from $(15, 10)$ to $(30, 10)$.

Answers to Warm-up Exercises

W 1.1: $15, $5, $20; **W 1.2**: $39, $20; **W 1.3**: $21, $20; Notice that here, regardless of the trading price, the *total* of buyer's profit and seller's profit is always $20. In general, the *sum* of the profits of the buyer and the seller depend only on their Buyer Values and Seller Costs and not on the trading price.

Answers to Exercises

Ex. 1.1: 30, 25, 10, 0; **Ex. 1.2**: 10, 20, 30, 0; **Ex. 1.3**: 10, 25; **Ex. 1.4**: 10, 20; **Ex. 1.5**: $15, $10; **Ex. 1.6**: $10, $15; **Ex. 1.7**: $25, $35; **Ex. 1.8**: $25, $35; **Ex. 1.9**: S, S, S, D, D; **Ex. 1.10**: $15, $15; **Ex. 1.11**: $15, 20.

Lab Notes for Experiment 1

Recording Transactions and Profits

In order to study and interpret the results of this experiment, you will need a set of "lab notes" that record the relevant information about what happened in the experiment. In particular, you will need a record of the transactions made in the last round of each session. This information can be copied into Tables 1.4 and 1.5.[7] The first three columns record *Sale Price*, supplier's *Seller Cost*, and demander's *Buyer Value*.

To complete Tables 1.4 and 1.5, you need to calculate and record **seller's profit**, **buyer's profit**, and **total profit** for each transaction. If your class has no more than 25–30 students, there will be only about 10 transactions per round, so it won't take you long to do these calculations by hand or with a calculator. For larger classes, we suggest that you use a computer spreadsheet. If you work with a spreadsheet, you may print out a copy of the spreadsheet rather than copy the numbers into these tables.

Recall that for any transaction, the seller's profit is $P - C$, where P is the price and C is her Seller Cost. The buyer's profit is $V - P$, where V is his Buyer Value and P is the price. Total profit in a transaction is the sum of the seller's profit and the buyer's profit in that transaction. When you have calculated the information in Tables 1.4 and 1.5, you can use this information to fill in the tables for Problem 1.1 of your homework.

Recording Market Fundamentals

At the end of the experiment, your instructor will announce the distribution of suppliers' Seller Costs and demanders' Buyer Values for all the participants in the experiment, including those who did not trade as well as those who did trade. (You will not be able to recover all of this information simply from the transaction sheets, because although these sheets tell you the types of the people who *did* trade, they give you no information about those who did not trade.) You should copy this information into Tables 1.6 and 1.7. You will need this information to draw supply and demand curves for the market and to make predictions using supply and demand theory.

---

[7]If your class is fairly small, you can copy this information directly from the blackboard at the end of the last round of each session. In large classes, your instructor may post this information for you on a class website or distribute it by other means.

Table 1.4: Transactions in the Last Round of Session 1

Trans-action	Price	Seller Cost	Buyer Value	Seller's Profit	Buyer's Profit	Total Profit
1						
2						
3						
4						
5						
6						
7						
8						
9						
10						
11						
12						
13						
14						
15						
16						
17						
18						
19						
20						
21						
22						
23						
24						
25						

Table 1.5: Transactions in the Last Round of Session 2

Trans-action	Price	Seller Cost	Buyer Value	Seller's Profit	Buyer's Profit	Total Profit
1						
2						
3						
4						
5						
6						
7						
8						
9						
10						
11						
12						
13						
14						
15						
16						
17						
18						
19						
20						
21						
22						
23						
24						
25						

Table 1.6: Distribution of Types in Session 1

Type of Agent	Number of Agents	Value	Cost
Low-Cost Supplier		▆	
High-Cost Supplier		▆	
High-Value Demander			▆
Low-Value Demander			▆

Table 1.7: Distribution of Types in Session 2

Type of Agent	Number of Agents	Value	Cost
Low-Cost Supplier		▆	
High-Cost Supplier		▆	
High-Value Demander			▆
Low-Value Demander			▆

Predictions of the Theory

The way that scientists evaluate a theory is to see how well it predicts outcomes in controlled experiments or in real-world situations that approximate
the conditions postulated by the theory. Supply and demand theory makes
detailed predictions about what will happen in each session of the Apple
Market experiment. Given the distribution of types of buyers and sellers in
the market, the theory predicts the price at which apples will be sold and
the number of bushels of apples traded. It also predicts the total amount
of profits made by suppliers and demanders and it predicts which types will
trade and which will not.

You are now in a position to evaluate supply and demand theory by
comparing its predictions with the outcomes in your classroom market. In
the discussion section of this chapter, you learned how to draw supply and
demand curves for a market given the distribution of Buyer Values and Seller
Costs. For your homework, you need to draw supply and demand curves for
the distribution of Buyer Values and Seller Costs found in your classroom
experiment. When you have drawn these curves, you will be able to find
the equilibrium prices, quantities, and profits predicted by the competitive
theory.

Experiment 2

Shifting Supply

A Village Fish Market

It is early morning at the fish market on a lonely Pacific island. The mist is rising, the gulls are calling, and the fishermen have just returned to the harbor with their catch. A noisy crowd of villagers have come to the fish market to gossip and buy their dinners.

There are no refrigerators on the island and day-old fish will spoil. One fish is enough to feed a family for a day, so each demander wants at most one fish. The number of fish that a fisherman catches will vary from session to session. Sometimes a fisherman may catch only one fish, sometimes two or three fish. Last night, before going out to sea, every fisherman had to pay $10 to fuel his fishing boat. This money has already been spent, and so every fisherman has costs of $10 regardless of how many fish he sells. Once a fish is caught, no other expenses are incurred in selling it. In contrast to the apple market in our previous experiment, fishermen cannot save any costs by not selling their fish.

The overall distribution of Buyer Values will be the same in both sessions, though individual Buyer Values change from one session to another. Because of changes in the weather, fishermen will catch more fish in the second session than in the first.

Instructions

You will be better prepared to participate profitably in this market if you read these instructions and complete the brief warm-up exercise before you come to class.

In this experiment, some of you will be fishermen with fish to sell and some will be fish demanders. Sellers and buyers must find each other and agree on a price. If they reach an agreement, the buyer and the seller should bring a sales contract to the market manager. The sales contract records the ID number of the buyer and seller, the price, and the Buyer Value. (You don't need to fill in the Seller Cost on the sales contract.)

If you are a fish demander and you buy a fish, you will receive your Buyer Value from the market manager. Your profit as a demander is the difference between your Buyer Value and the price you paid for the fish.

If you are a fisherman, you will have either one, two, or three fish to sell. If you have more than one fish, you must find a *different* buyer for each fish that you sell. After you have turned in a contract for the sale of a fish, if you still have some fish left, you can return to the market and look for another buyer. Your profits are equal to the total amount of money you get from selling your fish *minus* the $10 fuel cost. If you sell no fish at all, you will have a loss of $10.

Warm-up Exercise

After reading the instructions for this experiment, please check your understanding by answering the following questions.[1]

W 2.1 In the first session of this experiment, suppose that you catch two fish. You sell one fish for $15 and one fish for $6. How much is your total profit? $ __11__ Suppose that you sell the first fish for $15 and are unable to sell the second fish. How much is your total profit? $ __5__

W 2.2 Suppose that you have caught only one fish. The best offer that you are made for this fish is $4. What would be your profit (or loss) if you sell the fish for $4? $ __−6__ What would be your profit (or loss) if you don't sell your fish, but let it rot? $ __−10__ If you want to maximize your profit from this experiment, and you are faced with a choice between selling the fish for $4 or not selling the fish, what should you do? __Sell__

W 2.3 Suppose that you are a fish demander with a Buyer Value of $20, and you see that there are many fishermen still trying to sell fish, but only a few demanders left who have not already bought their fish. Assuming that

---

[1]Answers to these warm-up exercises can be found on page 47.

you want to maximize your profits, at what price would you offer to buy?

$ _11 - 13_

W 2.4 Suppose that you are a fisherman and you have one fish left to sell. You see that almost all of the fish demanders have already bought their fish, but there are several fishermen still trying to sell fish. The average price of the fish that have already been sold is about $10. Would you expect to be able to sell your fish for $10? **No** If somebody offered you $2 for your fish, would you take the offer? _Probably_ Explain. _better to take some money than no money_

What Do You Expect to See?

Before you conduct an experiment, it is useful to think about what you expect to happen and to to record your prediction. Then after the experiment you can look back at your earlier notes and compare what actually happened to what you expected. When the experiment presents you with a surprise, the next step will be to try to revise your theories of how things work in order to make sense of your new experience.

■ If fishing conditions improve so that more fish are caught, would you expect the price of fish to go up or down? _down_ Would you expect total profits of *all* fishermen to go up, go down, or stay the same? _up_

Discussion of Experiment 2

Shifting the Supply Curve

In the Apple Market experiment, you learned to draw supply and demand curves and to find competitive equilibrium prices and quantities. In this experiment, we apply supply and demand theory to explain the way that the price of fish and the revenue of fishermen respond to a change in the number of fish caught. Because of changes in the weather, fishermen caught many more fish in Session 2 than in Session 1. What prediction does competitive equilibrium theory make about the effect of a larger catch on the price of fish and on the profits of fishermen? We will answer this question by using a technique known to economists as **comparative statics**. Comparative statics is a tool for predicting the way that external causes such as the weather will affect economic variables. We will use this tool to study the effects of a change in the number of fish caught on market prices, on profits, and on consumers' surplus.

The recipe for comparative statics analysis is simple. First draw the supply and demand curves that apply before the change and look at the predicted equilibrium values of the economic variables of interest. Then draw the supply and demand curves that apply after the change and predict the new equilibrium values. Finally, compare the equilibrium values of these variables before and after the change.

The key to comparative statics analysis is to answer two questions: "What happened to the supply curve?" and "What happened to the demand curve?" Let us apply these two questions to the fish-market experiment.

What Happened to the Supply Curve?

Recall that the supply curve shows the number of fish that fishermen would be willing to sell at any possible price. In the Apple Market experiment, suppliers had to pay their Seller Cost only if they sold a bushel of apples. They did not have to pay this cost if they did not sell. In this experiment, the fishermen's only costs are for the fuel they purchased the night before. These costs are known as **sunk costs**, since fishermen must pay them even if they don't sell any fish. As you found in the warm-up exercises, fishermen are better off accepting any positive price for their fish rather than leaving the fish to rot on the beach.

So what does the supply curve for fish look like? At any positive price, every fisherman will want to sell all of his fish. Therefore the supply curve includes a vertical line segment that meets the horizontal axis at the total number of fish caught by fishermen. This vertical line is shown as the dashed line in Figure 2.1 for a case where 15 fish are caught. At a price of zero, fishermen will be just indifferent between selling their fish or not, so the supply curve also includes a horizontal segment running from the origin to the point on the horizontal axis where the vertical segment begins. In Figure 2.1, this is the line segment extending from the origin to the point $(15, 0)$.

Figure 2.1: Shifting Supply Curve

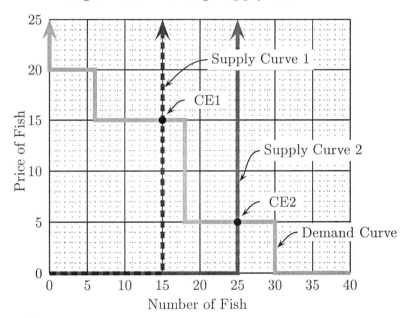

In Session 2 of our experiment, the total number of fish caught is different from that in Session 1, but fishermen will again want to sell all of their fish at any positive price. Therefore the new supply curve includes a vertical line segment that meets the horizontal axis at the number of fish caught in the second session, and a horizontal line segment extending from the origin to the bottom of the vertical segment. For example, if the new number of fish caught happened to be 25, then the supply curve would be as shown by Supply Curve 2. The vertical segment meets the horizontal axis at $(25, 0)$ and the horizontal segment extends from the origin to $(25, 0)$. The effect of the change in the size of the catch was to shift the vertical portion of the supply curve for fish outward by the number of additional fish caught.

What Happened to the Demand Curve?

In this experiment, although the number of fish caught in the two sessions differed, the number of demanders did not change, nor did the distribution of demanders' Buyer Values. This means that at any given price, the total number of fish demanded is the same in the two sessions. Therefore the demand curve did not change at all.

An Example

Let's work through a complete comparative statics exercise for the case depicted in Figure 2.1. Suppose that on Day 1 the total number of fish caught was 15, and on Day 2 the total number caught was 25. On Figure 2.1, the supply curve for Day 1 is given by the dashed line labeled *Supply Curve 1* and the supply curve for Day 2 is given by the solid line labeled *Supply Curve 2*.

The demand curve remains the same on both days. We see that competitive equilibrium on Day 1 is at the point $CE1$ and competitive equilibrium on Day 2 is at the point $CE2$. Thus when the number of fish caught increases from 15 to 25, the price of fish falls from $15 to $5 per fish, and total revenue of fishermen falls from $15 \times 15 = 225 to $5 \times 25 = 125.

Prices and Shifting Supply in Commodity Markets

Supply and Demand in the News

A story in the *Wall Street Journal* on September 4, 1996 reports events that are strikingly similar to the results of our fish-market experiment. The headline of this story is "Fishermen in Alaska, Awash in Salmon, Strive to Stay Afloat." According to this report,

> "Alaska is awash in salmon. Huge fish runs have been building here. Combined with the growing output from sources like Chilean fish farms and Russian fishing fleets, they are glutting the market and driving wholesale prices to record lows."

The story goes on to say that the price of salmon has fallen to five cents a pound from a peak price of eighty cents a pound eight years ago. It quotes a fisherman who

"figures he would have to catch nearly a million pounds of salmon
this summer to cover his boat payment and expenses for his
three-man crew."

Implicitly, the story suggests that he will be unable to catch enough fish to
pay all of these expenses. The same fisherman is quoted as saying

"Its a weird problem. You love to catch fish, but the more you
catch the less they're worth."

Stories like this are not rare. If you follow the business pages of any
major newspaper, in almost any week you will find a report on how external
events such as changes in the weather have changed the size of harvests in
agriculture or fisheries, and how commodity prices respond to these changes.
Here are some more examples from a single newspaper story.

The United States Department of Agriculture (USDA) issues monthly
estimates of the size of agricultural crops. These estimates are almost always
followed by news stories about their effects on prices. For example, in the
Wall Street Journal for September 12, 1996, there is a story with the headline
"Grain Prices Fall After Harvest Estimate." According to the story, on the
previous day the USDA released a new forecast for the size of the corn,
wheat, and soybean crops to be harvested in the fall of 1996.

- The forecast for the size of the corn crop was 1% higher than the
  amount forecast a month ago. The reason given was that growing
  conditions were better than expected. Because of the cool, rainy spring
  weather, the corn crop got off to a slow start, but in the last month
  warmer than normal weather in the Midwest helped the corn crop to
  catch up. Immediately after this announcement was made, the price
  of a contract to deliver corn in December dropped 7.6 cents to $3.27
  per bushel.

- The forecast for the size of the wheat crop was 2% higher than that
  of a month ago, due to better than expected weather in the Northern
  Plains. In response to this news the price of wheat to be delivered in
  the autumn fell by 5%.

- The USDA *reduced* its estimate of the year's soybean crop by 1.3%.
  According to the story, the soybean crop got off to a slow start this year
  and despite recent warm weather continues to lag behind in maturing.
  So what do you think happened to the price of soybeans after this
  announcement? The price of soybeans *rose* by 1.5 cents to $8.35 a
  bushel.

On the Economics of Farming and Fishing

In the short run, industries like agriculture and fishing are highly vulnerable to changes in the price of their product, caused by shifts in the total supply. Farmers face much the same problem that our fishermen did. Most of farmers' expenses are incurred in the spring, when they prepare the soil and plant and fertilize their crops. Their returns on this investment do not come until fall when they harvest their crops. When they plant, they do not know how large their harvests will be, nor do they know the price at which they can sell their product. This depends on unforeseeable events, like the weather.

When autumn comes, if the price of corn is low, farmers cannot get their expenses back by unplanting their corn. Their only choice is whether to harvest the crops and sell them for the going price or to leave them in the fields. As long as the price is higher than the cost of harvesting, farmers will want to sell their crops. The cost of harvesting is a small fraction of the total cost of producing a crop of corn. There are many years in which the price of a bushel of corn is high enough so that it is worthwhile for farmers to pick it and bring it in from the fields, but not high enough to repay all of the money that they have invested in the crop. In these years, farmers will harvest the crop and sell it for whatever it brings, despite the fact that they have lost money. They may wish that they hadn't planted corn in the spring, but it is too late to undo that decision. These farmers, like the fishermen in Session 2 of our experiment, cannot hope to recover their entire initial investment. The best that they can do to minimize their losses is to sell their output at the going price.

Costs that are already incurred and cannot be reduced by altering production are known as **sunk costs** or **fixed costs**. Costs that vary with the number of units sold are called **variable costs**. In the instance of the corn farmer, at harvest time the costs of planting the corn, caring for it, and fertilizing it are sunk costs. At this time, the only variable cost is the cost of harvesting, which could be avoided by leaving the crop in the fields.

Our experiment dealt with the supply of fish in the morning when fishermen's fuel costs from the night before were already sunk costs. Our discussion of farmers, so far, concerns their behavior in the fall after planting and fertilizing expenditures have become sunk costs. The choices made in situations like this are called **short-run decisions**.

Economists also study **long-run decisions**, by which we mean forward-looking decisions taken at a time when sunk costs are not yet sunk. For the fishermen of our experiment, in the morning when they come in with their fish, the cost of last night's fuel is a sunk cost. But in the afternoon, before fishermen refuel their boats, they may be able to decide whether or not to go fishing at all. At this time, their fuel costs are variable costs. When they make the decision of whether or not to go fishing, the fishermen can avoid fuel costs by leaving their boats in the harbor. Of course, if they do so they will catch no fish. For farmers, the cost of planting is a fixed cost at harvest time, but it is a variable cost in the spring. If the farmer chooses not to plant any crops he can avoid all of these costs. Of course, if he does so he will have no crops to sell in the fall.

Since weather conditions, the size of the harvests, and the price of output are unpredictable, we can expect there will be times when fishermen and farmers do not recover their sunk costs and also times when they get back more than they have spent. If on average, over the years, fishermen or farmers do not recover their sunk costs, then at least some of them will go out of business. Perhaps you can guess what the effects of this will be. A reduction in the number of fishermen or farmers will reduce the amount of product supplied at any price, thus shifting the supply curve to the left and causing the price to be higher in future periods.

It turns out that the principles that we have discussed for fishing and agriculture apply in much the same way to other industries, including manufacturing and service industries. We will study these principles in more detail in a later experiment, where we deal with short-run and long-run decision-making in the restaurant business.

Answers to Warm-up Exercises
W 2.1: $21 − $10 = $11, $5;   **W 2.2**: $4 − $10 = −$6, −$10, sell the fish;   **W 2.3**: Low offers could work;   **W 2.4**: No, there are many more fish available than buyers will buy. Every fisherman would rather sell for a positive price than give his fish away. Smart buyers will be able to get fish cheaply. The low price may be something to consider.

Lab Notes for Experiment 2

Recording Transactions, Prices, and Profits

In Tables 2.1 and 2.2, record the price and the buyer's Buyer Value for each transaction of the last round of Sessions 1 and 2. For each transaction, subtract price from Buyer Value to determine the Buyer's Profit.

Recording Market Fundamentals

At the end of the experiment, the instructor will post the distribution of demanders' Buyer Values and the number of students in the class who were designated as fishermen. The instructor will also post the number of fish that were caught in each session. Record this information in Tables 2.3 and 2.4.

Computing Market Statistics

In Table 2.5, for each session of the classroom experiment, record the average price at which fish were sold, the number of fish sold, total profits of fishermen, and total profits of demanders.

Table 2.1: Transactions in Session 1–Last Round

Trans-action	Price	Buyer Value	Buyer's Profit	Trans-action	Price	Buyer Value	Buyer's Profit
1				26			
2				27			
3				28			
4				29			
5				30			
6				31			
7				32			
8				33			
9				34			
10				35			
11				36			
12				37			
13				38			
14				39			
15				40			
16				41			
17				42			
18				43			
19				44			
20				45			
21				46			
22				47			
23				48			
24				49			
25				50			

Table 2.2: Transactions in Session 2–Last Round

Trans-action	Price	Buyer Value	Buyer's Profit	Trans-action	Price	Buyer Value	Buyer's Profit
1				26			
2				27			
3				28			
4				29			
5				30			
6				31			
7				32			
8				33			
9				34			
10				35			
11				36			
12				37			
13				38			
14				39			
15				40			
16				41			
17				42			
18				43			
19				44			
20				45			
21				46			
22				47			
23				48			
24				49			
25				50			

Table 2.3: Distribution of Buyer Values–All Sessions

Buyer Value	Number of Buyers
$25	
$20	
$5	

Table 2.4: Number of Fishermen and Fish Caught

	Number of Fishermen	Number of Fish Caught
Session 1		
Session 2		

Table 2.5: Market Statistics for the Fish Market

	Session 1	Session 2
Mean Price		
Number of Fish Sold		
Total Profits of Fishermen*		
Total Profits of Demanders		
Total Profits All Participants		

***Hint:** Every fisherman, whether or not he sells any fish, has total costs of $10. Therefore total costs of fishermen is $10 times the number of fishermen participating in the experiment (including those who sold no fish). Total revenue of fishermen equals the total amount of money that they received for fish. Find this from Table 2.1 (or 2.2). Total profits of fishermen equals total revenue minus total costs.

Part II

Market Intervention and Public Policy

Experiment 3

A Sales Tax

We are back at the Farmers' Apple Market. There is a hint of frost in the air and the leaves are changing colors. Today's market session is a little more complex. Instead of just two types of buyers and sellers, there will be several types of each. This should make shopping a bit more interesting than it was before. A new (and perhaps unwelcome) player, the Tax Collector, also makes his debut.

Instructions

You will be better prepared to participate profitably in this market if you read these instructions and complete the brief warm-up exercise before you come to class.

There will be three market sessions today. In the first session, there are no taxes. In the second session, *suppliers* will have to pay a sales tax of $15 if they make a sale. In the third session, *demanders* will have to pay a sales tax of $15 if they buy a bushel of apples. You are likely to play a different role in each of the three sessions, but the overall distribution of buyers and sellers in the market is the same in all three sessions; that is, the total number of buyers with each possible Buyer Value and the total number of sellers with each possible Seller Cost, will be the same in all sessions.

Procedures are similar to those used in the Apple Market experiment. In each session you will get a Personal Information Sheet that tells you whether you are a supplier or a demander and reports your Seller Cost or Buyer Value. In each round of a session, you can trade at most one bushel of apples. If you agree on a sale, you and your trading partner should fill in a Sales Contract and bring it to the market manager.

In the second market session, sellers have to pay a sales tax of $15. In this session, if you are a seller with Seller Cost C and you sell a bushel of apples for P, then your profit on the transaction will be $P - $C - 15.

In the third market session, buyers have to pay a sales tax of $15. If you are a buyer with Buyer Value V and you buy a bushel of apples for P, then your profit on the transaction will be $V - $P - 15.

If you make no transactions at all, you don't have to pay a tax and you have no costs or revenue, so your profit is zero.

Warm-up Exercise

After reading the instructions for this experiment, please check your understanding by answering the following questions.[1]

W 3.1 Suppose that sellers have to pay a sales tax of $15 when they sell a bushel of apples. If a supplier who has a Seller Cost of $5 sells a bushel of apples for $25 to a demander who has a Buyer Value of $45, the supplier will

make a profit of $___5___ and the demander will make a profit (consumer's

surplus) of $__20__.

W 3.2 Suppose that buyers have to pay a sales tax of $15 when they buy a bushel of apples. If a supplier who has a Seller Cost of $5 sells a bushel of apples for $25 to a demander who has a Buyer Value of $45, the supplier will

make a profit of $___20___ and the demander will make a profit (consumer's

surplus) of $__5__.

W 3.3 You are a supplier with a Seller Cost of $15. Sellers have to pay a sales tax of $15 when they sell a bushel of apples. What is the lowest price

at which you would not lose money by selling apples? $__30__.

W 3.4 You are a demander with Buyer Value of $30. Buyers have to pay a sales tax of $15 when they buy a bushel of apples. What is the highest

price at which you can buy a bushel of apples and not lose money? $__15__.

---

[1]Answers to these warm-up exercises can be found on page 77.

What Do You Expect to See?

These questions ask you to explore your beliefs about what will happen in the experiment before you know the experimental outcome and before you read the discussion in this chapter. After the experiment is done and you have finished the discussion and homework, you can look back to compare your prior answers with what you know when you finish this chapter.

■   In the experimental market, would you predict that the $15 tax paid by sellers in Session 1 will cause the average price paid by buyers to increase by more than $15, less than $15, or just about $15?   _less than $15_

■   Will demanders be better off if sellers pay the tax or if buyers pay the tax?   _Sellers_

Discussion of Experiment 3

If the government puts a sales tax on cigarettes, beer, luxury yachts, or hotel rooms, who pays the cost of the tax? When a new sales tax is proposed for some good, there are usually loud complaints from sellers, who believe that the tax will come out of their profits. Often there are also complaints from buyers of the good, who think that the tax will be passed on to them in the form of higher prices. Who is right?

In this experiment, we explore the effects of a sales tax on the price of the good that is taxed and on the profits of sellers and buyers. This experiment tests these effects for one particular distribution of Seller Costs and Buyer Values. Competitive equilibrium theory makes interesting *general* predictions about the effects of a sales tax on prices, quantities, and profits. The beauty of having a general theoretical model like competitive equilibrium theory is that it can give us a good idea of what the effects of a sales tax will be, not only under the specific conditions of our experiment, but in a wide variety of possible market environments.

The Effects of a Sales Tax–An Example

We begin to study the theory of sales taxes by working with a specific example, in which the distributions of Seller Costs and Buyer Values are as given in Table 3.1.

Table 3.1: Distribution of Types of Agents

Seller's Costs	Number in Market	Buyer's Value	Number in Market
3	2	45	2
8	2	40	2
13	2	35	2
18	2	30	2
23	2	25	2
28	2	20	2

We have drawn supply and demand curves for this example in Figure 3.1. Make sure that you understand how to use the data from Table 3.1 to draw

Figure 3.1: Supply and Demand with No Sales Tax

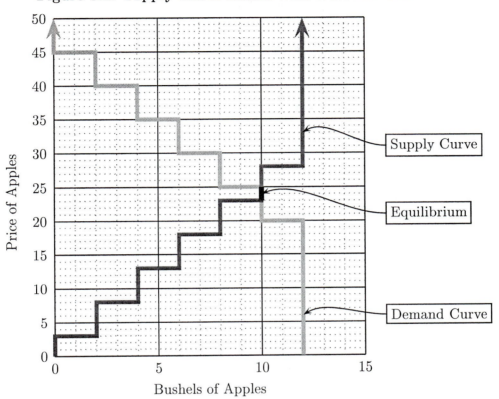

these curves. If you need help in seeing how supply and demand curves are drawn, turn to page 78, where there is a detailed explanation.

Notice that the supply and demand curves in Figure 3.1 do not cross each other at just a single point, but meet and run together along the interval from $(10, 23)$ to $(10, 25)$, where the number of trades is 10 and the price can be anything between $23 and $25.

At prices greater than $25, the supply curve lies to the right of the demand curve, meaning that there are more suppliers wanting to sell a bushel of apples than demanders wanting to buy a bushel of apples. At prices less than $23, the demand curve lies to the right of the supply curve, meaning that there are more demanders wanting to buy apples than suppliers wanting to sell them. But at any price between $23 and $25, there are 10 suppliers who want to sell a bushel of apples and 10 demanders who want to buy a bushel of apples. Therefore, at prices between $23 and $25, "supply equals demand" and the market is in competitive equilibrium. Thus the competitive model predicts that 10 bushels of apples will be sold. Instead of predicting a unique equilibrium price, the theory says only that the price will lie somewhere in the interval from $23 to $25.

Equilibrium with A Sales Tax Paid by Sellers

The way to find out the effect of a sales tax on competitive equilibrium prices and quantities is to study the effect of the tax on the supply and demand curves.

How does a $15 sales tax, charged to sellers, affect the supply curve? Any supplier who sells a bushel of apples will now have to pay a $15 tax in addition to her production cost. For example, with the tax, a supplier who has a Seller Cost of $8 would lose money if she sold a bushel of apples for less than $8+$15=$23. The effect of the tax is to *increase* by $15 the lowest price at which each seller would be willing to sell a unit. Since the supply curve plots the lowest prices at which suppliers are willing to sell, the introduction of the tax has the same effect on the supply curve as would a $15 increase in Seller Costs for each supplier. Therefore when the sales tax is imposed, each point on the supply curve must be drawn $15 higher than the corresponding point on the original supply curve. Economists describe this change by saying that the tax "shifted the supply curve upward" by $15. On Figure 3.2, we have drawn the pre-tax supply curve as a solid line and the post-tax supply curve as a dashed line.

How does this sales tax affect the demand curve? That's easy. Since Buyer Values do not change and buyers do not have to pay any tax, the tax does not change any demander's willingness-to-pay (reservation price) for apples. Therefore the demand curve will be the same as it was without taxes.

Looking at the supply and demand curves in Figure 3.2, we can find the effect of the tax on competitive equilibrium prices and quantities. The equilibrium without a tax is indicated by the darkened interval marked "Old Equilibrium." Without a sales tax, 10 bushels are sold and the price must be in the interval between $23 to $25. The competitive equilibrium with the tax is marked by the darkened interval marked "New Equilibrium," where the dashed supply curve meets the demand curve. On this interval, 6 bushels of apples are sold and the price must be somewhere in the interval between $30 to $33.

Thus the sales tax, when collected from sellers, decreases the number of trades from 10 to 6 and causes the price to rise from a price in the interval between $23 and $25 to a price in the interval between $30 and $33.

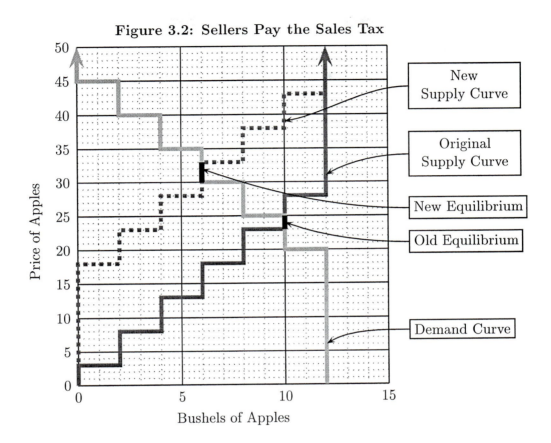

Figure 3.2: Sellers Pay the Sales Tax

Equilibrium with a Sales Tax Paid by Buyers

To find the effect of a sales tax charged to buyers instead of to sellers, we again ask our two questions: What happens to the supply curve? What happens to the demand curve?

How does this tax affect the supply curve? The tax does not change any supplier's Seller Costs. Since sellers do not have to pay any taxes directly to the government, the minimum price that any seller would be willing to accept for a bushel of apples does not change. Therefore the supply curve remains the same as it was without taxes.

How does this tax affect the demand curve? When a demander obtains a bushel of apples, he will receive his Buyer Value from the market manager, and he will also have to pay the $15 tax to the tax collector. Thus the tax reduces the value of the object to the buyer by the amount of the tax. For example, suppose that a demander with Buyer Value $40 buys a bushel of apples. He would collect his $40 from the market manager, but he would

Figure 3.3: Buyers Pay the Sales Tax

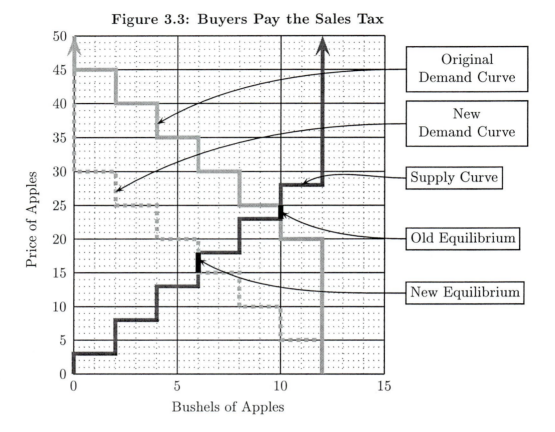

also have to pay the $15 tax. The most that he could pay to a seller and still make a profit is $40 − $15 = $25. Thus we see that the effect of a $15 sales tax collected from the buyer is to reduce each demander's willingness-to-pay by $15. The effect is the same as if every demander's Buyer Value were reduced by $15. This means that when the tax is paid by buyers, the demand curve must be drawn exactly $15 lower than the original demand curve. In the language of economists, the $15 tax has "shifted the demand curve downward" by $15. In Figure 3.3, we have drawn the pre-tax demand curve as a solid line and the post-tax demand curve as a dashed line.

We can find the effects of a tax collected from buyers by looking at the supply and demand curves in Figure 3.3. Without a sales tax, 10 bushels are sold and the price must be in the interval between $23 and $25. The competitive equilibrium with the tax is marked by the darkened interval marked "New Equilibrium," where the dashed demand curve meets the original supply curve. On this interval, 6 bushels of apples are sold and the price must be somewhere in the interval between $15 and $18. Thus the sales tax collected from buyers reduces the number of trades from 10 to 6 and causes the price to fall, from a price in the interval between $23 and $25 to a price in the interval between $15 and $18.

The Effects of Sales Taxes

Equivalence of Taxes Collected from Sellers and Buyers

Which leads to higher profits for buyers, a sales tax that is collected from sellers or a sales tax that is collected directly from buyers? At first blush, the answer seems to be obvious. Surely your profits will be higher if somebody else pays the tax than if you pay the tax.

Let us see what happens in the example that we have just discussed. For simplicity, we will assume that in each equilibrium, the competitive price falls exactly in the middle of the range of possible prices. Thus when there is no tax, the price would be $24; when the sellers pay the tax, the price would be $31.50; and when the buyers pay the tax, the price would be $16.50.

Now let us ask which is better for buyers. If sellers pay the tax, the equilibrium price is $31.50 and buyers don't have to pay any tax. If buyers pay the tax, the equilibrium price is $16.50, but they also have to pay a tax of $15 for each unit they buy. Therefore the total amount that buyers have to pay for a bushel of apples is $16.50 + $15 = $31.50. We see, therefore, that in equilibrium the cost of a bushel of apples to the buyers, including tax, is the same whether buyers pay the tax or sellers pay the tax.

Now consider the profits of suppliers. If sellers pay the tax, then the equilibrium price is $31.50, but a seller has to pay a tax of $15 for each bushel that she sells, so that after taxes she receives only $31.50 − $15 = $16.50 per bushel. If buyers pay the tax, the equilibrium price is $16.50. In this case, the seller receives $16.50 per bushel and is not obliged to pay any tax. Thus we see that the after-tax price received by sellers is the same regardless of who pays the tax.

The result found in this example illustrates a principle that holds in all competitive markets. For a given tax rate per unit sold, in competitive equilibrium, the *after-tax* prices paid by buyers are the same and the *after-tax* prices received by sellers are the same, whether the tax is collected from sellers or from buyers. Since the after-tax prices are the same, regardless of from whom the tax is collected, profits of sellers and of buyers are also the same whether sellers pay the tax or buyers pay the tax. Moreover, the total number of transactions is also the same in both cases. Thus we find that despite apparent differences:

Proposition 3.1 *The real effects of a per-unit sales tax are no different, whether the tax is collected from sellers or from buyers.*

Sharing the Burden of a Sales Tax

Who bears the burden of a sales tax? Do sellers simply pass the tax on to buyers, or do sellers absorb the tax and leave the price paid by consumers the same as it would be without the tax? Or is the answer somewhere in between? It turns out that if demand curves are downward sloping and supply curves are upward sloping, the burden of the tax will be shared between buyers and sellers. Without a sales tax, the price received by sellers is the same as the price paid by buyers. With a sales tax, regardless of whether the sales tax is collected from sellers or from buyers, the after-tax price received by sellers falls and the after-tax price paid by buyers rises. This means that typically the burden of a sales tax is shared between suppliers and demanders.

In the example just considered, without a sales tax there is an equilibrium where suppliers receive $24 per unit and demanders pay $24 per unit. With the sales tax, suppliers receive $16.50 for each unit they sell and demanders pay $31.50 for each unit they purchase. This means that the tax causes the price paid by demanders to increase by $7.50 and the price received by suppliers to decrease by $7.50. Thus the $15 per-unit "burden of the tax" is shared between suppliers and demanders, with demanders bearing a $7.50 increase in the price they have to pay and suppliers bearing a $7.50 decrease in the price they receive. Although in this example, suppliers and demanders share the burden of the tax exactly equally, this is not in general the case. In general, the way the tax burden is shared depends on the shapes of the supply and demand curves. Suppliers will bear a larger share of the burden of the tax the steeper is the supply curve relative to the demand curve.

Profits, Tax Revenue, and Excess Burden

A sales tax must reduce the total profits of buyers and sellers, since the tax causes the price paid by buyers to rise and the price received by sellers to fall. On the other hand, the government collects **tax revenue** that could be used to provide beneficial goods and services or could even be refunded to market participants. It would be interesting to know whether the tax revenue collected by the government is greater than, less than, or equal to the amount of profits lost by buyers and sellers because of the tax.

If supply curves slope up and demand curves slope down, the answer to this question is that a sales tax will reduce total profits of sellers and buyers by more than the amount of tax revenue collected. The difference between the loss in total profits of market participants and the amount of tax revenue is called the **excess burden** or **deadweight loss** of the tax. The reason that a sales tax causes excess burden is that the tax prevents some trades that would be profitable for both buyer and seller in the absence of a tax.

It is helpful to think about an extreme case. Suppose that the government imposed a sales tax of $1,000,000 on every quart of orange juice consumed. What do you think would happen to the price of orange juice? What do you think would happen to orange juice consumption? How much money do you think that the government would collect from this tax? Without this monstrous sales tax, the orange juice industry is large and prosperous. Orange juice suppliers make significant profits and orange juice consumers enjoy substantial consumers' surplus. With the $1,000,000 tax, almost no orange juice would be produced or sold. Almost the entire profit and consumers' surplus from orange juice would disappear. The lost profits and consumers' surplus would not be regained in the form of government revenue. With the tax, almost no orange juice would be bought or sold, and so the government would collect almost no revenue. The excess burden from this tax would be just about the entire amount of profits and consumers' surplus that existed without the tax.

We will explore the way to calculate the tax revenue and excess burden for a less dramatic case, namely, the $15 sales tax that was imposed on sellers in the example shown in Figure 3.2. The excess burden of a tax is found by first calculating the sum of sellers' and buyers' profits without the tax, then calculating the sum of sellers' profits, buyers' profits, and tax revenue when the tax is in place, and finally subtracting the latter sum from the former.

Total Profits of Sellers and Buyers with No Tax

First we calculate total profits of suppliers and demanders in competitive equilibrium before the tax. We see from Figure 3.2 that in competitive equilibrium with no tax, 10 bushels of apples are sold and the equilibrium price could be anywhere between $23 and $25. For our calculations, we assume that the price is $24, exactly in the middle of this range.[2]

---

[2]If we had chosen any other price in this interval, the distribution of profits between Suppliers and Demanders would have changed, but the number of units sold, total tax

The suppliers who sell apples in competitive equilibrium at a price of $24 are the ones with Seller Costs of $24 or lower, and the demanders who buy apples are the ones with Buyer Values of $24 or higher. From the supply curve, we see that there are 10 suppliers with Seller Costs of $24 or lower. These include two suppliers each with Seller Costs $3, $8, $13, $18, and $23. Since they sell a total of 10 bushels of apples for $24 a bushel, their total revenue is $24 × 10 = $240. Since there are two sellers of each type, the total of their costs is 2 × $(3 + 8 + 13 + 18 + 23) = $130. Therefore the total profit of sellers is $240 − $130 = $110.

From the demand curve we see that there are 10 demanders with Buyer Values of $24 or higher. These include two demanders each with Buyer Values $45, $40, $35, $30, and $25. The total profits that the buyers make will be equal to the sum of their Buyer Values minus the total amount that they pay for apples. Since there are two demanders of each type, the sum of their Buyer Values is 2 × $(45 + 40 + 35 + 30 + 25) = $350. Since they buy a total of 10 bushels of apples for $24 a bushel, the total amount that they pay for apples is $24 × 10 = $240. Therefore the total profit of buyers is $350 − $240 = $110.

The sum of sellers' profits and buyers' profits when there is no sales tax is therefore $110 + $110 = $220.

Total Profits of Sellers and Buyers with Tax Paid by Sellers

Next we calculate the total profits of suppliers and demanders when sellers must pay a $15 sales tax. We see from Figure 3.2 that in competitive equilibrium with the tax, 6 bushels of apples will be sold and the price will be in the range from $30 and $33. Let us calculate profits on the assumption that the price is in the middle of this range, at $31.50. We see from the graph that at a price of $31.50, the 6 suppliers who sell in competitive equilibrium include two sellers each with Seller Costs $3, $8, and $13. Since they sell a total of 6 units at a price of $31.50, these sellers will have total revenue of $31.50 × 6 = $189. The sum of the Seller Costs of these 6 sellers is 2 × $(3 + 8 + 13) = $48. In addition to their Seller Costs, the sellers must pay a total of $15 × 6 = $90 in sales taxes. Therefore their profit after taxes will be $189 − $48 − $90 = $51.

We see from Figure 3.2 that in equilibrium with the tax, there are 6 buyers, two each with Buyer Values $45, $40, and $35. Total profits of these buyers will be the sum of their Buyer Values minus the total amount of

---

revenue, total profits of all market participants, and excess burden would all have been exactly the same as the values that we calculate.

money that they spend on apples. The sum of the Buyer Values for the 6 buyers is $2 \times \$(45 + 40 + 35) = \$240$. The total amount of money they have to pay for the 6 bushels of apples that they purchase is $\$31.50 \times 6 = \$189$. Their total profit is therefore $\$240 - \$189 = \$51$.

Since sellers and buyers each make a profit of $51, the total profit of market participants with the tax is $\$51 + \$51 = \$102$.

Total Tax Revenue and Excess Burden

Since 6 bushels of apples are sold when the $15 tax is imposed, the government collects a tax revenue of $6 \times \$15 = \$90$. Therefore when the $15 sales tax is collected from sellers, the sum of suppliers' profits, demanders' profits, and tax revenue is $\$51 + \$51 + \$90 = \$192$. In the absence of the tax, we found that total profits of suppliers and demanders were $220. Since the excess burden is the difference between total profits without the tax and the sum of total profits and total tax revenue with the tax, it follows that the excess burden of the tax in this example is $\$220 - \$192 = \$28$.

In this example, suppliers and demanders suffered a loss in total profits of $\$220 - \$102 = \$118$. Of this lost $118, only $90 appeared in the government's treasury. Where did the other $28, the excess burden, disappear to? We can see what happened by looking back at the demand and supply curves in Figure 3.2. Before the tax was put into place, the suppliers with Seller Costs of $18 and $23 also sold apples and the demanders with Buyer Values of $30 and $25 also bought apples. If a Sales Tax of $15 is imposed, there is no way that any of these traders could make a trade with each other that would result in an after-tax profit for both parties.[3] In the absence of a tax, mutually profitable trades could be arranged to include the eight omitted suppliers and demanders. In fact, you will notice that the sum of the buyer values of the four omitted demanders is $110 and the sum of the seller costs of the four omitted suppliers is $82. The $\$110 - \$82 = \$28$ total profits that they could have made by trading in the absence of a tax, is precisely equal to the excess burden that we found in the previous paragraph.

A Geometric Treatment

In Figure 3.4 we show profits, tax revenue, and excess burden geometrically. In the absence of tax the competitive equilibrium price is $24 and the number of bushels sold is 10. Total profits of buyers and sellers is represented by the

---

[3]We can see this because the difference between the Buyer Values and Seller Costs of any two of these traders is less than $15.

area between the demand and supply curve to the left of the point marked "Old Equilibrium." This area is the sum of the areas of the four regions marked A, B, C, and D.

Figure 3.4: Profits and Tax Revenue

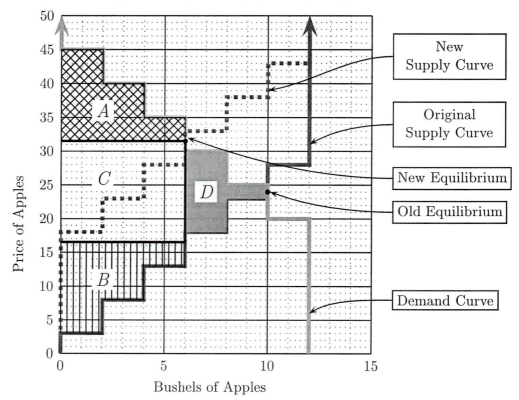

As we have discovered previously, when a $15 sales tax is collected from sellers, the equilibrium price rises to $31.50 and only 6 bushels of apples are sold. With the tax in place, the total profit of demanders is equal to the area of the region marked A. When suppliers have to pay the tax, although the price is $31.50, the after-tax revenue received by suppliers is only $31.50 − $15 = $16.50 per bushel of apples. Their total profit is equal to the area of the region labeled B.

Total tax revenue is the number of bushels sold with the tax times the tax rate. The height of the box labeled C is equal to the tax rate ($15) and the width of C is the number of bushels sold (6). f Therefore total tax revenue is equal to the area of region C.

We observed that total profits in the absence of a tax is the sum of the areas of regions A, B, C, and D. We found that when the tax is collected, total profits plus tax revenue is the sum of the areas of regions A, B, and C. The excess burden (deadweight loss) from the sales tax is the difference between these two areas, which is just the area of region D.

Tax Rates and Tax Revenue

It is interesting to notice that the amount of revenue that the government collects from a sales tax does not always increase when tax rates increase. The reason is that as a commodity is more heavily taxed, the number of units decreases and thus, although the government collects more tax per unit sold, it is able to collect taxes on fewer units. You can explore the relation between tax rates and tax revenue by working the following exercise.

Exercise: Tax Rates and Tax Revenue[4]

Exercise 3.1   Using the supply and demand curves for apples given in Figure 3.5:

a) Complete Table 3.2 to show how the government's tax revenue depends on the sales tax rate. **Hint:** To fill out this table, you might want to trace a copy of Figure 3.5 on scratch paper and draw the demand curve and some shifted supply curves for the various tax rates.

b) What is the greatest amount of revenue that the government can

get by choosing one of these tax rates?   _____

c) Of the tax rates listed in Table 3.2, the government will get the

most revenue from the rates $_____ and $_____ .

d) There are two different tax rates that raise the same maximum amount of tax revenue. Which of these two tax rates results in the

smaller excess burden?   _____

---

[4]Answers are found on page 77.

Figure 3.5: Supply and Demand for Apples

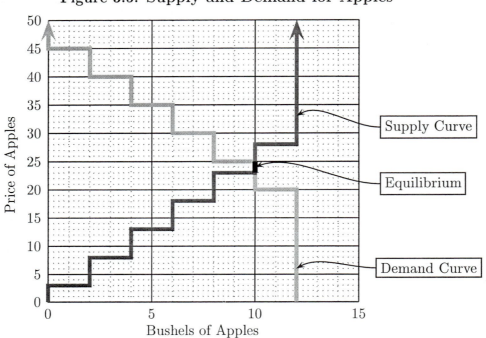

Bushels of Apples

Table 3.2: Revenue and Tax Rate

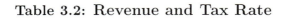

Tax Rate	Number of Sales	Tax Revenue
$0	10	$0
$5	8	$40
$10	8	$80
$15	6	$90
$20		
$25		
$30		
$35		
$40	2	$80
$50	0	$0

The Effects of a Subsidy

A **subsidy** is a negative tax. If the government pays a subsidy of $15 per bushel to apple suppliers, then any supplier who sells a bushel of apples gets the price from the buyer *plus* a $15 subsidy from the government. Similarly, if the government pays a $15 per bushel subsidy to apple demanders, then any apple demander who buys a bushel of apples receives his Buyer Value *plus* the $15 subsidy.

A good way for you to practice using supply and demand curves is to work out the predicted effects of a subsidy paid to apple buyers. To do this, you need to ask yourself two questions. You guessed it. What does the subsidy do to the supply curve? What does it do to the demand curve?

Exercise: Subsidies and Taxes

Exercise 3.2 Suppose that the government pays a subsidy of $15 to every demander who buys a bushel of apples.

a) How will the subsidy affect a demander's willingness to pay for

apples? _____

b) What will the subsidy do to the demand curve for apples? (**Hint:** Recall that a $15 *tax* paid by buyers shifted the demand curve *down* by $15.)

_____

c) How will the subsidy affect the lowest price that a supplier is willing

to accept for a bushel of apples? _____

d) Does the subsidy change the supply curve? _____

Exercise 3.3
a) On Figure 3.6, draw a dashed line to show the demand curve when a $15 per bushel subsidy is paid to demanders.
b) How does this subsidy affect the equilibrium quantity of apples

sold? _____

c) How does this subsidy affect the equilibrium price range?

_____

Figure 3.6: Supply and Demand with a Subsidy

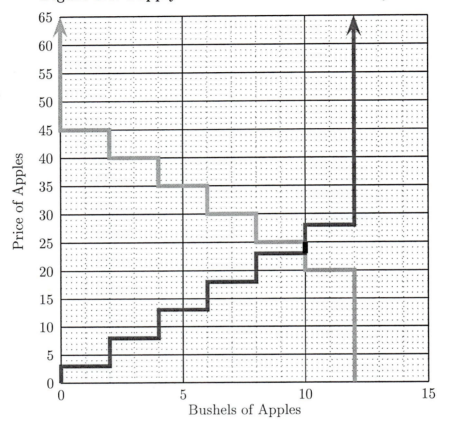

Bushels of Apples

Exercise 3.4 Suppose that in addition to paying a subsidy of $15 to buyers for every apple purchased, the government also collects a tax of $15 from sellers for every apple sold.
a) How would this tax affect the supply curve? the demand curve?

_____

b) Use a dashed red line to draw the supply curve when the tax is imposed.
c) Compare the equilibrium number of bushels of apples traded when the subsidy is paid and the tax collected to the number of bushels traded if there is no tax and no subsidy.

_____

d) Compare the equilibrium price range when the subsidy is paid and

the tax collected to the price if there is no tax and no subsidy. _____

e) Compare the (after-tax) total profits of suppliers when the subsidy is paid and the tax collected to total profits if there is no tax and no

subsidy. _____

f) Compare the (after-subsidy) total consumers' surplus when the subsidy is paid and the tax is collected to the total consumers' surplus if

there is no tax and no subsidy. _____

g) When the government pays a subsidy of $15 per bushel to every buyer and collects a $15 per bushel tax from every seller, compare the amount of money that the government pays out in the subsidy to the

amount that it collects from the tax. _____

Answers to Warm-up Exercises

W 3.1: $5, $20; **W 3.2**: $20, $5; **W 3.3**: $30; **W 3.4**: $15.

Answers to Exercises

Ex. 3.1: a) 6, $120; 4, $100; 4, $120; 2, $70; b)$120; c)$20, $30; d)$20; **Ex. 3.2**: a) Increase it by $15; b) It shifts up by $15; c) No change; d) No; **Ex. 3.3**: b) It rises from 10 to 12; c) It rises from $23–25 to $28–35; **Ex. 3.4**: a) Tax shifts supply curve up by $15, does not change the demand curve; c) They are the same; d) Price range moves from $23–25 to $38–40; e) Suppliers' profits are the same in both cases; f) Consumers' surplus is the same in both cases; g) They are the same.

Drawing the Curves in Figure 3.1

These are the details on how the demand and supply curves in Figure 3.1 were drawn.[5] At prices below $3, the supply is zero. This explains the vertical segment of the supply curve running from $(0,0)$ to $(0,3)$. At a price of $3, the two lowest-cost suppliers are just indifferent between supplying and not supplying their apples, so the supply can be any quantity between 0 and 2. This explains the flat part of the first step of the supply curve running from $(0,3)$ to $(2,3)$. According to Table 3.1, the second lowest-cost suppliers have costs of $8. At prices between $3 and $8, only the two lowest-cost suppliers would want to supply, so the supply schedule contains a vertical segment running from $(2,3)$ to $(2,8)$.

The top of the second step in the supply-curve stairway is drawn at a height of $8, the price where supply from the next lowest-cost group of suppliers kicks in. At a price of $8, the two lowest-cost suppliers would surely want to sell apples and the two suppliers with the second-lowest costs would be just indifferent between selling and not selling. So at this price, the supply can be anything between 2 and 4. This gives us the flat top of the second step, a segment running from $(2,8)$ to $(4,8)$. In the same way as we drew the first two steps, we add more steps to the supply curve as the price rises and more sellers enter the market. This continues until we have reached a price of $28, at which each of the 12 sellers in the market is willing to supply a bushel of apples. Since every supplier in this market has only one bushel to sell, increasing the price above $28 will not bring in any more supply. Thus, at prices higher than $28, the supply curve is vertical with 12 bushels of apples being provided.

The demand curve is constructed in a similar fashion. At prices higher than $45, nobody wants to buy. At prices between $45 and $40, only the two highest-value demanders want to buy. At prices between $40 and $35, the four highest-value demanders will want to buy, and so on.

---

[5]If you already understand how to draw these curves, there is no need for you to read this section.

Lab Notes for Experiment 3

Recording Transactions, Prices, and Profits

For the last round of each session, use Tables 3.3, 3.4, and 3.5 to record the price, Seller Cost, and Buyer Value in each transaction. Complete these tables by calculating the seller's profit, the buyer's profit, and total profits in each transaction. The profits to be recorded are *after-tax* profits. When the seller has to pay the tax, if the price is P and the seller's Seller Cost is C, then the seller's profit is $P - C - 15$. When the buyer has to pay the tax, if the buyer pays a price of P and the buyer's Buyer Value is V, the buyer's profit is $V - P - 15$. Total profits for any transaction is the sum of the seller's profit and the buyer's profit on that transaction.

Recording Market Fundamentals

After trading is completed your instructor will post the number of suppliers and demanders of each type and their Seller Costs and Buyer Values. In this experiment, the number of suppliers and demanders of each type will be the same in all three sessions. Copy this information into Table 3.6.

Computing Market Statistics

The information needed to complete Table 3.7 can be obtained from Tables 3.3, 3.4, and 3.5. For Session 1, no taxes are collected. To calculate total taxes collected in the last rounds of Sessions 2 and 3, multiply the number of transactions in the session by the tax on each transaction. Total Profits of sellers and of buyers in Sessions 2 and 3 should be calculated as after-tax profits.

Table 3.3: Transactions in Session 1–Last Round

(No Taxes)

Trans-action	Price	Seller Cost	Buyer Value	Seller's Profit	Buyer's Profit	Total Profit
1						
2						
3						
4						
5						
6						
7						
8						
9						
10						
11						
12						
13						
14						
15						
16						
17						
18						
19						
20						
21						
22						
23						
24						
25						

Table 3.4: Transactions in Session 2–Last Round

(Sellers Pay Sales Tax)

Trans-action	Price	Seller Cost	Buyer Value	Seller's Profit	Buyer's Profit	Total Profit
1						
2						
3						
4						
5						
6						
7						
8						
9						
10						
11						
12						
13						
14						
15						
16						
17						
18						
19						
20						
21						
22						
23						
24						
25						

Table 3.5: Transactions in Session 3–Last Round

(Buyers Pay Sales Tax)

Trans-action	Price	Seller Cost	Buyer Value	Seller's Profit	Buyer's Profit	Total Profit
1						
2						
3						
4						
5						
6						
7						
8						
9						
10						
11						
12						
13						
14						
15						
16						
17						
18						
19						
20						
21						
22						
23						
24						
25						

Table 3.6: Distribution of Types of Agents

Seller Cost	Number in Market	Buyer Value	Number in Market
28		20	
23		25	
18		30	
13		35	
8		40	
3		45	

Table 3.7: Market Statistics

	Session 1	Session 2	Session 3
Mean Price			
Number of Transactions			
Total Taxes Collected			
Total Profit of Sellers			
Total Profit of Buyers			
Total Profits Plus Taxes Collected			

Experiment 4

Prohibition

You are in a seedy neighborhood; it is past midnight and a cold drizzle is falling. You see three kinds of people on the street. There are demanders, hoping to buy drugs, suppliers, hoping to sell drugs, and police, hoping to arrest drug sellers and confiscate drugs.

This experiment concerns a partially successful government effort to suppress trade in drugs. In Session 1 of the experiment, the drug market is not illegal and there is no police interference. In Session 2, buying and selling drugs is made illegal. The police are not able to prevent all trades, but they do manage to intercept half of the trades made and to destroy the confiscated material. In Session 3 the drug trade is outlawed as in Session but in this session, instead of destroying the drugs that they confiscate, police resell them to the original buyers at prevailing market prices.[1]

Instructions

In experiment, some participants will be drug suppliers and some will be demanders. Some of the drug demanders will be casual users and some l be addicts.

Suppliers' Instructions

In ns of this experiment, suppliers can produce at most two units of cluding drugs that are confiscated by police. Suppliers have a Sel of $10 for each unit that they produce. Since each buyer can

_____

[1] unt of class time available is short, your instructor may choose not to run Sess

buy at most one unit of drugs, a supplier who wants to sell two units must deal with two different buyers.

In Session 1 the drug market is free from police intervention. Each supplier can sell zero, one, or two units of drugs. Sellers who want to sell two units must find two different buyers and fill out separate sales contracts with each of them.

In Session 2 the police intercept half of the sales contracts as they are brought to the market manager. In Session 2, sellers must make at least two sales before they can turn them in to the market manager. After a seller has signed up his first buyer, he or she must find a second buyer and then turn in the two sales contracts simultaneously. When a seller brings two contracts to the market manager, the police will randomly select one of these contracts and confiscate the drugs that were sold with that contract. The seller will have to pay the $10 Seller Cost for each of the two units that she sold, and she will also have to pay a $5 fine. The buyer whose contract was confiscated will not have to pay the sales price that he agreed to pay the seller, and he will not get the drugs. The sale that was recorded on the unconfiscated drug contract will go through without interference. Buyers whose contracts were seized by the police can return to the market and try to make another deal.

In Session 3, the police confiscate drugs and fine the sellers, just as they did in Session 2, but in this session the police resell the confiscated drugs. They will sell the confiscated item to the original buyer at the same price that was originally contracted between buyer and seller.

Demanders' Instructions

There are two kinds of demanders in this market:

- *Addicts* have a Buyer Value of $30. An addict who buys a unit of drugs for price P will have a profit of $30 − P$. Addicts who *do not* buy a unit of drugs will suffer severe withdrawal systems which result in a *loss* of $20.

- *Casual users* have Buyer Values of $15. A casual user who buys a unit of drugs for price P will have a profit of $15 − P$. A casual user who *does not* buy a unit of drugs will have a profit of $0.

As in previous markets, demanders can buy either zero or one unit. In Session 2, there is an extra complication for demanders. Half of the sales contracts are intercepted by the police. If a buyer's contract is intercepted, the police will tell him that his seller got caught. When this happens, the buyer does not get the unit that he agreed to buy, but he also does not have to pay the amount that he agreed to pay on that contract. When a contract is intercepted, the buyer is free to try to make another purchase from another supplier.

In Session 3, half the sales are again intercepted by the police. In this session, however, when the police seize the drugs, they do not destroy them, but simply sell them to the buyer at the price the buyer had agreed to pay the drug dealer. The drug dealer gets no money for the confiscated drugs and has to pay a $5 fine.

Warm-up Exercise

After reading the instructions for this experiment, please check your understanding by answering the following questions.[2]

W 4.1 In Session 2 you are a supplier and you agree to sell two units of drugs, each at a price of $40. You bring the contracts to the market manager. The police confiscate one of the units and fine you $5. You have to pay the $10 Seller Cost for each of the two units of output. What are

your total profits?_____

W 4.2 In Session 2 you are a supplier and you sell two units of drugs, one for $50 and one for $20. Your production costs are $10 per unit and when the police catch you they make you pay a $5 fine. If the police confiscate

the unit you sold for $20, how much profit (or loss) do you make?_____
If the police had confiscated the unit you sold for $50, how much profit (or

loss) would you have made?_____

W 4.3 You are an addict. You have searched the marketplace and the lowest price at which you can get a unit of drugs is $40. What would your

profit (or loss) be if you bought at $40? _____What would your profit

(or loss) be if you did not buy any drugs? _____

W 4.4 An addict is better off buying a unit of drugs rather than not buying

any drugs, as long as the price is lower than _____.

---

[2]Answers to these warm-up exercises can be found on page 107.

What Do You Expect to See?

■   Would you expect that making it illegal to sell a drug would cause the street price of that drug to increase or to decrease? _____

■   Do you think that making it illegal to sell a drug would increase or decrease the amount of money spent on this drug: by addicts? _____

_____ by casual users? _____ in total?

_____

■   Suppose that the police confiscated drugs whenever they caught a drug seller, but then resold the drugs to users at the going street price. How do you think the police activity will affect the amount of drugs consumed?

_____

Discussion of Experiment 4

Illegal Markets

Governments sometimes attempt to regulate trade by taxing certain markets or by enforcing price floors or ceilings. Sometimes they take more dramatic measures by passing **prohibition laws** that make trade illegal in certain markets. Here are some examples of markets in which governments have attempted to enforce prohibition.

- In the period from 1920 to 1933, the United States government prohibited the purchase and sale of alcoholic beverages.

- In almost all states in the United States, it is currently illegal to sell alcoholic beverages to minors.

- Federal and local governments in the United States (and many other countries) prohibit the purchase and sale of certain drugs that are believed to be addictive and/or otherwise harmful.

- In many states and countries gambling is illegal (except through state-sponsored lotteries).

- In most states and localities in the United States prostitution is illegal.

- It is illegal in most countries to buy or sell animals (or body parts of animals) belonging to endangered species.

- In the 1950s, the sale of yellow-dyed margarine was illegal in the states of Minnesota and Wisconsin.

- In the United States and in many other countries, until relatively recently, it was illegal to perform abortions.

- In the 1980s a law was passed in the United States prohibiting the sale of human body organs to transplant recipients.

- In most countries it is illegal to buy and sell children for adoption.

- In most countries, including the United States since 1863, it is illegal to buy and sell human slaves.

A variety of motives impel governments to pass prohibition laws. Some lawmakers reason that consumers do not realize the harm caused by drugs, alcohol, and gambling. Such lawmakers support prohibition of these goods in hopes of protecting consumers from making ill-advised choices. Lawmakers who favor endangered species legislation aim to protect the endangered animals from being captured or killed for the market. The prohibition against yellow-dyed margarine in Minnesota and Wisconsin was maintained by political pressure from dairy farmers who feared that the availability of colored margarine would reduce the demand for butter.[3] We leave it to you to speculate about the motives for the other prohibitions mentioned.

Whatever the motives for suppressing certain markets, prohibitions typically fail to *eliminate* trade in the prohibited good. Prohibition of alcohol did not eliminate alcohol consumption. In the 1950s "oleo-smugglers" would sneak truckloads of colored oleo-margarine into Minnesota and Wisconsin to be sold to eager consumers. The War on Drugs has not eliminated the consumption of marijuana, cocaine, or heroin. Prohibition of gambling and prostitution are only partially effective.

Supply and Demand of Illegal Goods

In order to determine the effects of a policy designed to discourage sales of a commodity, we need to look at the way that this policy influences the supply and demand curves for the commodity.

How Does Confiscation and Destruction Affect the Supply Curve?

In Session 2 the police intercept half of all transactions, and when they intercept a transaction they confiscate and destroy the goods that the supplier was trying to sell and fine the supplier.

How does this policy affect the supply curve? In Session 1 the Seller Cost was $10 per unit. At prices below $10 per unit, drug dealers would not want to sell any drugs. At prices above $10, each drug dealer would supply two units. Thus, the supply curve will have a horizontal portion at a price of $10 running from a quantity of zero to a quantity of twice the number of drug dealers. In Session 2 every supplier realizes that for each unit that she is able to sell, she will have to supply *two* units and pay a fine. Since

---

[3]Margarine is made primarily from vegetable oils, while butter is made from milk.

the cost of producing a single unit is $10 and the fine is $5,[4] the cost to a supplier of making a successful sale is $25 per unit. Therefore, with the drug-enforcement policy, drug dealers would not want to supply any drugs at prices below $25, but each drug dealer would try to sell two units at prices higher than $25. Thus we see that the drug-enforcement policy pushes the flat part of the supply curve up from $10 to $25.

This upward shift is not the only effect on the supply curve. Remember that when a drug dealer tries to sell two units, only one of these units gets to the demanders and the other unit is destroyed. In our previous experiments, the amount of a good that demanders get is the same as the amount that suppliers produce. A supply curve is intended to show the quantity of goods that *reaches the demanders* at any price. If police confiscate and destroy half of the drugs produced, then only half of the drugs produced reach the demanders. At prices above $25, each drug dealer tries to sell two units, but succeeds in selling only one unit to demanders. Thus the total amount of drugs supplied at prices above $25 is only one unit per drug dealer rather than two units. The enforcement policy shifts the vertical portion of the supply curve inward, toward the vertical axis.

So far we have discussed cases where the police are always able to seize exactly half of the drugs that each dealer tries to sell. In the real world each drug dealer faces uncertainty about whether the police will catch him. For any sale, there will be some probability, π, that the sale is intercepted. In deciding whether to sell drugs, suppliers who are trying to maximize their expected profits will sell only if the price of drugs is high enough so that on average they will make a profit. We can make calculations very similar to those we made for the case where the police intercept exactly half of all sales. When we do so, we will find that the threat of confiscation and a fine shifts the supply curve upward, and that the larger the fine and the higher the probability of getting caught the further upward the supply curve is shifted.[5]

An example will help us to see how the supply curve shifts.

---

[4] In the experiment we use a fine rather than imprisonment, since the latter seems impractical for a classroom experiment. If the punishment is a prison term, we can analyze the problem by attributing a money cost to the harm that one suffers by being sent to prison.

[5] With some calculations, one can show that if the probability that a supplier is caught is π, the fine is F, and the Seller Cost is C, then the supplier's expected payoff from trying to sell a unit of the illegal good at price P is $(1 - \pi)P - \pi F - C$. Trying to sell drugs is profitable on average only if $(1 - \pi)P - \pi F > C$ or, equivalently, only if $P > \frac{C}{(1-\pi)} + \frac{\pi F}{(1-\pi)}$.

Figure 4.1: Confiscation and Destruction

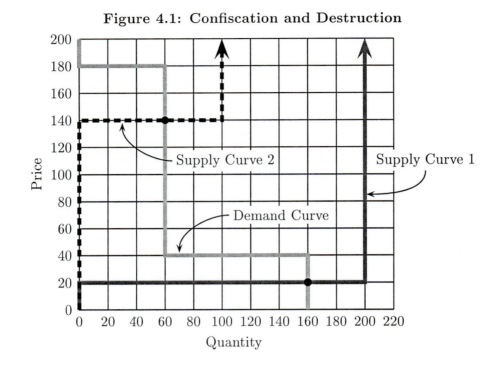

Example:

Consider a market with 20 suppliers, each of whom can produce up to 10 units of output, and suppose that the cost of producing a unit is $C = \$20$. If the police do not interfere with sales, suppliers will want to supply nothing at prices below \$20, but at prices above \$20, each of the 20 suppliers will want to supply 10 units, so the total supply would be 200 units. The resulting supply curve is shown as *Supply Curve 1* in Figure 4.1. Now suppose that half of the sales that a supplier tries to make are intercepted by the police, who confiscate and destroy the unit that the supplier is trying to sell, and make the supplier pay a fine of $F = \$100$. Then for every unit that she successfully sells, a supplier has to produce two units and pay a fine of $\$F$. It will be profitable for a seller to produce and try to sell output only if $P > 2C + F = \$140$. Therefore the drug enforcement policy pushes the horizontal part of the supply curve up to \$140. At prices above \$140, each supplier will produce and try to sell 10 units, but half of these units will be confiscated and destroyed, so that only 5 of the units she produces will reach consumers. Therefore at prices higher than \$140, each of the 20 suppliers will supply 5 units to consumers, so that the total amount supplied is $20 \times 5 = 100$. The resulting supply curve is shown as *Supply Curve 2* in Figure 4.1.

How Does Confiscation and Resale Affect the Supply Curve?

Now let us see what happens to the supply curve of goods reaching consumers if, as in Session 3 of our experiment, the police resell the goods that they confiscate instead of destroying them.

As in the case where confiscated goods are destroyed, suppliers must take into account the fact that some of their attempted sales will be confiscated and they will be fined. As before, this causes the supply curve to shift upward, where the amount of the upward shift is greater, the higher the probability that they are caught and the larger the fine. In contrast to the case where police destroy the confiscated goods, all goods that are produced ultimately get to the consumers. It is only a question of whether they pass through the hands of the police on the way. At first you might think that confiscating illegal goods will have no effect on consumption, since all of the goods produced wind up in the hands of the consumers, whether or not they are confiscated. But when you think about how this policy affects the supply curve, you will realize that despite the fact that the confiscated goods are resold, the enforcement policy raises each supplier's costs. This pushes the supply curve upward and as a result, the equilibrium price will be higher, and consumption will be lower, than would have been the case if there had been no police interference.

Example:

> Supply and demand in the absence of police interference are the same as in our previous example. We redraw these curves in Figure 4.2, where the supply curve in the absence of police interference is labeled *Supply Curve 1*. Suppose that the police intercept half of the sales that suppliers attempt to make, and that when they intercept a sale they confiscate the goods from the seller, fine the seller $100, and resell the confiscated goods to demanders at the same price that the suppliers were charging. What does the resulting supply curve look like? Suppliers will not want to supply any drugs unless their expected profit is positive. This will be the case only if the price is greater than $140. So no drugs are available at prices below $140 per unit. However, at prices above $140, each of the 20 suppliers will try to sell 10 units of the good. Since the police resell everything that they confiscate, all 20 units can reach consumers. So the quantity supplied to consumers is 200 units at all prices above $140. The supply curve with confiscation and resale is drawn as *Supply Curve 3* in Figure 4.2.

How Does Punishing Suppliers Affect Demanders?

If the police punish the suppliers only, as we postulated in Sessions 2 and 3, then their enforcement policy has no effect on the amount that demanders

Figure 4.2: Confiscation and Resale

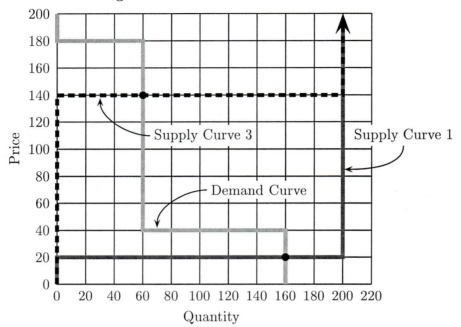

are willing to pay for a unit of the illegal commodity, and so the demand curve remains unchanged.

Although the demand curve remains unchanged, an upward shift of the supply curve will result in a higher price and a lower total amount consumed. In our experimental sessions, the price of drugs rose sufficiently that casual users stopped using drugs while addicts continued to purchase them.

These observations from our experiments illustrate some general principles about policies that attempt to reduce drug consumption by punishing suppliers. Harsh enforcement policies can be expected to have the following effects.

- The street price of drugs will increase as punishment becomes harsher.

- Harsher enforcement will reduce consumption by casual users, but will have little effect on consumption by addicts.

- The higher price of drugs makes drug addiction a much more serious problem for addicts than it would be if drugs were available at competitive prices without police intervention. Being addicted to something expensive is much worse for addicts than being addicted to something cheap.

- Harsher drug enforcement may increase, rather than decrease, *total* expenditure on drugs. If drug users use illegal means such as theft or prostitution to acquire money for purchases, than harsh drug enforcement is likely to increase the frequency of these crimes.

These effects can be illustrated for the market with the supply and demand curves shown in Figure 4.1. Suppose that in this economy there are 60 addicts, each of whom is willing to pay up to $180 for a unit of drugs, and there are 100 casual users, each of whom is willing to pay up to $40 for a unit of drugs. The resulting demand curve is shown in Figure 4.1. When drugs are legal, the supply curve is given by *Supply Curve 1*. In this case, the competitive equilibrium price is $20 per unit and drugs are purchased by all 60 addicts and all 100 casual users. With the police policy of confiscation and fines, the supply curve becomes *Supply Curve 2*, and the price is pushed up to $140. At this price the casual users no longer buy drugs, but all 60 of the addicts continue to do so. The total amount of money spent on drugs *rises* from $20 × 160 = $3200 to $140 × 60 = $8400.

Drug Policies that Affect the Demand Curve

In our experiment, the policy of punishing suppliers affected the supply curve but did not influence the demand curve. In the real world, anti-drug policies can, and do, influence the demand curve. Two quite different types of policies can cause the demand curve to shift downward. There are policies that reduce demanders' willingness to pay for drugs by persuasion or by the provision of substitute goods. There are also policies that punish drug buyers and hence increase the cost of buying drugs above the price paid to suppliers.

Information and Treatment

Let us first consider policies that reduce demanders' willingness to pay. For people who are not addicts, such policies include dispersal of reliable information on the dangers of drug use and provision of alternative recreational activities. Addicts' cravings for drugs will probably not be much reduced by further information on the health consequences of drug addiction. On the other hand, the availability of treatment facilities and of less harmful substitutes for the drug to which they are addicted may help them reduce their dependence and return to normal lives. Expenditures on research into the nature and possible cures of drug addiction are likely to lead to improved ways to help addicts to escape their addiction.

Demand and supply analysis suggests an important lesson about drug intervention policies, which we ask you to demonstrate to yourself in the following exercise.[6]

Exercise: Alternative Drug Interventions

In Figure 4.3 we have drawn an upward-sloping supply curve and a downward-sloping demand curve for drugs. As you see from the graph, the competitive equilibrium in this market has a price of $50 and a quantity of 150 units sold.

Exercise 4.1 Suppose that the government introduces a policy of punishing suppliers, and that this policy shifts the supply curve upward by $60 at every quantity. Draw the new supply curve on Figure 4.3.

With the shifted supply curve, the new equilibrium price is $_____

and the new equilibrium quantity is _____.

Exercise 4.2 Suppose that instead of punishing suppliers, the government offers an information and treatment program that reduces the willingness to pay of every demander by $60, but leaves the supply curve as originally shown on the graph. Draw the new demand curve that applies after the introduction of the information and treatment program. With the shifted demand curve, the equilibrium price

is $_____ and the equilibrium quantity is _____.

If you drew your curves correctly, you will find that both of the policies reduced consumption from 150 units to 100 units. The enforcement policy of punishing suppliers resulted in a competitive equilibrium price of $100 per unit, while the demand-reduction policy of information and treatment resulted in a much lower competitive equilibrium price of $40.

If the two policies were equally expensive, which would you prefer? Both accomplish the same reduction in consumption, but one increases the price paid by drug users and the other decreases this price. People who take a

---

[6]Answers to this exercise can be found on Page 107.

Figure 4.3: Alternative Drug Policies

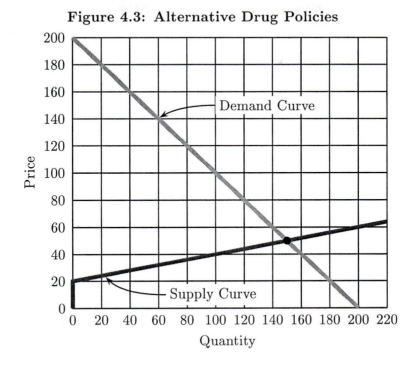

punitive view might favor the enforcement approach on the grounds that drug users are the enemy and deserve to be made miserable. People who think that drug addicts are unfortunate, much like those with an illness, may prefer the demand-reduction strategy on the grounds that if drug prices are high, addicts are likely to suffer from both poverty and ill health. One of the major social costs of drug-addiction is thought to be the fact that many addicts commit crimes in order to raise enough money to buy drugs. A policy that results in lower prices with the same amount of consumption would be preferable on this account.

Punishing Demanders

In our experiment, the police punished people trying to sell drugs, but did not directly punish people trying to buy drugs. In many markets for prohibited goods, police will punish both suppliers and demanders. In most places in the United States, possession of marijuana, cocaine, or heroin is a felony. Buyers who have purchased these commodities can be arrested and imprisoned. The effect of such punishment is to make the cost of drugs to a buyer higher than the price he pays the seller. This in turn causes the demand curve to shift downward. In the resulting equilibrium, the price that the buyer pays to the seller is lower than it would be if demanders were not punished. But the total cost to the buyer of buying drugs must include the cost that the buyers place on the probability of punishment. This effect can be illustrated in Figure 4.3. Suppose that demand and supply are as originally drawn on this figure, and that instead of punishing drug sellers, the police imprison drug buyers whenever they catch them. If with each purchase, the risk of getting caught and imprisoned is equivalent to a loss of $60, then the demand curve would shift down by $60 and would be in the same position as the demand curve that you drew for the case where the government reduced demand by persuasion and treatment. Just as in the case of the other demand-reducing policy, the resulting equilibrium consumption would be 100 units and the equilibrium price that buyers pay sellers would be $40. But when buyers are punished, this is not the only cost that they pay. They also bear the risk of prison, which is equivalent to a cost of $60. This means that the actual cost of purchasing drugs is equivalent to $100. Thus the outcome where demanders are punished directly is neither worse nor better for drug users than the outcome where suppliers are punished.

It is worth noticing that the policy of punishing drug buyers shifts the demand curve for drugs in the same way that it would be shifted by a sales tax of $60 paid by buyers. There is, however, an important difference. With the sales tax, the government collects revenue. With imprisonment, the government has costs, but no revenue.

Effects of the "War on Drugs" in the United States

In the past 20 years, the federal, state, and local governments in the United States have dramatically increased expenditures on enforcement of laws against the use and sale of such illegal drugs as marijuana, cocaine, and heroine. A recent article by Ernest Drucker, a professor of epidemiology and public medicine,[7] reports a wealth of statistical information.

Federal expenditures on drug control enforcement increased from about $1 billion in 1981 to more than $10 billion in 1998. The federal government spends more than twice as much money on enforcement as they do on treatment, prevention, and research in drug-related areas. In 1980, approximately 50,000 people were in prison for drug law violations. In 1995, this number had grown to more than 400,000. Drug offenders constitute 60% of all federal prisoners and more than 25% of state and local prisoners. More

---

[7] *Public Health Reports*, vol 114, no. 1, January/February, 1999.

than 90% of drug offenders are arrested for possession or low-level drug deals to support their personal use.[8]

The National Household Survey on Drug Abuse reports annually on the percentage of a large sample population who report using illegal drugs in the month before being surveyed. The percentage of the adult population reporting use of marijuana has declined from 13% in 1979 to less than 5% in 1996. The percentage using cocaine rose from just over 2% in 1979 to nearly 5% in 1988, but declined to less than 1% in 1996. Reported use of heroin has remained roughly constant at less than 0.1% throughout this period.

Although the fraction of the population that uses illegal drugs has greatly diminished since 1979, the number of persons suffering severe or fatal consequences from drug overdoses has risen during the same period. The number of drug-related admissions to hospital emergency rooms rose by 60% from 1978 to 1994, and the number of deaths from overdoses more than quadrupled over the same period. More than 90% of the deaths are due to overdoses of heroin and cocaine. The increase in the death rates from overdoses has taken place over all age ranges of users.[9]

The fact that reported use of illegal drugs has fallen while drug-related emergency room admissions and deaths have risen suggests that casual use of illegal drugs has diminished while the amount of severe addiction has increased. This result is roughly consistent with the predictions of supply and demand theory, which suggests that a harsh enforcement policy increases the price of drugs, causing casual use of drugs to fall without significantly reducing consumption by addicts. Although demand and supply theory do not suggest that harsh enforcement would actually *increase* the number of persons addicted to drugs, the theory does suggest that such policies, by making addiction extremely expensive, will force many drug addicts into lives of poverty, crime, and prostitution, which in turn are likely to increase the risk of severe health consequences from addiction.

Politicians have often claimed success in the "war on drugs." For example, in the preface to the *National Drug Control Strategy, 1998*, President Clinton announced that

> "We are making a difference. Drug use is down 50% in the last decade."

---

[8]The prison and arrest statistics reported in Drucker's article come from U.S. Department of Justice publications.

[9]The statistics on drug usage, emergency-room visits, and fatalities are reported in Drucker's article, and are taken from publications of the U.S. Department of Health and Human Services.

Certainly the drug enforcement policies of the last twenty years have "made a difference." The number of people in prison for drug offenses has increased by more than 350,000, and every year $10 billion dollars are being spent on police enforcement of the drug laws. There are indications that this effort has contributed to a reduction in casual drug use. But if the war on drugs is intended to reduce the *damage* from drugs, then it is hard to see that the difference that government intervention has made is a difference for the better. If we take as indicators of the damage done by drugs the number of hospitalizations caused by severe drug addiction, the number of deaths from drug overdoses, and the number of persons put in prison for drug offenses, then a plausible case can be made that the war on drugs has done more harm than good.

In the light of the comparison that we made between the effects of enforcement and those of demand reduction, it is interesting to notice that the federal government spends twice as much money on drug enforcement as it does on treatment, prevention, and research. Most people would probably agree that if the costs were the same, a downward shift of the demand curve is preferable to an equal-sized upward shift of the supply curve. Of course there is no reason to believe that an extra dollar spent on demand-reduction would move the demand curve down by as much as an extra dollar spent on enforcement moves the supply curve up. It would be useful to know more about this tradeoff. Unfortunately questions like this are rarely raised in political discussions.

Topics for Discussion

The issue of when governments should prohibit voluntary transactions is of major social importance. Thinking about which goods should or should not be prohibited and predicting the economic effects of prohibition policy is an excellent way to develop your understanding of economic theory.

■ What argument(s) would you make in favor of a prohibition on addictive drugs, knowing that any such prohibition will be imperfectly enforced?

■ Suppose that the government decided to legalize trade in marijuana, cocaine, and heroin, but in order to reduce consumption it imposed a sales tax that was about as large as the difference between current seller costs and the current street price of these drugs. Assuming that the collection of the tax could be costlessly enforced, how do you think the amount of drugs consumed would be affected?

■   If there were no police enforcement of the tax described in the previous question, some suppliers would certainly sell the material illegally, without paying the tax. But if the same police effort that is currently devoted to confiscating illegal sales were devoted to punishing suppliers who did not pay their tax, how much tax evasion do you think there would be?

■   Compare the effects on government budgets of a policy of imprisoning drug buyers as contrasted to taxing them. (To do this carefully, you might want to investigate the annual cost to taxpayers of keeping a prisoner in jail and estimate the number of people that need to be put in jail in order to maintain the current level of enforcement.)

■   Are there any commodities that are currently legally sold that you think should be prohibited? Explain why.

■   Discuss some commodity (other than drugs) that the government currently makes it illegal to sell. Explain why you think prohibition of this market is either a good or a bad idea.

■   Can you think of illegal markets where sellers are punished more frequently or severely than buyers? where buyers are punished more frequently than sellers? where both parties are punished with similar frequency and severity?

Answers to Warm-up Exercises

W 4.1: $40 - $25 = $15; **W 4.2**: $50 - $25 = $25, $20 - $25 = -$5; **W 4.3**: loss of $10, loss of $20; **W 4.4**: $50.

Answers to Questions

Ex. 4.1: $100, 100; **Ex. 4.2**: $40, 100.

Lab Notes for Experiment 4

Recording Market Fundamentals

After the experiment has been run, the market manager will inform you of
the number of suppliers, addicts, and casual demanders who participated.
Record this information in Table 4.1.

Table 4.1: Number of Suppliers and Demanders

Participant Type	Number
Suppliers	
Addicted Demanders	
Casual Demanders	

Recording Prices and Buyer Values

In Table 4.2, for the last round of each session, record the price and the
Buyer Value for each sale that was actually carried out. Recall that addicts
have Buyer Values of $30 and casual users have Buyer Values of $15.

For Session 3, enter sales by police as well as by dealers. Put an asterisk
next to sales that were made by the police.

Computing Market Statistics

Complete Table 4.3 by recording the average price paid for drugs, the number of units of drugs sold to addicts and nonaddicts, and the profits of
buyers, sellers, and the police.

Table 4.2: Drug Sales—Last Round, All Sessions

Trans-action	Session 1		Session 2		Session 3	
	Sale Price	Buyer Value	Sale Price	Buyer Value	Sale Price	Buyer Value
1						
2						
3						
4						
5						
6						
7						
8						
9						
10						
11						
12						
13						
14						
15						
16						
17						
18						
19						
20						
21						
22						
23						
24						
25						

Table 4.3: Market Statistics

	Sess. 1	Sess. 2	Sess. 3
Mean Price			
Number of Sales			
Number of Units Consumed by Addicts			
Number of Units Consumed by Casual Users			
Total Amount of Money Demanders Spent on Drugs			
Total Revenue of Suppliers			
Total Profit of Suppliers			
Total Profit of Demanders			
Total Revenue of Police			

Hints for Completing Table 4.3

- The price at which each unit of drugs was sold is found in Table 4.2. From this information you can calculate the mean price and count the number of sales in each session. In Session 3, sales include sales from the police to consumers.

- Since addicts have Buyer Values of $30, you can find the number of units consumed by addicts in each session from Table 4.2 by counting the number of units purchased by buyers with Buyer Values of $30. Similarly, the number of units consumed by casual users is the number of units purchased by buyers with Buyer Values of $15.

- The total amount of money spent on drugs by consumers is the sum of the prices in each session reported in Table 4.2.

- In Sessions 1 and 2, Total Revenue of Suppliers is equal to the Total Amount of Money Demanders Spent on Drugs. In Session 3, some of the money that consumers spent on drugs went to the police. Total Revenue of Suppliers is the sum of the prices that appear in Table 4.2 without asterisks.

- Profits of Suppliers are equal to their revenue minus their costs. In Session 1, the total costs of suppliers are $10 times the number of units sold. In Sessions 2 and 3, every drug dealer who successfully sold a unit of drugs must have produced two units of drugs, one of which was confiscated. The cost of producing two units of drugs is $20. A drug dealer also had to pay a fine of $5 when she was caught selling. Therefore every drug dealer who sells one unit of drugs has costs of $25 and the total costs of drug dealers are equal to $25 times the number of units of drugs sold by dealers.

- Total Profit of Demanders is equal to the total profit of the buyers who bought a unit of drugs, minus the losses sustained by addicts who did *not* buy drugs (the $20 withdrawal costs). Each demander who bought a unit of drugs earned a profit equal to his Buyer Value minus the price that he paid for drugs. (Addicts who bought drugs do not have to pay the withdrawal cost.) To find the number of addicts who did not buy drugs, first find the total number of addicts participating in the market from Table 4.1. Then from Table 4.2, count the number of addicts who bought drugs (they have $30 Buyer Values). The difference between these two numbers is the number of addicts who did not buy drugs. Each addict who did not buy drugs has a loss of $20. Subtract the total losses of addicts who did not buy drugs from the sum of profits of those who did buy drugs to get total profits of demanders.

- In Sessions 2 and 3, the police revenue includes the amount of money they collect in fines. In Session 3, their revenue also includes the money that they get from reselling confiscated drugs. Sales by police are marked with an asterisk in Table 4.2.

Experiment 5

A Minimum Wage

People are often dissatisfied with the prices that emerge from competitive markets. Farmers think the price of corn is too low. Laborers would like higher wages. Renters want lower rents for their apartments. Borrowers believe that interest rates are too high. Party animals think that beer is too expensive...and so on. Occasionally, governments intervene in markets in the hope of changing market prices in one direction or the other. What is the effect of such intervention?

This lesson concerns government efforts to raise wages by minimum-wage legislation. The good that will be traded in this experiment is "labor." The suppliers are workers and the demanders are firms. The "price" in this market is the wage rate that firms pay their workers. In the second and third sessions of this experiment, a **minimum wage law** is introduced. A minimum wage law makes it illegal to hire anyone at a wage lower than the mandated minimum wage. In our experiment, the market manager will not honor any contract in which a worker is paid less than the minimum wage.

Instructions

Some participants in this experiment will be workers and some will be employers. As in previous markets, workers and employers can circulate around the trading floor, trying to make a deal.

Workers' Instructions

If you are a laborer, you can either take a job or remain unemployed. If you remain unemployed, you will get a payment equal to the **reservation wage** listed on your Personal Information Sheet. In the real world, a person's reservation wage represents the lowest wage at which he or she is willing to take a job rather than remain unemployed.[1]

In each round of the experiment, if you agree to take a job, you should record your ID number, wage, and reservation wage on your employer's employment record sheet. Your profit will be the wage that you agree to.

If you do not take a job, you should put your identification number and type on the List of Unemployed which is maintained by the market manager, and you will be credited with a profit that is equal to your reservation wage.

Employers' Instructions

In the first two sessions, each employer can hire zero, one, or two laborers. In the third session, each employer can hire up to four laborers. In the first two sessions, if you are an employer, the total value of your output will be 0 if you hire no laborers, $20 if you hire one laborer, and $30 if you hire two laborers. In Session 3, the total value of your output will be 0 if you hire no laborers, $30 if you hire one laborer, $55 if you hire two laborers, $75 if you hire three laborers, and $95 if you hire four laborers. Your profits are equal to the total value of your output minus the total amount of wages that you pay. In each round of each session, you will be given an *employment record* on which you should record the ID number and type of each laborer that you hire, as well as the wage that you pay this laborer.

Example:

> Suppose that your personal information sheet tells you that the value of your output will be $20 if you hire one laborer and $30 if you hire two laborers. You find somebody who will work for you for $6. You record that person's ID and reservation wage on your employment sheet, and return to the trading floor where you find somebody else who agrees to work for you at a wage of $9. Since you have hired two people, the value of your output is $30. Your total labor costs are $6 + $9 = $15. So your profits are $30 − $15 = $15. If you had hired only the first laborer and not the second, the value of your output would have been $20, your total labor costs would have been $6, and your profits would have been $20 − $6 = $14.

---

[1]Typically a person's reservation wage is influenced by the amount of unemployment benefits that she could earn if unemployed, the amount or earnings that she could make in self-employed activities, and the value that she places on leisure.

A Tip for Employers

A general rule to apply is this: Hiring one more laborer will increase profits if the amount of money that an additional laborer *adds* to your revenue is more than the amount of money it costs to hire her.

Warm-up Exercise

The first part of this exercise is designed to help you think about the best strategy to use in the experiment. Please answer these questions before you come to class.[2]

For the next three questions, suppose that you are an employer who can hire either 0, 1, or 2 laborers. If you hire 0 laborers, you will produce no output. If you hire 1 laborer, you will produce $30 worth of output. If you hire 2 laborers, you will produce $50 worth of output.

W 5.1 You run a firm and you have to pay a wage of $35 for each laborer that you hire, what will your profits (or loss) be if you hire:

0 laborers? $ _____, 1 laborer? $ _____, 2 laborers? $ _____

How many laborers should you hire in order to maximize profits? _____

W 5.2 You run a firm and you have to pay a wage of $25 for each laborer hired, what will your profits (or loss) be if you hire:

0 laborers? $ _____, 1 laborer? $ _____, 2 laborers? $ _____

How many laborers should you hire in order to maximize profits? _____

W 5.3 You run a firm and you have to pay a wage of $15 for each laborer that you hire, what will your profits (or loss) be if you hire

0 laborers? $ _____, 1 laborer? $ _____, 2 laborers? $ _____

How many laborers should you hire in order to maximize profits? _____

W 5.4 Assuming that you have to pay the same wage to each employee, it will be more profitable to hire 1 worker than to hire 0 workers, as long as

the wage is less than $ _____.

W 5.5 Assuming that you have to pay the same wage to each employee, it will be more profitable to hire 2 workers than 1 worker, as long as the wage

---

[2]Answers to these exercises are found on page 139.

is less than $ _____.

W 5.6 You are a laborer and your reservation wage is $12. You are offered a job at a wage of $10. What will be your profit if you take the job?

$ _____ What will your profit be if you do not take the job? $ _____

W 5.7 You are a laborer and your reservation wage is $5. You are offered a job at a wage of $10. What will be your profit if you take the job?

$ _____ What will be your profit if you do not take the job? $ _____

What Do You Expect to See?

■ Do you think that doubling the legal minimum wage would increase, decrease, or have no effect on the number of people who want jobs but cannot find them?

_____

■ Do you think that doubling the legal minimum wage would increase, decrease, or have no effect on the total income of employed laborers?

_____

Discussion of Experiment 5

Labor Markets and Derived Demand

In our experiment, students who played the role of firms had to decide how many workers to hire in order to maximize profits. Firms wanted to hire workers because they produced valuable output. In the experiment, a firm's profits were equal to the value of the its output minus the wages that it paid to workers.

In real-world labor markets, much as in our experiment, firms hire labor because they can use it to produce marketable goods. In a competitive labor market, all firms must pay the going wage rate in order to attract workers. Given the wage, profit-maximizing firms will hire the amount of labor that results in the highest profits. This gives us a demand curve for labor, where the "price" of labor is the wage and the demanders are firms. Since a firm's demand for labor is "derived" from the value of the output that it can produce, the study of the demand for labor by profit-maximizing firms is known as the **theory of derived demand** for labor.

The Marginal-Value Product Rule

Economists have a technical name for the amount of extra output produced by an extra unit of labor. We call this the **marginal product** of labor.[3] The reason that firms are interested in extra output is that they can sell it for extra revenue. The extra revenue that a firm receives from the output produced by an extra unit of labor is known as the **marginal value product** of labor. If a firm can sell all of its output for a fixed price, then the marginal value product of labor is equal to the price of output times the marginal product of labor. For example, if the marginal product of a worker is 10 units of output and if each unit of output can be sold for $5, then the marginal value product of labor is $50.

Given the size of its current workforce, a competitive, profit-maximizing firm will want to know whether it can increase its profits by either increasing or decreasing the number of workers that it hires. If the marginal value

---

[3]For those of you who know some calculus, if we write the total amount of output as a function of the amount of labor used holding constant the amounts of other inputs, then the marginal product of labor is the *derivative* of the total amount of output with respect to the amount of labor used.

product of an additional worker is larger than the wage, then the firm can increase its profits by hiring one more worker, since the extra revenue that the firm gets from the output added by one more worker exceeds the cost of hiring this worker. On the other hand, if the marginal value product of the last worker hired is smaller than the wage, then the firm would have higher profits if it reduced its labor force by one.

We have the following general principle, which we call the **marginal-value-product rule**:

> If a firm must produce a positive amount of output, then it will maximize its profits by hiring enough labor so that the marginal value product of the *last* worker hired is at least as large as the wage, and the marginal value product of hiring an *additional* worker is less than or equal to the wage.

The statement of the marginal-value-product rule includes the phrase "if it must produce a positive amount," because at high enough wage rates the firm may be better off hiring no labor at all.

Two Definitions and a Warning

A concept that is sometimes confused with the marginal value product of labor is the **average value product** of labor. The average value product of labor is also known as **labor productivity**. Labor productivity is equal to the total value of output divided by the number of workers. It is important to understand that labor productivity is not the same thing as the marginal value product. A firm using the decision rule "hire an additional worker so long as labor productivity (the *average* value product of labor) exceeds the wage," would not behave in the same way as a firm using the marginal-value-product rule. Indeed, as we will show in the next example, a firm using an average productivity rule would in general make lower profits than a firm that used the marginal productivity rule.

A Working Example

Consider a firm for which the relation between the number of workers hired and the total revenue is given by the first two columns of Table 5.1. In the third column of this table, we show the average value product of labor, which is calculated by dividing the value of output by the number of workers. In the fourth column, we show the marginal value product of the last laborer hired when the number of workers is given in the first column. For example, when there are 3 workers, the marginal product of the third worker is the extra revenue gained by increasing the number of workers from 2 to 3, which is $8 = $20 − $12.

Table 5.1: Labor and Output Measures–Example 1

Number of Workers	Total Value of Output	Average Value Product of Labor	Marginal Value Product of Labor
0	$0	-	-
1	$2	$2.00	$2.00
2	$12	$6.00	$10.00
3	$20	$6.67	$8.00
4	$26	$6.50	$6.00
5	$30	$6.00	$4.00
6	$32	$5.33	$2.00
7	$32	$4.57	$0.00
8	$30	$3.75	−$2.00

This example satisfies the definition of (eventually) diminishing marginal value product. Although the marginal value product of the second worker is higher than that of the first worker, the marginal product of each additional worker after the second worker decreases as the number of workers increases.[4]

Suppose that the firm in this example could hire labor at a wage rate of $5 per worker. How many workers should it hire in order to maximize its profits? We have argued that it should hire enough labor so that the marginal value product of the last worker hired is at least $5, and that the marginal value product of hiring one more laborer is no more than $5. As we see from Table 5.1, the marginal value product of hiring the fourth worker is $6, but the marginal value product of hiring a fifth worker is only $4. The marginal-value-product rule tells us that at a wage of $5, the firm should hire exactly 4 workers in order to maximize its profits.

Let us verify by direct calculation that if the wage is $5, the firm will maximize its profits by hiring 4 workers. Table 5.2 shows revenue, total wage costs, and profits for each possible number of workers. As we see from the

---

[4]Notice that the marginal product of the 7th worker is zero, and the marginal product of the 8th worker is negative. This might happen because the workplace gets so crowded that adding an extra worker actually reduces total ouput. For a restaurant, this would be the case where "too many cooks spoil the broth."

fourth column of this table, the firm makes the most profits ($6) by hiring 4 workers.

Table 5.2: Revenue, Costs, and Profits–Example 1

Number of Workers	Firm's Revenue	Firm's Total Wage Costs	Firm's Profits
0	$0	$0	$0
1	$2	$5	-$3
2	$12	$10	$2
3	$20	$15	$5
4	$26	$20	$6
5	$30	$25	$5
6	$32	$30	$2
7	$32	$35	−$3
8	$30	$40	−$10

It is interesting to ask how much profit the firm would make if instead of using the marginal-value-product rule, it used an average-value-product rule and continued to hire additional workers so long as the *average* value product of labor was larger than the wage. As we see from Table 5.1, the average value product of labor is greater than wage until the firm has more than 6 employees. Thus, if the firm used the average-value-product rule it would hire 6 workers and its profits would be only $2, which is clearly less than the $6 that it would make if it used the marginal-value-product rule.

A Firm's Labor Demand Curve

You can use the marginal-value-product rule to figure out the number of workers that a firm will demand at any wage. This will allow you to draw the market demand curve for labor. For drawing the market demand curve for labor, it is helpful to construct a demand table for a single firm. This table will show the number of workers that the firm would demand at all possible wages. The marginal-value-product rule turns out to be just what we need for this task. According to the marginal-value-product rule, if a firm is going to produce a positive amount, it will make the highest possible profit by hiring labor up to the point where the marginal value product of one more worker falls below the wage.

Let us look at an example to see how to do this. Consider a firm whose only variable input is labor and where the number of workers is related to output as in Table 5.3.

Table 5.3: Labor and Output Measures–Example 2

Number of Workers	Total Value of Output	Marginal Value Product of Labor
0	$0	-
1	$12	$12
2	$21	$9
3	$27	$6
4	$30	$3
5	$30	$0

The highest marginal value product of labor found in Table 5.3 is $12, which is the marginal value product of the first laborer hired. If the wage rate is higher than $12, the firm's profits will be highest if it hires no labor at all. Therefore at wages higher than $12, the firm would demand zero units of labor. We see from Table 5.3 that the marginal value product of the first worker hired is $12, while the marginal value product of the second worker is $9. Thus at any wage rate between $9 and $12 it is profitable for the firm to hire one worker, but hiring any additional workers would reduce its profits. Therefore the firm's demand for labor at wages between $9 and $12 is one worker. According to Table 5.3, the marginal value product of a second worker is $9, while the marginal value product of a third worker is $6. If the wage rate is greater than $6, but less than $9, the firm will find it profitable to hire a second worker, but will not find it profitable to hire a third worker. So the firm's demand for labor at wages between $6 and $9 is two workers. Similar reasoning shows that the firm's demand for labor is three workers at wages between $3 and $6, and four workers at wages between $0 and $3. We record all of these results in Table 5.4.

Now that we have constructed the demand table, we can draw the firm's demand curve for labor in Figure 5.1. At every price between $9 and $12, the firm demands one worker, so we draw a vertical line from $(1, 9)$ to $(1, 12)$. At every price between $6 and $9, the firm demands two workers, so we draw a vertical line from $(2, 6)$ to $(2, 9)$. Similar reasoning tells us that the demand curve includes vertical line segments corresponding to a demand of three workers at prices between $3 and $6, and a demand of four workers at prices between $0 and $3. With the vertical segments drawn, we must

Table 5.4: Labor Demand Table of Firm–Example 2

Wage Rate (w)	Number of Workers Demanded
$w > \$12$	0
$\$9 < w < \$12$	1
$\$6 < w < \$9$	2
$\$3 < w < \$6$	3
$\$0 < w < \$3$	4

ask ourselves about the firm's demand at wages of exactly \$12, exactly \$9, exactly \$6, and exactly \$3. If the wage is exactly \$9, then a firm that has one worker would increase its revenue by \$9 (from \$12 to \$21) by adding a second worker. Therefore the firm's extra revenue from hiring a second worker would exactly equal the cost of hiring this worker, and so the firm would be indifferent between having one worker or having two workers. The points $(1, 9)$ and $(2, 9)$ are both on the firm's demand curve. The points on the horizontal line between $(1, 9)$ and $(2, 9)$ would also be on the firm's demand curve if the firm can hire part time workers at a wage proportional to the amount of time they work, and if the extra output from a part time worker is in the same proportion to the extra output from a full time worker. We draw this horizontal line segment as a dashed line in the figure. Similar reasoning explains the dashed horizontal line segments at wages of \$12, \$6, and \$3.

Figure 5.1: Labor Demand Curve of a Firm–Example 2

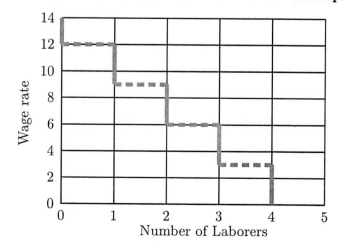

The Market Demand Curve for Labor

At any wage rate, the total amount of labor demanded in the market is the sum of the amounts demanded by all the firms in the market.

Suppose, for example, that there are 10 firms in the market, all of which have the same demands as the firm we have just studied. Then the Demand Table for the entire market can be obtained from Table 5.4 simply by multiplying the number of workers demanded at each wage by 10. The demand curve in this case is given by Figure 5.2.

Figure 5.2: Market Demand Curve for Labor–10 Firms

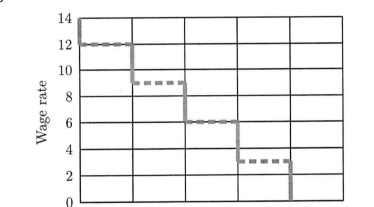

Labor Supply, Unemployment, and Income

A worker's **reservation wage** is defined to be the lowest wage at which he or she would be willing to accept employment. Another name for the reservation wage is the **opportunity cost** of labor time. Economists define the opportunity cost of any resource to be the money value of putting that resource to its best alternative use. Time spent working on a job could alternatively be spent at leisure, working at home, or getting formal or informal education. A worker's reservation wage is the money value that he or she attributes to the most attractive of these alternatives.

In a competitive labor market, the labor supply at any wage is defined to be the number of workers who want to work at that wage. All workers whose reservation wages are lower than the wage rate will want to supply labor at that wage rate, and all workers whose reservation wages are higher than the wage rate will not want to supply labor. Workers whose reservation wage equals the wage rate will be indifferent about working or not.

Economists define two kinds of unemployment: **involuntary unemployment** and **voluntary employment**. A laborer who is not employed, but would willingly work at the average wage paid to other laborers is involuntarily unemployed. A laborer who is not employed and would choose not to work at the average wage paid to other laborers is voluntarily unemployed.

Being unemployed is not the same thing as working for zero income. If they did not receive any wages, most workers would prefer to spend their time doing something other than working for their employers. In this discussion, we will count the income of those who are unemployed as equal to their reservation wages—the opportunity cost of their time. The income of employed laborers is equal to the wages that they receive. The total income of all laborers is therefore measured as the total wages received by employed laborers *plus* the total of reservation wages of all unemployed laborers.[5]

Market Equilibrium with a Minimum Wage

A minimum wage law does not change the marginal value product of labor for any firm, nor does it change any worker's reservation wage. Therefore it does not change either the supply curve or the demand curve for labor. But if the minimum wage is set higher than the competitive equilibrium wage, then more workers will want to be employed than the number of workers that firms are willing to hire. So what happens?

Let us explore the effects of a minimum wage law by looking at a specific example. Consider a competitive labor market in which there are 14 workers with reservation wages of $5, and 14 workers with reservation values of $12. At wages above $12, all 28 workers will want jobs; at wages between $5 and $12, only the 14 workers with $5 reservation wages will want jobs; and at wages below $5, no workers will want jobs. These facts enable us to draw the supply curve shown in Figure 5.3.

Suppose that this market has 9 firms, each of which can hire up to two laborers. The value of a firm's output will be $0 if it hires no labor, $20 if it hires 1 laborer, and $30 if it hires 2 laborers. At wages higher than $20, no firm will want to hire any labor and the demand for labor is 0. At wages

---

[5]If part of the income received by unemployed workers consists of "unemployment benefits" or public assistance, then it would be appropriate when adding up the social costs of a minimum wage law to include the extra costs born by taxpayers to support additional unemployment payments.

between \$10 and \$20, every firm will maximize its profits by hiring 1 worker and total demand for labor by the 9 firms is 9 workers. At wages below \$10, every firm will maximize its profits by hiring 2 laborers. Total demand for labor by the 9 firms would then be 18 workers. The resulting demand curve for labor appears in Figure 5.3

From Figure 5.3, we see that in the absence of a minimum wage law, there is a competitive equilbrium in which the wage rate is \$10 and 14 workers are employed. Suppose that a law is passed making it illegal to hire labor for any wage lower than \$15. What do we expect will happen?

Figure 5.3: A Labor Market with Minimum Wage

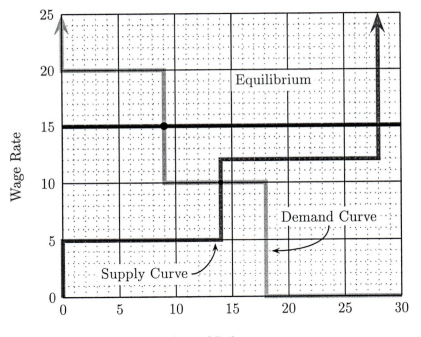

Number of Laborers

Although the minimum wage law makes it illegal to pay less than the minimum wage, it does not require firms to hire more workers than they want at these wages. Looking at the labor demand curve in Figure 5.3, we see that at a wage of \$15 firms are willing to hire only 9 workers. Looking at the labor supply curve, we see that all 28 workers will want to work at a wage of \$15. Since firms are not required to hire more workers than they want, we predict that at this wage, 9 workers will be hired and the other $28 - 9 = 19$ workers would like to get jobs at the going wage rate but will be unable to do so. No firm will offer a higher wage than $15, since firms can get as much labor as they want at this wage. Thus the outcome in which the wage is $15 and 9 workers are employed can be called a **market equilibrium with a minimum wage**.

In the absence of a minimum wage, supply and demand theory makes a strong prediction about which workers will be employed and which will not, and about the total income of workers. At the competitive equilibrium wage of $10, all 14 of the workers with reservation wages of $5 would be employed and all 14 workers with reservation wages of $12 would be voluntarily unemployed. The total income of all employed workers would be $10 × 14 = $140, and the total income of all unemployed workers would be $12 × 14 = $168. Therefore the total income of all workers would be $308.

For an economy in market equilibrium with a minimum wage, we cannot predict which workers will get jobs simply by knowing their reservation wages. In this example, at a minimum wage of $15 all 28 workers in the market would like to have jobs, but only 9 jobs are available. Which workers will get these jobs? This may be decided by which workers were able to sign up first, on friendships between workers and employers, or on pure luck. (What do you think happened in your experiment?) Since 14 workers of each type are seeking jobs at the minimum wage, it could happen that the 9 workers who get jobs all have reservation wages of $12, or that they all have reservation wages of $5, or some combination in between these extremes.

The fact that we cannot predict the exact distribution of the reservation wages of the unemployed means that we will not be able to make an exact prediction of the total income of unemployed workers in a market equilibrium with a minimum wage. We can, however, predict a range for this income. At one extreme, suppose that all 9 of the workers who get jobs have reservation wages of $12, then there will be 14 unemployed workers with reservation wages of $5 and 5 unemployed workers with reservation wages of $12. In this case, the total income of unemployed persons is $(14 × \$5) + (5 × \$12) = \$130$. At the other extreme, suppose that all 9 of the workers who get jobs have reservation wages of $5. Then there will be 5 unemployed workers with reservation wages of $5 and 14 unemployed workers with reservation wages of $12. The total income of unemployed workers will be $(5 × \$5) + (14 × \$12) = \$193$. If the unemployed include some workers with $5 reservation wages and some with $12 reservation wages, then total income of unemployed workers will be somewhere between these two extremes.

To find the total income of all workers, we add the total income of unemployed workers to the total income of employed workers. Since 9 workers will be employed at the minimum wage of $15, the total income of employed workers will be $9 \times \$15 = \$135$. Therefore in market equilibrium with a minimum wage of $15, total income of all workers will be in the range from $\$135 + \$130 = \$265$ to $\$135 + \$193 = \$328$.

Market Equilibrium with a Nonbinding Minimum Wage

In Session 3 of our experiment, the competitive equilibrium wage rate turns out to be higher than the legal minimum wage. The minimum wage law forbids firms from paying *less* than the minimum wage, but it does not forbid them from paying more. With the labor demand curve found in Session 3, if firms offered to pay only the minimum wage, then the number of workers that firms would like to hire would be greater than the number of workers available. In order to acquire the workers that they want to hire, firms will bid up the market wage as long as it is lower than the competitive wage. Therefore we would expect the wage and amount of employment to be the same as it would be in the absence of a minimum wage law. A minimum wage that is below the competitive equilibrium wage, and which therefore does not influence the actual wage paid, is said to be a **nonbinding minimum wage**.

Minimum Wage Laws in the News

The February 4, 1995, edition of *The New York Times* reported that President Clinton was seeking to increase the legal minimum wage from $4.25 to $5.15 an hour.[6] The President declared that "the only way to grow the middle class and shrink the underclass is to make work pay." According to National Public Radio, Presidential Assistant Leon Panetta asserted that an increase in the minimum wage would give people an incentive to take jobs instead of collecting welfare benefits.

The Republican Speaker of the House, Newt Gingrich, reacted as follows: "I personally am very skeptical of it, and I think it will kill jobs." According to the *Times*, the House Majority Leader, Dick Armey (who is a former economics professor from the University of North Texas in Denton) intended to fight the increase with "every fiber of his being." The president of the National Federation of Independent Business, a small-business lobbying group, said that the proposal was "a regressive and job-killing scheme which would put a big dent in small-business hiring."

---

[6]Legal minimum wage legislation does not apply to employees of firms in trade and services with sales less than $250,000, to farm workers working for small farms, or to domestic servants.

Which of these claims should we believe? It turns out that people on both sides of this argument were at least partially correct. The question of which side gets more partial credit is ultimately empirical rather than ideological. And, as you may have suspected, the empirical matter on which the answer turns is the shape of the supply and demand curves for labor.

Losers and Gainers from the Minimum Wage

In our minimum-wage experiment, we found that when a minimum wage was imposed, the number of workers employed decreased. Moreover, **involuntary unemployment** increased by even more than the decrease in employment. This happened because some laborers who were unwilling to work at the old equilibrium wage want to take jobs at the minimum wage.

Some people in the experiment were "harmed" by the minimum wage legislation. The most obvious losers were the firms. The minimum wage forced them to pay higher wages, although the revenue they received from their output did not change. It is not, then, very surprising that the small-business lobby quoted in the *Times* opposed an increased minimum wage.[7] Those laborers who were employed before the minimum wage was introduced, but who could not find jobs at the minimum wage, were also made worse off.

The gainers from the minimum wage increase are the workers who were able to keep their jobs and take advantage of the higher wage rate. If you believe that those who received the minimum wage belonged to the "underclass," but were able to join the "middle class" once they got the new minimum wage, then you will probably think that President Clinton was right.

Leon Panetta presented a less convincing argument. He was probably right in saying that higher wages for unskilled labor would influence some people to work instead of collecting welfare. But an increased minimum wage, even in the most favorable case, is not likely to *increase* the total amount of employment. If employment is to increase, firms must want to hire more labor. But if the wage has increased, firms will demand less, not more, labor. If the total demand for labor has not increased, then for every previously unemployed worker who chooses to work after an increase in the minimum wage, at least one previously employed worker will lose her job.

---

[7]Lobbyists do not seem to be bred for truth-telling. You are unlikely to hear a lobbyist say in public that he opposes Proposal X because it reduces the profits of the people who pay him. This is why the guy who is *paid by small business interests* claims he opposes an increased minimum wage because it will harm *labor* by "killing jobs."

Minimum Wages–Another Look

With the distribution of supplier and demander types present in our experiment, the minimum wage had a relatively small effect on total employment. If the demand curve is flatter, an increase in wages will have a larger effect on total employment. We now ask you to work an exercise with a flatter demand curve. In this case, the effect of an increased minimum wage rate is more like that predicted by Representatives Gingrich and Armey than like that predicted by President Clinton.

Exercise: Effects of a Minimum Wage[8]

Figure 5.4: Minimum Wage–Another Look

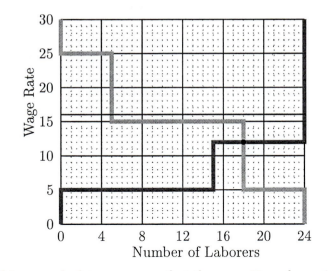

Number of Laborers

For this example, let us suppose that there are 15 workers with reservation wages of $5, and 9 workers with reservation values of $12. The supply and demand curves for labor are as drawn in Figure 5.4.

Exercise 5.1 Suppose that labor supply and demand are as given in Figure 5.4 and that there is no minimum wage legislation.

a) What will be the equilibrium wage rate? $_____

b) How many laborers will be employed?   _____

---

[8]Answers to this exercise are found at the bottom of page 139.

c) How many laborers will be voluntarily unemployed?   _____

d) How many laborers will be involuntarily unemployed?   _____
Hint: An unemployed worker whose reservation wage equals the market wage is indifferent about working or not, and is therefore voluntarily unemployed.

Exercise 5.2 Suppose that in the market depicted by Figure 5.4 a minimum wage of $16 is enforced. At the minimum wage

a) how many people will want jobs?   _____

b) how many laborers will firms want to hire?   _____

c) how many jobs are eliminated by the minimum wage?   _____

d) how many workers are voluntarily unemployed?   _____

e) how many workers are involuntarily unemployed?   _____

Exercise 5.3 If there is no minimum wage, total

a) wage earnings of all employed workers are $ _____ .

b) income of unemployed workers is $ _____ .

c) income of all workers is $ _____ .
Hint: Remember that we count an unemployed worker's income as equal to her reservation wage.

Exercise 5.4 With a minimum wage of $16, total

a) wage earnings of all employed workers is $ _____ .

b) income of unemployed workers is between $_____ and $_____ .

c) income of all workers is between $ _____ and $ _____ .
Hint: Total income of unemployed workers depends on which types of workers get jobs. The lowest possible total income occurs if all of the workers who get jobs have $12 reservation wages; the highest occurs if all of the workers who get jobs have $5 reservation wages.

Price Floors in General

A minimum wage is an example of a **price floor**. A price floor for a good is
a legal minimum price such that no one is allowed to buy or sell the good at
any lower price. If the price floor is *lower than* the competitive equilibrium
price, it will have *no effect* since competition will force prices to rise above
the floor. If the price floor is *higher than* the competitive equilibrium price,
then at any legally permitted price the quantity that suppliers will want to
sell is greater than the quantity that demanders will want to buy.

Figure 5.5: A Price Floor

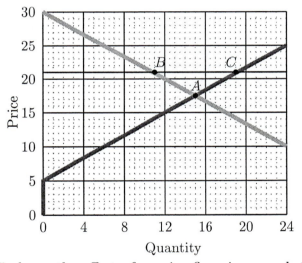

Figure 5.5 shows the effect of a price floor in a market with smooth
supply and demand curves. Without a price floor, the equilibrium price and
quantity are found at the point labeled A, where the price is $17.50 and the
quantity is 15 units. If there is a price floor of $21, then suppliers will want
to sell 19 units (point C) and demanders will want to buy only 11 units
(point B). Since demanders cannot be forced to buy if they don't want to,
the total number of units traded at the floor price of $21 is only 11, even
though at this price suppliers would like to sell 19 units. The difference
between the amount supplied and the amount demanded is known as the
excess supply of a good. Thus, we see that at a price of $21 there is an
excess supply of 8 units (an amount equal to the length of the line segment
BC).

A price floor set above the equilibrium point presents suppliers with some
good news and some bad news. The good news is that those who can make

a sale will receive a higher price. The bad news is that at the higher price, they will be able to sell fewer units. If the demand curve is very steep, then the bad news will not be very bad, because an increase in price will cause only a slight decrease in the number of units demanded. If the demand curve is very flat, then the bad news *will* be very bad, because a small increase in the price will cause a big decrease in the number of units demanded.

Rent Control and Price Ceilings

In the case of minimum wage legislation, sellers (laborers in this case) want the government to enforce a price floor to keep prices high. In other markets, buyers seek laws to keep prices *low*. Sometimes buyers are able to convince a government to establish a **price ceiling** on some good. To impose a price ceiling, the government makes it illegal to buy or sell a good at any price higher than some legal maximum. Some governments attempt to control the price of rental housing by legislating a maximum monthly rental rate on houses or apartments. During World War II, the United States government imposed price ceilings on many "essential" commodities. During the mideast oil embargo of the early 1970s, the United States imposed a price ceiling on gasoline.

The effects of these price ceilings have been just as the economic models would have predicted. Rent controlled housing has caused, and continues to cause, long waiting lists for renting homes. World War II's price controls resulted in "shortages" of foods, consumer durables, and clothing. Price controls on gasoline led to closed gasoline stations and long lines at the pumps.

Let us turn to the supply and demand analysis of a price ceiling. Consider the market depicted in Figure 5.6. If there is no price ceiling, the equilibrium price and quantity are found at point A, where the price is $18 and the quantity is 15 units. Suppose that the government enforces a price ceiling of $13. At a price of $13, demanders will want to buy 21 units (point C) and suppliers are willing to supply only 9 units (point B). While a price ceiling makes it illegal for suppliers to sell the good at a price higher than $13, it *cannot force* them to provide more units than they are willing to supply at this price. Therefore, with a price ceiling of $13 the quantity supplied is only 9 units. The difference between the quantity demanded and the quantity supplied at the ceiling price is known as the amount of **excess demand**. At the ceiling price of $13, there is an excess demand of 12 units. This quantity is represented in the diagram by the length of the line segment BC.

Figure 5.6: A Price Ceiling

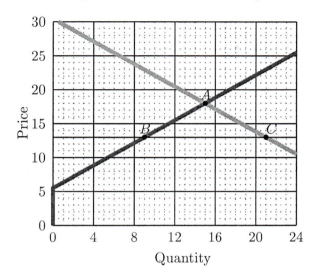

When a good is in excess demand, there is said to be a **shortage** of the good. At the ceiling price, not everyone who wants to buy a unit of the good will be able to find a supplier willing to sell. In the absence of a price ceiling, demanders who cannot get the good at the current price would offer a higher price. The market price would be bid up until the quantity that suppliers want to sell is equal to the quantity that demanders want to buy. If there is a price ceiling, competition among demanders for a scarce good cannot be resolved by bidding up the price. The problem of who gets the scarce good has to be decided in other ways, such as waiting-lines, favoritism toward relatives or friends, under-the-table payments, or brute force.

Answers to Warmup Exercises
W 5.1: $0, −$5, −$20, 0; **W 5.2**: $0, $5, $0, 1; **W 5.3**: $0, $15, $20, 2; **W 5.4**: $30; **W 5.5**: $20; **W 5.6**: $10,$12; **W 5.7**: $10, $5.
Answers to Other Exercises
Ex. 5.1: $12, 18, 6, 0; **Ex. 5.2**: 24, 5, 18 − 5 = 13, 0, 19; **Ex. 5.3**: $12 × 18 = $216, $12 × 6 = $72, $288; **Ex. 5.4**: $80, ($5 × 15) + ($12 × 4) = $123 and ($5 × 10) + ($12 × 9) = $158, $203 and $238.

Lab Notes for Experiment 5

Recording Wages, Profits, and Unemployment

Your instructor will post a listing of the wages paid by each firm to its workers in the last round of each session. Copy this information into Tables 5.5, 5.6, and 5.7, and then calculate total wages paid by each firm. Since these tables also record the total number of workers hired by each firm, you can determine each firm's total revenue. In Sessions 1 and 2, a firm's revenue is $20 if it hires one worker and $30 if it hires two. In Session 3, a firm's revenue is $30 if it hires one, $55 if it hires two, $75 if it hires three, and $95 if it hires four workers. Subtract total wages paid from total revenue to find each firm's profit.

Your instructor will also inform you of the number of unemployed laborers and their reservation wages. Record this information in Table 5.8.

Recording Market Fundamentals

After the experiment is over, your instructor will supply you with the number of employers and the number of laborers of each type who participated in each session. Copy this information into Table 5.9.

Calculating Market Statistics

Complete Table 5.10, which summarizes wages and profits in the last round of each session. All of the information that you need to complete this table is found in Tables 5.5, 5.6, 5.7, and 5.8. *Total Employment* is the number of workers who were hired by firms.

Table 5.5: Wages and Firm Profits in Session 1

Firm ID	Wages Paid to		Total Wages	Firm's Revenue	Firm's Profits
	Worker 1	Worker 2			

Table 5.6: Wages and Firm Profits in Session 2

Firm ID	Wages Paid to		Total Wages	Firm's Revenue	Firm's Profits
	Worker 1	Worker 2			

Table 5.7: Wages and Firm Profits in Session 3

Firm ID	Wages Paid to Workers					Firm's Revenue	Firm's Profit
	No. 1	No. 2	No. 3	No. 4	Total		

Table 5.8: Unemployment by Reservation Wages

| | Number of Unemployed Workers with: | |
	$5 reservation wage	$12 reservation wage
Session 1		
Session 2		
Session 3		

Table 5.9: Distribution of Types: Firms and Workers

	Session 1	Session 2	Session 3
Firms			
Laborers with $5 Reservation Wage			
Laborers with $12 Reservation Wage			

Table 5.10: Experimental Results–Wages and Profits

	Session 1	Session 2	Session 3
Average Wage Rate			
Total Employment*			
Total Profits of Firms			

*Number of workers hired.

Part III

Imperfect Markets

Experiment 6

Externalities

A Polluting Economy

The Isle of Effluvia has many small factories that make beautiful, hand-crafted bronze lawn ornaments, much cherished by Effluvians. The coal-fired furnaces used in these factories produce a fetid gray smoke that leaves a residue of grime all over the island. Effluvians trade only with other Effluvians.

The market for lawn ornaments has suppliers and demanders, much as in our previous experiments, but every lawn ornament that is supplied imposes a pollution cost on all Effluvians. Because of this pollution, trades that benefit both the buyer and seller can cause harm to third parties and, consequently, unrestricted trade in lawn ornaments leads to an inefficient outcome. This experiment shows how appropriate public policies designed to reduce pollution damage can increase the profits of all Effluvians.

Instructions

You will receive a Personal Information Sheet that informs you of your Buyer Value or Seller Cost in each session. At the beginning of the experiment, the market manager will tell you the amount of damage imposed on each participant by pollution from the production of each lawn ornament. If, for example, the market manager announces that producing one lawn ornament causes $1 damage to each participant, and if 15 lawn ornaments are sold, then all participants in the experiment, including those who make no trades, will *each* have to pay a "pollution cost" of $15.

In the first session of the experiment, there is no government interference in the market for lawn ornaments. Buyers and sellers who agree on a price can sign a contract and bring it to the market manager. As in earlier experiments, if a supplier with Seller Cost C sells a lawn ornament to a demander with Buyer Value V for price P, the seller will earn a profit of $(P - C)$ and the buyer will earn a profit of $(V - P)$ from the transaction. But in this experiment, everyone in Effluvia, whether they buy, sell, or do not transact at all, will have to pay the pollution cost. If 15 lawn ornaments are sold, and if each lawn ornament that is produced causes $1 worth of pollution damage to every Effluvian, then the profits of each participant in the experiment will be reduced by $15.

In the second session the market manager imposes a **pollution tax** on sellers. The revenue collected from the pollution tax will be redistributed in equal shares to all Effluvians. In this session, if a supplier with Seller Cost C sells a lawn ornament to a demander with Buyer Value V for price P, and if the tax per lawn ornament is T, then the seller's after-tax profit from the transaction is $(P - C - T)$ and the buyer's profit is $(V - P)$. In addition to any profits that they may make from buying or selling lawn ornaments, every Effluvian will receive an equal share of the government's tax revenue, and every Effluvian will suffer a loss of income equal to the amount of pollution damage imposed on each person by the production of lawn ornaments.

In the third session, a supplier is allowed to sell a lawn ornament only if she has a **pollution permit**. At the beginning of the session, some participants will receive marketable pollution permits. The original owner of a pollution permit can resell this permit to anyone else. When a lawn ornament supplier buys a pollution permit, the buyer and the seller of the permit must write their ID numbers and the sales price on the permit. The seller of the pollution permit receives a profit equal to the price at which the permit was sold. Having acquired a pollution permit, a lawn ornament supplier is allowed to sell a lawn ornament to a demander. When a supplier has completed the sale of a lawn ornament, she and the buyer should fill in a sales contract and bring it to the market manager, along with a pollution permit that entitles the seller to supply the lawn ornament.

A lawn ornament seller's total profit from her production activities is the price she receives for the lawn ornament, minus her Seller Cost, minus the price she pays for the pollution permit. A lawn ornament buyer's total profit from a purchase is his Buyer Value minus the price he pays for the lawn ornament. In addition to profits (or losses) that they make from transactions, all Effluvians also suffer a loss of profits equal to the amount of pollution damage imposed on each person by the production of lawn ornaments.

Warm-up Exercise

For all questions in this exercise, make the simplifying assumption that your own decision about whether to buy or sell a lawn ornament has *no* effect on the total number of lawn ornaments produced in Effluvia.[1]

W 6.1   Suppose that each lawn ornament that is produced in Effluvia imposes pollution costs of \$.50 on every Effluvian. If 20 lawn ornaments are

sold in Effluvia, each Effluvian will suffer pollution costs of \$ _____ . If there are 45 people in Effluvia, the total cost of pollution to all Effluvians

is \$ _____ .

W 6.2   In Session 1 you are a supplier with a Seller Cost of \$20. The best offer you have for a lawn ornament is \$27. A total of 20 ornaments will be sold, regardless of whether or not you sell one. Each lawn ornament imposes costs of \$.50 on all Effluvians. If you sell a lawn ornament for \$27, your total

profit (or loss) in this session will be \$ _____ . If you do not sell one, your

total profit (or loss) from the session will be \$ _____ . (Don't forget to account for pollution costs.)

W 6.3   Suppose that in Session 2 Effluvia has a population of 100 people. Each lawn ornament that is produced imposes a cost of \$.20 on each citizen of Effluvia. The government imposes a pollution tax of \$10 on every lawn ornament produced, and a total of 40 lawn ornaments are sold. If you make

no transactions, you will pay a pollution cost of \$ _____ and your share

of the total revenue collected from the tax will be \$ _____, so that your

profit (or loss) will be \$ _____ .

W 6.4   Suppose that the government collects a \$10 tax from the seller of each lawn ornament. A supplier with a Seller Cost of \$10 meets a demander with a Buyer Value of \$30 and sells a lawn ornament to the demander at a price of \$25. Ignoring pollution costs, the seller's after-tax profit from this

transaction is \$ _____ and the buyer's profit is \$ _____ .

W 6.5   In Session 3 you are a lawn ornament supplier with Seller Cost of \$25 and you received a pollution permit with your Personal Information Sheet. The most that anyone will pay you for a lawn ornament is \$32, and

---

[1] Answers to these questions are found on Page 170.

another seller has offered to buy your pollution permit for $10. What are your profits if you sell a lawn ornament, using your pollution permit to allow

the sale? $ _____ What are your profits if you do not sell a lawn ornament,

but sell your pollution permit for $10? $ _____ Which should you do to

maximize your profits? _____

W 6.6 In Session 3, Alice, who is a supplier with Seller Cost $15, buys a pollution permit for $20 from Bill and sells a lawn ornament for $50 to Charlie, who is a demander with Buyer Value $60. None of these three people makes any other transactions. A total of 20 lawn ornaments are sold in Effluvia, each of which imposes a pollution cost of $.20 on all residents.

Alice makes a profit of $ _____ , Bill makes a profit of $ _____ , and

Charlie makes a profit of $ _____ .

Discussion of Experiment 6

In previous experiments, a transaction affected the profits of only the buyer and the seller who were directly involved and not the profits of other participants in the marketplace. In this experiment, every lawn ornament that is sold imposes pollution costs on everybody in Effluvia. When economic activities affect the profits of persons who are not directly involved in the activity, we say that there is an **externality**. If these activities impose *costs* on others, the externality is said to be a **negative externality**. Air and water pollution in manufacturing are familiar examples of negative externalities. Highway congestion is another important negative externality. When an extra car enters an already crowded highway, all other drivers are forced to slow down, which costs each of the other drivers a loss of valuable time. The story is much the same with congestion on the internet. When the number of messages sent is close to capacity, every extra message sent will slow down the messages of all other users.

Some economic activities confer *benefits* on people not involved in the activity. These activities are said to produce a **positive externality**. Someone who spends resources on painting her house or planting a beautiful garden benefits her neighbors as well as herself. Someone who acquires education for herself is likely to confer positive externalities, since better educated people are likely to communicate more useful information to those around them, and are also likely to participate more intelligently in public decisions.

Competitive Markets and Externalities

When individuals decide to trade in a competitive market, they are motivated by *their own* costs or benefits, and tend to ignore the costs or benefits that their participation may impose on others. In general, this leads to inefficient outcomes.

An example will help us to understand the reason for this inefficiency. Consider a market in which the distribution of Buyer Values and Seller Costs is given in Table 6.1. For every bushel of apples that is produced, farmers spray insecticide that imposes a negative externality, costing each person in the market $1.

Everyone must bear the pollution costs imposed by others, regardless

Table 6.1: Buyer Values and Seller Costs

Seller Cost	Number of Persons	Buyer Value	Number of Persons
15	4	50	5
25	10	30	5
		20	6

of his or her own decision to buy or sell. Therefore, as with sunk costs in previous experiments, these costs have no effect on a buyer's willingness-to-pay for apples or on the lowest price that a seller is willing to accept. This means that supply and demand curves for apples are drawn in the same way that we drew these curves in the absence of externalities.[2] These supply and demand curves are shown in Figure 6.1.

Figure 6.1: Supply and Demand for Apples

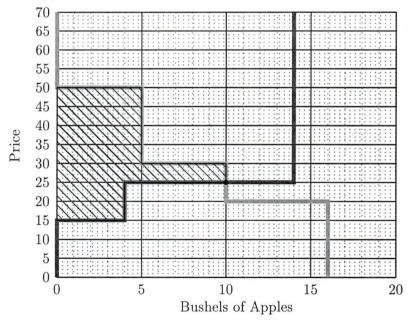

<hr />

[2]Almost all of the pollution that an individual experiences is caused by others, rather than by himself or herself, so it is reasonable to make the simplifying assumption that buyers or sellers ignore the effect of their own trading on the total amount of pollution.

From Figure 6.1 we see that the competitive equilibrium price of apples is $25 per bushel and the competitive equilibrium quantity is 10 bushels. As we discovered in Chapter 1, total profits made by buyers and sellers are equal to the shaded area between the supply and demand curves to the left of the competitive equilibrium quantity. In this case, the total profits that buyers and sellers make on apple transactions are $190.[3] But this is not the end of the story. Every bushel of apples that is produced imposes a cost of $1 on everybody in the market (whether or not they made a purchase or a sale). Since 10 bushels are sold, this means that each of the 30 people in the market has to pay a pollution cost of $10. Therefore the total cost of pollution to people in the market is $10 × 30 = $300. When we subtract the $300 in pollution costs from the $190 in profits made on transactions, we find that the total amount of profit earned by people in this market is −$110! Remarkably, it turns out that total profits are *lower* when people are allowed to trade to a competitive equilibrium than they would have been if there was no trade at all.

How can it be that although everybody who trades makes a profit (or at least no loss) on the trade, total profits of all persons in the market are negative? The answer is that traders take account of their own costs, but do not account for the costs that they impose on others through negative externalities. Consider, for example, a supplier with Seller Cost $25 who sells a bushel of apples to a demander with Buyer Value $30 for a price between $26 and $29. Both the buyer and the seller make a profit, and the total of the buyer's profit and the seller's profit is $5. But producing this bushel of apples imposed a pollution cost of $1 on each of the 30 people in the market. Although the buyer and seller together make a profit of $5 on the transaction, they impose a negative externality of $30, so that this sale reduced total profits in the market by $25.

One might first think that since total profits are negative when apples are traded competitively, the way to maximize total profits is to prohibit all trading in apples. But this turns out not to be the answer. To see why, consider a trade between a demander with Buyer Value $50 and a supplier with Seller Cost $15. Total gains of the seller and buyer from trading are $50 − $15 = $35, and the total costs imposed by the externality are $30. So this trade increases the total amount of profits in the market by $35 − $30 = $5.

---

[3]You can find this value by breaking up the shaded area into rectangles and adding the areas of these rectangles. One way to calculate this area is as follows: $35 × 4 + $25 × 1 + $5 × 5 = $190.

In general, it may be economically efficient for the economy to allow some transactions, even if they impose negative externalities. The transactions that are consistent with efficiency are those in which the total profits to buyer and seller are greater than the total costs imposed by the associated externality. For such trades, the traders would still make a profit even if they had to compensate everyone in the market for the negative externality caused by their trade. On the other hand, trades in which the profits of buyer and seller are smaller than the total amount of externalities caused by these trades will result in a reduction in total profits in the economy and are not economically efficient.

While trades between demanders with Buyer Values of $50 and suppliers with Seller Costs of $15 are economically *efficient*, you may well think that they are not *fair*. Why should individuals who make trades that impose negative externalities on others not have to pay their victims for damage done? Is it fair that trading between some individuals leaves others worse off than they would have been if no trades were allowed? We will demonstrate that with a pollution tax like the one in Session 2 of our experiment, it is possible to achieve efficiency while at the same time compensating those who are damaged by negative externalities.

A Pollution Tax to Regulate Externalities

We have seen that in a market with negative externalities and no controls on trader behavior, too many trades are made. One way to improve on this outcome is to introduce a pollution tax, just as we did in Session 2 of our experiment. In this session, sellers were taxed for each unit sold and all participants in the market received an equal share of the tax revenue. The effect of such a tax is that the supplier (at least partially) compensates everyone in the market for the pollution costs that her sales impose on others.

Suppose that the pollution tax on each sale is set equal to the total cost of the negative externalities that the sale imposes. Since the seller must pay the tax, she will be willing to sell a unit of output only if the price she is paid is at least as great as her Seller Cost *plus the tax*. Where the tax equals the total pollution costs imposed by producing one unit, she will sell only for a price that is greater than the sum of her production cost and the total pollution costs that she imposes by producing a unit.[4]

---

[4]A careful reader may notice that since 1/30 of the total amount of taxes collected will be rebated to each supplier, the true cost to a supplier of paying a $30 tax is only $29. The

In our previous example, the total cost of externalities generated in the production of a bushel of apples was $30. Suppose that the government imposed a pollution tax of $30, to be collected from the seller for each bushel of apples sold. As we learned in our earlier experiment with sales taxes, this tax will have the same effect on the supply curve as a $30 increase in Seller Costs for all suppliers. The tax would therefore shift the supply curve vertically by $30. This shifted supply curve is shown in Figure 6.2.

Figure 6.2: Supply and Demand With a Pollution Tax

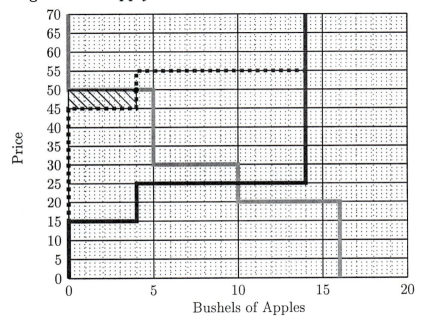

In Figure 6.2, we see that the shifted supply curve meets the demand curve where the price of apples is $50 per bushel and the number of bushels sold is 4. These are the competitive equilibrium price and quantity with a $30 pollution tax. Total profits made by buyers and sellers from apple transactions are given by the area between the shifted supply curve and the demand curve. These total profits are $5 × 4 = $20. Since each unit sold is

---

same careful reader might also notice that a clever supplier would be aware that her *own* production will cost her $1 in pollution damage, and hence the profits that she gets from selling a unit are $1 less than we have posited in drawing the supply and demand curves. These two effects exactly counterbalance each other, so that the outcome is precisely the same as if each supplier ignored the fact that she would share in the proceeds of the taxes that she paid and also ignored the cost to herself of her own pollution.

taxed at $30, total tax revenue is $30 × 4 = $120. Since each of the 4 units produced causes $1 worth of negative externalities to each of the 30 persons in the market, the total cost of externalities is $30 × 4 = $120. To find total profits in the market, we add buyers' and sellers' profits to the amount of tax revenue (which is returned to the market participants) and subtract the total externality costs. Thus we have total profits of $20+$120−$120 = $20.

Let us see how these profits are distributed in the population. The only people who *bought* apples were four of the demanders who had Buyer Values of $50 and who each paid $50 for a bushel of apples. Since the price equals their Buyer Values, these buyers made zero profits. The only people who *sold* apples were four suppliers who had Seller Costs of $15, and who paid a tax of $30. Since they received a price of $50 for their apples and had costs of $15 + $30 = $45, each of these sellers made $5 on the transaction. Every participant in the market suffered negative externalities of $4 ($1 from each of the four bushels of apples produced), but everyone got an equal share of the tax revenue. Since there was $120 in tax revenue to be divided among 30 people, each person received $4 as their share of tax revenue; this exactly cancels the $4 costs imposed on each person by the externality. When both the externalities and the divided tax revenue are taken into account, nobody is worse off than they would have been if production of apples had been prohibited, and the four sellers who sold apples are each better off by $5. Therefore total profits of all market participants would be $20.

In general, total profits in a market will be maximized if all individuals must pay the full costs, including externalities, of their actions. If suppliers must pay a pollution tax equal to the total cost of the externalities they impose, then they will sell their output only when someone is willing to pay the full social costs of producing it. In the apple market example, if apple producers must pay a $30 tax, they will sell a bushel of apples only if they can get a price that is at least $30 higher than their Seller Costs, which means that they will be able to make a sale only if the demander's Buyer Value exceeds the supplier's Seller Costs by at least the total cost of the negative externalities imposed by the production of a bushel of apples.

We found in an earlier experiment that when there are no externalities, introducing a sales tax will reduce market efficiency and result in a dead weight loss. In this experiment, we have discovered that the introduction of a of sales tax on the good that causes negative externalities can improve the efficiency of the market. In the example discussed here, a sales tax of $30 per bushel would increase total profits of market participants from a loss of $110 to a profit of $20.

Marketable Pollution Permits

In Session 3, we tried another method of controlling externalities. Each seller was required to have a pollution permit before being allowed to produce a unit of output. A fixed number of pollution permits was issued, and people were allowed to buy and sell these permits. Since suppliers must present a pollution permit for every unit of output that they produce, the total number of units produced cannot be greater than the number of permits issued.

Total profits made by buyers and sellers will depend not only on the number of permits sold, but also on which suppliers are using the permits. If pollution permits were not marketable, the only suppliers who would be permitted to sell lawn ornaments would be the ones who happened to own pollution permits. If some high-cost suppliers had pollution permits and some low-cost suppliers did not have permits, the outcome would be wasteful since output that could have been produced by low-cost suppliers would be produced by high-cost suppliers. If the government authorities know in advance which are the lowest-cost suppliers, they can achieve efficiency by awarding pollution permits to only the lowest-cost suppliers. But it is often difficult for policy-makers to determine who has the lowest costs. A simple way to ensure that pollution permits will ultimately find their way into the hands of the lowest-cost producers is to allow the holders of pollution permits to resell them.

To see that marketable permits will ultimately be used by the group of suppliers with the lowest Seller Costs, let us consider an example. Suppose that the market price for apples is $50 per bushel and that Supplier A, who has Seller Cost $35, has a permit, while Supplier B, who has Seller Cost $15 does not. If Supplier A uses her permit to sell a bushel of apples for $50, she will make a profit of $15. In this case, Supplier B cannot make a sale because she has no pollution permit. If Supplier B had a permit, she could produce a lawn ornament for a cost of $15 and sell it for $50, thus making a profit of $35. Therefore Supplier B would be willing to pay up to $35 for a permit. Since A makes a profit of only $15 from using the permit herself, it must be that *both* A and B could increase their profits if A sold her pollution permit to B for any price between $15 and $35.

Supply and Demand for Pollution Permits (Optional)

The market for pollution permits works much like the market for any other good. We should therefore be able to predict the equilibrium price of pollution permits using the tools of supply and demand. The "demanders" in the *permit market* are the suppliers of final goods who need pollution permits in order to be allowed to produce. In Effluvia, the demanders for permits are the suppliers of lawn ornaments. In our apple market example, the demanders for permits are the suppliers of apples.

Regardless of the price of permits, the total supply of permits in the market is fixed at the number of permits issued by the government. This means that the supply curve for permits is a vertical line.

Plotting the demand curve for permits is a little more complicated. The demand for permits is a "derived demand" that arises from the fact that you need a permit in order to sell the polluting good. In the case of our apple market example, we need to figure out the amount that each apple supplier would be willing to pay for a pollution permit. This will depend on the price that they can get for apples if they have a permit. The price of apples, in turn, will depend on the number of permits that are issued. Suppose, that the government issues 4 pollution permits. Knowing this, everyone will realize that only 4 bushels of apples can be brought to market with pollution permits. Looking at the demand curve for apples in Figure 6.1, we see that if the supply of apples is 4 bushels, the competitive equilibrium price of apples is $50 per bushel. Given that they expect to be able to sell apples for $50 a bushel, what would suppliers be willing to pay for a pollution permit?

Figure 6.3: Supply and Demand for Pollution Permits

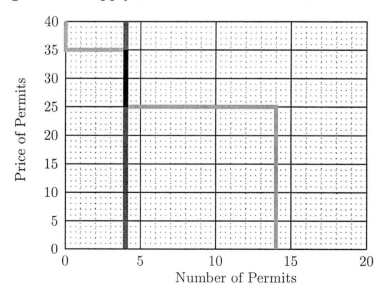

Consider a supplier with Seller Cost $15. If she had a pollution permit, she could make a profit of $35 by selling a bushel of apples for $50. Therefore she would be willing to pay up to $35 for a pollution permit. Now consider a supplier with Seller Cost $25. If she had a pollution permit, she could make a profit of $25 by selling a bushel of apples for $50. Therefore she would be willing to pay up to $25 for a pollution permit. It follows that in our example, the four suppliers with Seller Cost $15 would be willing to pay up to $35 and the ten suppliers with Seller Cost $25 would be willing to pay up to $25. These willingnesses-to-pay imply that the demand curve for pollution permits is as drawn in Figure 6.3.

Since the government makes exactly 4 pollution permits available, the supply curve for permits is a vertical line, corresponding to a fixed supply of 4 permits. From Figure 6.3, one can see that when 4 permits are available, the supply curve meets the demand curve along the line segment running from $(4, 25)$ to $(4, 35)$. This means that the market for pollution permits is in equilibrium at any price between $25 and $35 per permit.

A Remark on Information

In order to achieve full efficiency, either with a pollution tax or with pollution permits, the government needs to have far more detailed information about supply, demand, and externalities than it is likely to be able to obtain. If it is going to set a pollution tax equal to the total cost of the negative externalities generated, the government needs to know these costs. If it is going to issue pollution permits, the government needs to know the optimal number of permits to issue. Although full efficiency may not be attainable with available information, it is likely that significant movements in the direction of efficiency can be made using policies based even on approximate information.

If the government knew the supply and demand curves perfectly, it would always be possible to attain the same goals of pollution reduction either by taxing pollution or by distributing a limited number of marketable pollution permits. But if the government is not sure about these curves, then it faces a choice between setting the tax at a certain level without knowing the resulting level of pollution, or of issuing a fixed number of pollution permits, so it knows the amount of pollution reduction in advance, but does not know the price of permits, and hence does not know in detail the effects on the price of goods produced. One of the benefits that governments have discovered when they issue marketable pollution permits is that they are able to observe the prices of these permits and thus make better estimates of the costs and benefits of changing environmental standards.

Positive Externalities

Let us consider a happier story. The distribution of Buyer Values and Seller Costs remains the same as in Table 6.1, but the apple orchard uses no harmful chemical sprays. Instead, the beauty and fragrance of the orchard generates *positive* externalities. For every bushel of apples that is produced, every participant gets a *benefit* worth $.50. In this example, there are 30 participants, so the total value of the positive externalities generated by each bushel produced is $.50 \times 30 = $15. We ask you to work through the following exercise to determine the effects of a *subsidy* when there are positive externalities.[5]

Exercise: A Subsidy for Positive Externalities

Exercise 6.1 The distribution of Buyer Values and Seller Costs is given by Table 6.1. Suppose that the government pays a subsidy of $15 to each supplier who sells a bushel of apples. The government finances this subsidy by requiring everybody in the market, whether or not they bought or sold apples, to pay 1/30 of the total cost of the subsidy. On Figure 6.4, draw the demand and supply curves for apples that would apply if there is no subsidy. Then use a dotted red line to show the supply curve that applies with the subsidy.

Part a) With no subsidy, the competitive equilibrium price of apples

is $_____, and the competitive equilibrium quantity is _____ .

Part b) With the subsidy the competitive equilibrium price of apples

is $_____, and the competitive equilibrium quantity is _____ .

Part c) With no subsidy, total profits of buyers and sellers, not count-

ing externalities, are $_____. The total value of externalities pro-

duced is $_____, and total profits of all persons in the market, when

the value of externalities is included, is $_____ .

---

[5] Answers to this exercise can be found at the bottom of page 170

Figure 6.4: Supply and Demand With a Subsidy

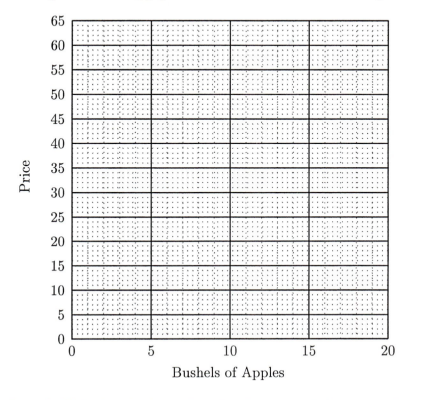

Part d) With the subsidy, total profits of buyers and sellers, including subsidy payments, but not including externalities, are $_____. The total amount of subsidy paid is $_____. The total value of externalities received by all participants is $_____. Total profits of all persons in the market, taking into account the value of positive externalities, and subtracting the amount of taxes that have to be paid to support the subsidy is $_____ .

Part e) If the cost of the subsidy is paid for by taxing each participant in the experiment for 1/30 of its total cost, then the introduction of the subsidy will (increase? decrease?) total after-tax profits of all buyers and sellers by $_____ .

Answers to Warm-up Exercises

W 6.1: $10, $450;   **W 6.2**: loss of $3, loss of $10;   **W 6.3**: $8, $4, loss of $4 ;   **W 6.4**: $5, $5;   **W 6.5**: $7, $10, sell the permit;   **W 6.6**: $50 − $15 − $20 − $4 = $11, $20 − $4 = $16, $60 − $50 − $4 = $6.

Answers to Exercises on Positive Externalities

Ex. 6.1: a)$25,10; b) $20,14; c) $190, $150, $340; d) $380, $210, $210, $380+$210−$210 = $380; e) increase, $40.

Lab Notes for Experiment 6

Recording Market Fundamentals

After trading is completed, the market manager will report the number of suppliers and demanders of each type and their Seller Costs and Buyer Values. Copy this information into Table 6.2.

Table 6.2: Distribution of Types of Agents

Seller Cost	Number in Market	Buyer Value	Number in Market
28		20	
23		25	
18		30	
13		35	
8		40	
3		45	

- Before the experiment began, the market manager announced the pollution cost that the production of each lawn ornament imposed on each individual Effluvian. Record this amount here. _____

- In Session 2, the market manager announced the amount of pollution tax charged to each seller of a lawn ornament. Record this amount here. _____

- In Session 3, the market manager announced the number of pollution permits that were issued. Record this number here. _____

In Table 6.3 record the price, Seller Cost, and Buyer Value in each transaction of the last round of Session 1. Then complete the table by calculating sellers' and buyers' profits from transactions. *These are profits before pollution damage is subtracted.*

Table 6.3: Prices and Transaction Profits in Session 1

Trans-action	Price	Seller Cost	Buyer Value	Seller's Profit*	Buyer's Profit*
1					
2					
3					
4					
5					
6					
7					
8					
9					
10					
11					
12					
13					
14					
15					
16					
17					
18					
19					
20					
21					
22					
23					
24					

*Profits before pollution damage is subtracted.

In Table 6.4 record the price, Seller Cost, and Buyer Value in each transaction of the last round of Session 2. Complete this table by calculating the buyer's profit for the transaction and the seller's *after-tax* profit. Calculate these profits *without* subtracting pollution costs or adding redistributed tax revenue.

Table 6.4: Prices and Transaction Profits in Session 2

Trans-action	Price	Seller Cost	Buyer Value	Pollution Tax	Seller's Profit*	Buyer's Profit*
1						
2						
3						
4						
5						
6						
7						
8						
9						
10						
11						
12						
13						
14						
15						
16						
17						
18						
19						
20						

*Profits recorded here are *after-tax* profits on transactions. Pollution damage is not yet subtracted and rebates from tax revenue are not yet added.

In Table 6.5 record the price, Seller Cost, Buyer Value and the amount that
the supplier paid for a pollution permit for each sale of a lawn ornament in
the last round of Session 3. Calculate each seller's and each buyer's profit.
To calculate seller's profits on transactions, subtract the seller's Seller Cost
and the price the seller paid for a permit from the price the seller got for the
lawn ornament. Do not include revenue received from the sale of permits in
calculating profits.

Table 6.5: Lawn Ornament Transactions and Profits–Session 3

Trans-action	Price	Seller Cost	Buyer Value	Price Paid for Permit	Seller's Profit*	Buyer's Profit*
1						
2						
3						
4						
5						
6						
7						
8						
9						
10						
11						
12						
13						
14						
15						
16						
17						
18						
19						
20						

*Profits recorded here do not include pollution damage suffered or any rev-
enue from sale of pollution permits.

Calculating Pollution Damage

Use Table 6.6 to calculate the total cost of pollution in the last round of each session of the experiment. In the first row enter the pollution cost that each resident of Effluvia suffered from the production of a single lawn ornament. (This cost was posted by the instructor and you recorded it on page 171.) In the second row record the number of lawn ornaments sold in each session. In the third row record the total pollution cost for each resident (which is equal to the number of lawn ornaments that were produced multiplied by the per-resident damage caused by each lawn ornament.) In the fourth row record the total number of participants in the experiment (including any who did not buy or sell). You can determine this number from the information in Table 6.2. In the last row, record the Total Cost of Pollution, which is equal to the total number of residents of Effluvia times the total pollution cost per resident.

Table 6.6: Pollution Damage, Sessions 1-3

	Session 1	Session 2	Session 3
Per-Resident Damage by Each Lawn Ornament			
Number of Lawn Ornaments Produced			
Total Pollution Cost Per Resident			
Number of Residents			
Total Cost of Pollution			

Experiment 7

Monopolies and Cartels

I'll Scratch Your Back

The industry chieftains are gathered in a luxurious hideaway, somewhere in the sunny Caribbean.

The chairman lifts his brandy glass and declares: "It is time to put an end to ruinous competition and price wars. From now on, we will work together. We will maintain a profitable price by restricting output. Each firm in our industry will get an output quota. Any firm that produces more than its quota will be severely punished."

"Hear! Hear!" roar his former competitors.

Session 1–Finding the Monopoly Output

A **monopoly** is a market that is served by only one supplier. This supplier is called a **monopolist**. A monopolist can typically increase its profits by charging a price higher than the competitive equilibrium price and selling less of its product than would be supplied in a competitive market.

Imagine that you run the only airline available to the demanders in your class. The cost to you of providing an airplane flight is $5 for each ticket you sell. Demanders will buy from you if your price is no greater than $1 below their Buyer Values; otherwise they will not buy. Your instructor will post the demanders' distribution of Buyer Values for airline tickets. On your Personal Information Sheet, write the price that you wish to charge and the number of units that you can sell at that price, and calculate your profits.

Session 2–Cartel Behavior

A group of firms in the same industry that agree to raise prices and restrict output is known as a **cartel**, and such behavior is known as **collusion**.[1] If a cartel can enforce its agreement, each of its members can make higher profits than they otherwise would. A cartel will maximize the total amount of profits made by its members if it chooses the same total industry output and price that a monopolist would set. The cartel can then agree to divide these profits among the firms in such a way that every cartel member gets more profits than it would have made without the cartel agreement.

This experiment simulates a market for airline tickets in a country where the airlines have managed to form a cartel. Six[2] members of the class will be designated as ticket suppliers (airlines), and the remaining class members will be ticket demanders.

Ticket Demanders' Instructions

Demanders receive Personal Information Sheets that indicate their Buyer Values for each session. The overall distribution of Buyer Values will be the same throughout all sessions of the experiment. At the beginning of the experiment, the market manager will announce the distribution of Buyer Values in the class and sketch the demand curve on the blackboard.

Demanders should make their purchases according to the following rule. Buy a unit of the good if you can find a price that is at least $1 below your Buyer Value; otherwise don't buy. If more than one firm posts a price lower than your Buyer Value, buy from a firm that is charging the lowest price. Your profits will be the difference between your Buyer Value and the price that you pay.

Suppliers' Instructions

Ticket suppliers will be given Firm Record Sheets on which they should record their own ID numbers, each customer's ID number and Buyer Value, and the price charged to that customer. Each supplier can supply up to 100 tickets. Each ticket sold costs $5 to produce.

In this session the suppliers will meet as a *cartel* and set output quotas for its members. If a 2/3 majority of cartel members agrees to a system of

---

[1]In the United States, cartels are illegal. If the U.S. Department of Justice discovered a meeting of the type described above, it would try to sentence the persons involved to prison terms.

[2]In small classes, your instructor may choose to have a smaller number of sellers.

quotas, the output quotas will be enforced on all members by the market manager (who will not accept sales by any firm that exceeds the quota assigned to it by the cartel). In addition to assigning quantity quotas, the cartel may also recommend a *price* to be charged by each cartel member. The price recommendation, however, will not be enforced by the market manager.

When the quotas have been set, suppliers are allocated locations near the blackboard where they can post their prices. Prices must be posted in dollar units, and suppliers are not allowed to change their prices, once they are posted. A supplier can sell any number of units that does not exceed its quota. A supplier's profits are equal to its total revenue minus the cost of producing the number of units that it sells.

Session 3–Can the Cartel Endure Secrecy?

In the previous session, the cartel agreement was enforced by the market manager. In more realistic situations, such outside enforcement may not be available. The cartel may find it very expensive or even impossible to keep track of the activities of its members and to punish overproduction and price-cutting.

In Session 3, the distribution of Buyer Values is the same as in Session 2. Cartel members again meet to discuss quotas and pricing requirements. They can make any agreement they wish. This time, however, the market manager will not enforce the quotas, so that compliance is voluntary.

Firm locations are scattered (if convenient, some firms may be located outside of the classroom). Suppliers can post prices and can change their posted prices whenever they like. Suppliers are also allowed to negotiate "private discounts" for individual buyers. For each sale, the supplier should record the identification number and Buyer Value of the buyer and the price at which the sale is made.

Session 4–The Cartel Offers Student Rates

Sometimes a cartel or a monopoly deals with demanders who can be divided into two groups with two different distributions of Buyer Values. When a cartel can determine who belongs to each of these two groups, it may profit by charging different prices to members of the two different groups. This practice is known as **price discrimination**. In Session 4, the cartel finds that students tend to have lower Buyer Values for airline tickets than nonstudents, and may find it profitable to charge lower prices to students.

As before, there are six firms and the remaining students are demanders. In this session, as in Session 2, the market manager *will* enforce cartel agreements.

Demanders' Instructions

In Session 4, there are two kinds of demanders, students and nonstudents. Those demanders who are designated as students will have the words "I AM A STUDENT" printed at the top of their Personal Information Sheets. Although firms will not be allowed to look at demanders' actual Buyer Values, they will be permitted to charge lower rates to demanders who can identify themselves as students. At the beginning of the session, the instructor will report to the class the distribution of Buyer Values among students and nonstudents.

A demander will be able to buy either zero or one unit of the good. A demander should buy a unit from a supplier if and only if the supplier's price is the lowest available and is at least $1 lower than the demander's Buyer Value.

Suppliers' Instructions

As in Session 2, producers meet as a cartel to set production quotas. The cartel will seek to agree on quotas for the number of units each producer can sell to students and to nonstudents. Again a 2/3 majority is required for agreements on quotas, which will be enforced by the market manager. The cartel can also suggest prices to the firms to charge each type of buyer.

Firms can post separate prices for students and for nonstudents, and can require customers to show student identification cards in order to qualify for student prices. Prices must be in dollar units and, once posted, can not be changed.

Warm-up Exercise

Profit Maximization for a Monopoly

Suppose that you are the only seller of airline tickets between two cities. You can produce as many units as you wish at a cost of $5 per unit. In the market there are 40 demanders with Buyer Values of $26, 10 demanders with

Buyer Values of $16, and 10 demanders with Buyer Values of $11. Assume that a demander will buy a ticket if and only if the price is at least $1 below his Buyer Value.[3]

W 7.1 If you set a price higher than $25, how many units would you sell?

_____

W 7.2 If you set a price of $25 you could sell _____ tickets and your total revenue would be $ _____ . The total cost of producing this number of units is $ _____, so your total profits would be $ _____.

W 7.3 If you set a price of $15, you could sell _____ tickets and your total revenue would be _____. The total cost of producing this number of units is $ _____, so your total profits would be $ _____ .

W 7.4 If you set a price of $10, you could sell _____ tickets and your total revenue would be _____. The total cost of producing this number of units is $ _____, so your total profits would be $ _____ .

W 7.5 At what price would you maximize total profit? $ _____ How many units can you sell at this price? _____

Suppose that you have the same costs as before, but suppose that the market now has 12 demanders with Buyer Values of $26, 18 demanders with Buyer Values of $16, and 6 demanders with Buyer Value of $11. As before, a demander will buy a ticket if the price is at least $1 below his Buyer Value and otherwise he will not buy.

W 7.6 If you set a price of $25, you could sell _____ tickets and your total revenue would be _____. The total cost of producing this number of units is _____, so your total profits would be _____.

---

[3]Answers to these exercises can be found on page 211.

W 7.7 If you set a price of $15, you could sell _____ tickets and your total revenue would be _____. The total cost of producing this number of units is _____, so your total profits would be _____.

W 7.8 If you set a price of $10, you could sell _____ tickets and your total revenue would be _____. The total cost of producing this number of units is _____, so your total profits would be _____.

W 7.9 At what price would you maximize total profit? _____ How many units can you sell at this price? _____

Profit Maximization for a Cartel

For all of the questions in this section assume that there are 6 firms in an airline cartel, and that each of these firms can produce as many units as it likes at a cost of $5 per unit.

As before, the market has 12 demanders with Buyer Values of $26, 18 demanders with Buyer Values of $16, and 6 demanders with Buyer Value of $11. Demanders will buy a ticket if and only if the price is at least $1 below their Buyer Values.

W 7.10 Total profit for the cartel will be maximized if everyone sets a price of $ _____ . At this price, a total of _____ tickets would be sold.

W 7.11 If cartel members decide to allocate to each firm an equal-sized quota of tickets to sell, how many tickets should each be allowed to sell if they want to maximize their profits? _____ If they choose profit-maximizing equal-sized quotas, what is the highest price at which each cartel member could sell her entire quota? $ _____ How much profit would each firm make? $ _____

Student Discounts

Suppose that customers can be reliably identified as students or nonstudents. There are 12 nonstudents with Buyer Values of $26 and 6 nonstudents with

Buyer Values of $16. There are 12 students with Buyer Values of $16 and 6 students with Buyer Values of $11. The market is controlled by a monopolist who can produce as many units as she likes at a cost of $5 per unit.

W 7.12 What price charged to nonstudents would yield the most profit from nonstudents? $ _____ At this price, what would be the total profits made from sales to nonstudents? $ _____

W 7.13 What price charged to students would yield the most profit from students? $ _____ At this price, what would be the total profits made from sales to students? $ _____

W 7.14 If the monopolist chose its most profitable price for students and its most profitable price for nonstudents, what would be its total profits?

$ _____ Compare these profits with the profits that it could make if all customers had to be charged the same price.

What Do You Expect to See?

■ If cartel agreements are enforced by the market manager, would you expect total output of cartel members to be greater, smaller, or about the same as when cartel agreements are voluntary? _____

■ If the cartel can make agreements but they are not enforced by the market manager, what do you think will happen to prices?

■ Do you think that the *sum* of firms' profits *plus* total consumers' surplus will be greater with an effective cartel or with an ineffective cartel?

Discussion of Experiment 7

Monopoly

In previous experiments we studied markets in which there were many sell-ers. We were able to make good predictions of market prices and quantities by finding the intersection of the competitive supply and demand curves. The competitive theory does not, however, do a good job of predicting the price and quantity in a market where there is only one seller. The reason for this difference can be explained by a simple theory of monopoly behavior.

Profit Maximization and Demand

The economic theory of monopoly relies on the assumption that a monopolist takes whatever actions are necessary to maximize its profit. If a monopolist could independently choose both price and quantity, it could make itself very rich indeed. All it would have to do would be to sell one unit at a price of, say, eighty billion dollars. In general, however, a monopolist is able to choose *price or quantity* but not both. If you owned the only taxicab company in town, you could set a price of $10,000 per ride, but at that price you wouldn't sell very many cab rides. Ordinarily, the number of units that a monopolist can sell will be smaller the higher the price that it charges. Or, to say the same thing in another way, the more units that a monopolist chooses to sell, the lower the price it will be able to charge for each unit.

The relation between the price that a monopolist charges and the number of units that it sells is determined by the *demand curve*.[4] Remember from previous experiments that the demand curve tells us the number of units demanders will buy at a given price. Consider, for example, a monopolist that faces the demand curve drawn in Figure 7.1.

From the demand curve, we can read off the number of units that the monopolist can sell at any price. It cannot sell any output at a price above $20. At a price of $20 it can sell one unit. At a price of $18 it can sell two units. At a price of $16 it can sell three units, and so on. From the same demand curve, we can also read off the best price that it could get as a function of the number of units it sells. That is to say, if it wants to sell exactly one unit, the highest price it can charge is $20. If it wants to sell

---

[4]Here, unlike the way we ran our experiment, we will assume that demanders will buy even if the price is exactly equal to their Buyer Values.

Figure 7.1: A Monopolist's Demand Curve

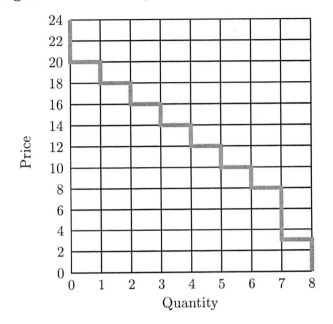

two units, the highest price that it can charge per unit is $18, and so on. Either way that we read the demand curve, we see that the monopolist can not independently choose both price and quantity, but in choosing one of these variables, it is forced to accept the other.

The first two columns of Table 7.1 record quantities and the highest price at which the monopolist can sell each quantity, given the demand curve in Figure 7.1.

Total and Marginal Revenue

A monopolist's **total revenue** is equal to the price it charges times the number of units it sells at that price. A monopolist's **marginal revenue** is the *increase* in total revenue that it gets from selling one more unit. The third column of Table 7.1 reports total revenue for each possible quantity sold. In the fourth column, we record marginal revenue. If the monopolist increases its sales from zero units to one unit of output, total revenue changes from $0 to $20, so marginal revenue is $20−$0 = $20. When it increases sales from one to two units, total revenue changes from $20 to $36, so marginal revenue is $36 − $20 = $16, and so on. When the monopolist increases sales from five to six units, its total revenue remains at $60, so marginal revenue

Table 7.1: Quantity, Price, Costs, and Profits

Quantity Sold	Price	Total Revenue	Marginal Revenue	Marginal Cost	Total Cost	Total Profit
0	–	0	-	-	0	0
1	20	20	20	5	5	15
2	18	36	16	5	10	26
3	16	48	12	5	15	33
4	14	56	8	5	20	36
5	12	60	4	5	25	35
6	10	60	0	5	30	30
7	8	56	−4	5	35	21
8	3	24	−32	5	40	−16

is \$0. When it increases sales from six to seven units, total revenue *falls* from \$60 to \$56, and so marginal revenue is −\$4.

Marginal Costs, Total Costs, and Profits

Since each unit that it produces costs the monopolist \$5 to make, the monopolist's total costs are equal to \$5 times its output. Thus its marginal cost, which is the extra cost of producing an additional unit, is always equal to \$5. We record marginal cost in the fifth column of Table 7.1, and total cost for each quantity of output in the sixth column.

The monopolist's profits are found by subtracting total costs from revenue. These are recorded in the last column of Table 7.1. As we see from the table, the monopolist achieves a maximum profit of \$36, which it accomplishes by selling 4 units at a price of \$14 per unit.

Marginal Revenue, Marginal Cost, and Profit-Maximization

In the example considered here, it is easy enough for the monopolist to find the most profitable number of units to sell and the corresponding price, simply by calculating profits for each amount of output that can be sold for a positive price. In more complicated and realistic environments, it may be easier for a firm to determine the marginal revenue and the marginal cost of a change in output than to determine total revenues and total costs for all possible quantities. Decision-making is simplified by the fact that information about marginal revenue and marginal cost is sufficient to determine whether small changes in the number of units sold will increase or decrease profits. In particular, we are able to apply the following principle:

Proposition 7.1 The Marginal Principle for a Monopolist. *If the marginal revenue from selling one more unit is greater than the marginal cost of producing that unit, then a monopolist can increase its profits by increasing its output. If the marginal revenue gained by selling its last unit is less than the marginal cost of producing the last unit, then a monopolist can increase its profits by decreasing its output.*

When a firm is selling the profit-maximizing number of units, it must not be able to increase its profits either by *increasing* or by *decreasing* its output. If the marginal revenue from selling one more unit is *greater* than the marginal cost of producing that unit, then the firm can increase its profits by producing and selling one *more* unit. Similarly, if the marginal revenue from the last unit of the current output is *smaller* than the marginal cost of producing that unit, then the firm can increase its profits by producing and selling one *less* unit.[5]

For example, in Table 7.1 one sees that if the monopoly is selling 3 units of output, its marginal revenue from increasing its output to 4 units is $8, which is greater than its marginal cost of $5. It can therefore increase its profits (by $3) if it sells 4 units rather than 3 units. On the other hand, if the monopoly is selling 5 units, its marginal revenue from selling the fifth unit is $4, which is *less than* its marginal cost of $5. Therefore, it could increase its profits (by $1) if it reduces its output by one unit. When the number of units sold is 4, however, profits cannot be increased either by lowering the price and selling 5 units or by raising the price and selling 3 units.

Comparing Marginal Revenue and Price

If the price that a firm could get for its output did not depend on the number of units it sold, then the extra revenue that it would get from selling one more unit would be just equal to its current price. But if the demand curve for a monopolist's product is downward sloping, then in order to increase its sales the monopolist has to lower the price that it charges. As it lowers price, it loses revenue on the units that it had been selling previously at

---

[5]Those who are familiar with elementary calculus will recognize that this condition corresponds to the "first-order condition" for a local maximum and that this is only a *necessary* condition for profit-maximization and not a *sufficient* condition. It may, for example, be that at some quantities no *small* change would increase profits, but some large change might do so.

the higher price. This loss in revenue has to be subtracted from the gain in revenue that it gets from selling an extra unit. This means that the *marginal revenue* from selling an extra unit is less than the *price* at which that unit is sold. In the example described in Table 7.1, suppose that the monopolist is selling 4 units at a price of $14. If it wants to increase its sales to 5 units, it will have cut its price to $12 per unit. The monopolist's marginal revenue is less than $12 because if it sold only 4 units, it could get $14 per unit. Thus to sell the extra unit, the monopolist has to cut its price on each of the first 4 units by $2. This means that although the monopolist gets $12 for its fifth unit, in order to make this sale it has to reduce its revenue from the first four units by $2 × 4 = $8. Therefore its marginal revenue is only $12 − $8 = $4. In general, we have the following useful fact:

Proposition 7.2 Marginal Revenue Is Less Than Price. *If a monopolist sells at a single price in a market with a downward-sloping demand curve, then marginal revenue at any amount of output is always less than the price at which that amount of output can be sold.*

Comparing Monopoly and Competition

We found that the profit-maximizing monopolist in our example would sell 4 units at a price of $14 each and would make a total profit of $36. Let us see what would happen if this same market had many competitive firms, each of which could produce the good at a cost of $5 per unit.

The market demand curve would be the same as that in Figure 7.1. What about the (competitive) supply curve? At prices below the marginal cost of $5, no firm would want to sell any output. At prices above $5, all firms would want to produce as much as possible so supply would be very large. At a price of exactly $5, firms would be willing to supply any positive amount. The resulting supply curve is a horizontal line at a height of $5, running all the way across the graph, as shown in Figure 7.2.

In Figure 7.2 the supply curve meets the demand curve at a price of $5 and a quantity of 7 units. Since the price is $5, and costs are $5 per unit, all firms make zero profits. At a price of $5, the demander with Buyer Value $20 makes a profit of $15, the demander with Buyer Value $18 makes a profit of $13, and so on, down to the demander with Buyer Value $8, who makes a profit of $3. The total amount of buyers' profits (consumers' surplus), which is measured by the area between the demand curve and the supply curve, is $63.

Figure 7.2: Competitive Supply and Demand

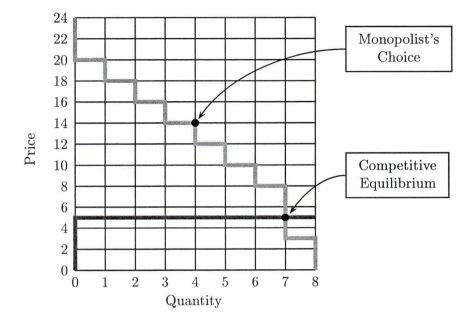

We can now compare the monopoly and the competitive outcomes. Table 7.2 shows prices, quantities, and profits for our example, when the market is a monopoly and when the market is competitive with several firms, each with a marginal cost of $5.

Table 7.2: Comparing Monopoly and Competition

	Price	Quantity	Sellers' Profits	Buyers' Profits	Total Profits
Monopoly	14	4	36	12	48
Competition	5	7	0	63	63

Differences Between Monopoly and Competition

In general, the following differences are found between a monopoly (where the monopolist must charge the same price for each unit sold) and the outcome in a market with the same demand curve and same marginal costs, but with many competitive firms:

- A profit-maximizing monopolist charges a higher price than the competitive equilibrium price, and sells a smaller quantity than the competitive equilibrium quantity.

- A profit-maximizing monopolist makes greater profits than the total profits that all firms in the industry would make under competition.

- The sum of demanders' profits and suppliers' profits is lower under monopoly than under competition.

Since a monopolist charges a price that is higher than the competitive price, it is not surprising that the profits of demanders are lower under monopoly than under competition. What is more interesting is the fact that *total* profits, which are the sum of demanders' profits and suppliers' profits, are in general higher if the market is competitive than if it is a monopoly. Why is this the case? Wouldn't you think that the buyers' loss from the higher price would be exactly matched by the seller's gain?

The sellers' gain from acting like a monopolist would equal the buyers' loss if the number of transactions did not change when the price rose. In fact, for those demanders who continue to buy from the monopolist, the effect of the monopolist's higher price is simply to reduce the demanders' profits by the same amount as the monopolist's profits increase. The sum of profits of demanders and suppliers from these transactions would therefore be the same under monopoly as under competition. But this is not the end of the story. The monopolist's higher price typically eliminates some trades that would be made at competitive prices. In our example, increasing the price from $5 to $14 eliminates three trades that would have been made under competition. At the competitive price of $5, buyers with Buyer Values $12, $10, and $8 would all have made purchases, and each of these purchases would have been profitable for the buyer and caused no loss to the sellers. At the monopoly price of $14 these three buyers make no purchases, and so neither buyer nor seller makes a profit. Therefore *total* profits of demanders and suppliers are lower with monopoly than with competition.

Cartels

Recall that a *cartel* is a group of firms, all in the same industry, who agree to produce less than they would in a competitive environment in an effort to increase their profits. In order to maximize the total profits of its members, a cartel would like to produce the same total quantity and charge the same price as a monopolist. The cartel will also have to work out an arrangement to coordinate the activities of its members and divide total profits.

Where cartel members all have the same costs of production, one simple way of maximizing total profits is to calculate the profit-maximizing quantity for a monopolist, and then give each firm a *production quota* equal to the monopoly output divided by the number of firms in the industry. If all firms produce their quotas, then total output will be the same as the monopoly output, each firm can sell its entire quota at the monopoly price, and all firms will get equal profits. For example, in the market discussed in the previous section, the profit-maximizing output for a monopoly is 4 units, which the monopoly would sell at a price of $14 per unit. If this industry had 4 firms, and the firms agreed to collude, they could assign a production quota of $4/4 = 1$ unit to each firm and recommend a price of $14. As long as each firm stuck to its quota, it would be possible for every firm to sell its single unit of output at a price of $14. Each of the four firms would then make a profit of $9, and total profits of all firms would be $36.

While a cartel agreement would be very profitable for its members, it is not easy to enforce. The problem is that any one firm could gain by violating its production quota and producing more output. Attempts to maintain industry prices by collusive agreements frequently break down. To see why, consider the four firms who agreed to production quotas of one unit of output for each firm. Suppose that one of these firms secretly chose to produce 2 units and to offer these units for sale at $12. It would be able to sell these two units for a total revenue of $24, and since its costs are $5 per unit it would have a profit of $14, which is $5 better than the $9 that it would make if it stuck to the agreement. But when this firm violates its quota, it reduces the profits of all other cartel members. If the other three firms each produce one unit, and the violator produces two units, then total industry output is five units, and we see from the demand table that in order for all five units to be sold, the price must fall to $12. The three firms that produced one unit, would therefore each get a revenue of $12 and a profit of $7. But this is not the worst of it. The other firms would realize that they too could gain by cheating on the cartel agreement, and the price would soon be driven close to the competitive price. You most likely saw this happen quite dramatically in Session 3 of the experiment.

In most countries, since cartels are illegal, cartel agreements have to be made in secret and certainly cannot be enforced by legal contracts. Cartels may still be able to get their members to restrain production by threatening punishment to those who produce too much, but in order to enforce these threats they would need to observe the output and/or pricing behavior of each cartel member. Thus we are more likely to see cartel behavior when it is easy for firms to monitor each others' pricing and output decisions than when it is difficult to do so.

Price Discrimination

In a story in the *New York Times*[6] Robert E. Mertens, the vice president of pricing and product planning at American Airlines, was quoted as saying:

> "Its a sophisticated guessing game. You don't want to sell a seat to a guy for $69 when he's willing to pay $400."

In the example that we discussed above, a monopolist with the demand curve given by Figure 7.1 will maximize her profit by charging a price of $14 and selling 4 units. If she sets her price at $14, the monopolist is faced with a tantalizing possibility. There are three buyers who still have not bought her output, but who are willing to pay $12, $10, and $8. Her marginal cost is only $5 per unit. If she could identify these three buyers, she could increase her profits by charging each of them a price of, say, $7, while maintaining a price of $14 to the other buyers. Selling these 3 units for $7 would give her an additional revenue of $21 and an additional cost of only $15, so she would add $6 to her profits. But she can only do this if she can identify the groups with higher and lower Buyer Values, and sell at different prices to each group. Selling the same goods at different prices to different buyers is called **price discrimination**.

Perfect Price Discrimination

Let us first consider an extreme form of price discrimination in which the monopolist knows the Buyer Value of every demander and is able to set a different price for each of them. If a profit-maximizing monopolist could do this, how would she behave? A demander is willing to pay any price that is less than his Buyer Value, and no price that is higher. Therefore the most the monopolist can expect to extract from any demander is an amount slightly less than his Buyer Value. To maximize her total profit, the monopolist should sell the good to all buyers who have Buyer Values that are greater than her marginal cost, and she should charge each buyer a price slightly less than his Buyer Value. A monopolist who does this is said to practice **perfect price discrimination**, which is also known as **first-degree price discrimination**.

---

[6] *New York Times*, March 4, 1987.

Figure 7.3: Discriminating Monopolist's Demand and Costs

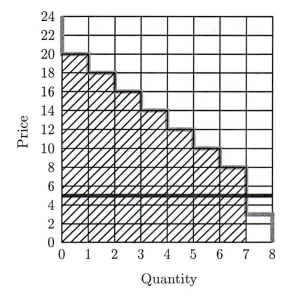

Consider a monopolist who faces the same demand curve that we studied in our earlier example and who is able to practice perfect price discrimination. We have redrawn this demand curve in Figure 7.3. With this demand curve, a monopolist who is able to practice perfect price discrimination could charge just under \$20 for the first unit sold, just under \$18 for the second, and so on down to the seventh unit, which could be sold for just under \$8. The monopolist's total revenue would then be slightly less than \$20 + 18 + 16 + 14 + 12 + 10 + 8 = \$98. This is equal to the area of the shaded region in Figure 7.3. Since it is selling 7 units, its total costs would be \$35, and its profit would be slightly less than \$98 − 35 = \$63. (This is equal to the area of the part of the shaded region above the horizontal line that we have drawn at a height of \$5.) In comparison, recall that a monopolist who must charge the same price to all consumers would charge a price of \$14 to everyone, would sell only 4 units, and would make a profit of \$36.

This example illustrates several facts that are true in general for perfectly discriminating monopolists.

Proposition 7.3 *A monopolist practicing perfect price discrimination:*

- *sells to every demander whose Buyer Value is greater than the monopolist's marginal cost.*

- *charges each buyer a price that is just slightly below his Buyer Value.*

- *sells the same number of units that would be sold in competitive equilibrium.*

- *sells more units and makes higher profits than a monopolist who charges a single price.*

- *leaves all demanders with consumers' surplus of almost zero.*

- *makes profits that are almost as high as the total of firms' profits and consumers' surplus in competitive equilibrium.*

Since a monopolist practicing perfect price discrimination makes even more profits than a monopolist who charges a single price, you may wonder why all monopolists don't do this. There are at least two important limitations on a monopolist's ability to charge different prices to different buyers. The first is the possibility of resale. If a monopolist sells at a lower price to some buyers than to others, then one of the buyers who can get the good cheaply can make profits by buying the good and reselling it to someone who would have to pay the monopolist a higher price. For example, suppose that the demander with Buyer Value $8 buys a unit from the monopolist for $8 and resells this unit to the demander with Buyer Value $20 for $15. If he does so, the demander with Buyer Value $8 makes a profit of $7 and the demander with Buyer Value $20 makes a profit of $5, while the monopolist loses the opportunity to sell a unit to the demander with Buyer Value $20 for $20. For this reason, price discrimination is not likely to be successful for commodities, like clothing or computers, that are easy to resell. On the other hand, goods and services like restaurant meals, haircuts, appendectomies, or taxicab rides are difficult, if not impossible, for the original purchaser to resell. For such commodities the possibilities for price discrimination are greater.

Even if a good is not resellable, a monopolist's ability to price discriminate is limited by the fact that although she may have a good estimate of the overall market demand curve, she is unlikely to know which *individuals* are the ones with high and low willingness-to-pay. In our example, the monopolist may know that one of the demanders has a Buyer Value of $20, another has a Buyer Value of $18, and so on, but may not know which demander is which. Nor is the monopolist likely to get this information by asking potential customers. Suppose that you are a demander and a monopolist asks you to report your Buyer Value. If you know that the monopolist is going to charge you a price just below your reported Buyer Value, what will your answer be? Buyers would have every incentive to report Buyer Values below their true willingness-to-pay.

Pricing in Separate Markets

Although monopolists are rarely, if ever, able to practice perfect price discrimination, they can sometimes divide their demanders into two or more separate groups and charge different prices to members of each group. For example, book publishers charge different prices for the same book in different countries. Restaurants and movie theaters charge different prices to senior citizens or students than to other demanders. Software sellers charge different prices to new customers and customers who own an earlier, less elaborate version of the same product, and so on. Price discrimination of this kind is known as **third-degree price discrimination**.

Third-degree price discrimination can be successfully practiced only in markets in which resale from one type of customer to another is impossible, or at least inconvenient, and in which demanders can be divided into easily identifiable groups with different distributions of Buyer Values.

If a firm is able to separate its demanders into distinct groups with different distributions of Buyer Values, then it typically can increase its profits by charging a different price to members of each group. The monopolist can treat each group as a separate market and charge the price that maximizes profits from that market. We encourage you to work through the following exercise on the practice of third-degree price discrimination.[7]

Exercise: A Price Discriminating Barber

A very small town has just one barbershop. The barber's costs are $5 for each haircut that he gives. He discovers that the four red-haired people in town have Buyer Values of $18, $12, $10, and $3, and that the other four people in town have Buyer Values $20, $16, $14, and $8.[8] Citizens of this town will buy a haircut if the price is *less than or equal to* their Buyer Values, and will not buy a haircut for any price above their Buyer Values.

Exercise 7.1   The barber is trying to decide on prices to charge to redheads and to others. To help him make this decision, complete Table 7.3. In the second column of the Redheads box record the number of haircuts that he could sell to redheads at each price. In the third column calculate the total revenue (price times quantity) from redheads at each price. In the fourth column record the profit that

---

[7]Answers are found on page 211.

[8]He doesn't know which of the redheads has which of these values, or which non-redhead has which of the non-redhead Buyer Values.

he would make from cutting redheads' hair at each price. His profit from redheads will be his revenue minus his total costs, which are $5 for each haircut that he gives. When you have completed the table for redheads, complete the other table for Other Residents.

Table 7.3: Splitting Hairs

Redheads				Other Residents			
Price	Quant.	Rev.	Profit	Price	Quant.	Rev.	Profit
$20				$20			
$18				$18			
$16				$16			
$14				$14			
$12				$12			
$10				$10			
$8				$8			
$3				$3			

Exercise 7.2 In order to maximize his profits, what price should the barber charge redheads? _____ What price should he charge the other residents? _____

Exercise 7.3 If he charges the profit-maximizing prices to redheads and to others, how much profit does he make from the redheads?

_____ How much profit does he make from others?_____ How much profit does he make in total? _____

Exercise 7.4 Suppose that the barber must charge the same price to redheads as to others. Complete Table 7.4 to help him find the price that maximizes his profits.

Exercise 7.5 In order to maximize profits, if he must charge everyone the same price, what price should the barber charge? _____ How

Table 7.4: One Price For All

Price	Quantity	Revenue	Profit
$20			
$18			
$16			
$14			
$12			
$10			
$8			
$3			

much are his profits when he charges this price? _____

Exercise 7.6 The barber's profits when he can charge different prices

to redheads and to others are $_____ (higher?, lower?) than when he must charge the same price to everyone.

Exercise 7.7 If the barber price-discriminates between redheads and others in the profit-maximizing way, which people will not get haircuts?

_____

Exercise 7.8 If the barber must charge the same price to everyone and chooses his profit-maximizing price, which people will not get

haircuts?_____

Monopoly with Smooth Curves

So far we have dealt with the behavior of monopolists that faced staircase demand functions. Now we will explore the theory of a monopolist that faces a smooth, downward-sloping demand curve. Where the demand curve is smooth, a profit-maximizing monopolist will choose a quantity at which marginal revenue is exactly equal to marginal cost.

A monopolist's marginal revenue is always less than the price because in order to sell an extra unit it has to reduce the price for every unit it sells. If $P(q)$ is the price at which the firm can sell q units, then a monopolist's marginal revenue curve is given by the equation

$$MR(q) = P(q) - (\text{Price cut needed to sell one more unit}) \times q. \qquad (7.1)$$

Let us see how this works in the special case of a linear demand curve. If the demand curve is given by the equation $P(q) = a - bq$, then we see from the demand equation that for each additional unit that it sells, the firm has to cut its price by b. Therefore the firm's marginal revenue must be $MR(q) = (a - bq) - bq = a - 2bq$. The equation for $MR(q)$ is therefore a straight line with the same vertical intercept (a) as the demand curve, but with a slope $(-2b)$ that is exactly twice as steep. We restate this fact, which is quite useful to remember, as follows.

Proposition 7.4 *If the demand curve is a straight line with the equation $p = a - bq$, then the marginal revenue curve is also a straight line. The marginal revenue curve has the same vertical intercept as the demand curve, but is twice as steep, and its equation is $p = a - 2bq$.*

Let us look at a specific example of how a monopolist's profit-maximizing price and quantity are determined. Demand is given by the equation $p = 45 - .15q$, as shown in Figure 7.4. The marginal revenue curve then has the equation $p = 45 - .30q$, and is drawn as a dashed line in Figure 7.4.

Let us assume that the monopolist can produce as many units as it likes at a cost of $15 per unit. Then its marginal cost is $15 for all quantities and its marginal cost curve is a horizontal line as shown in the figure.

The marginal revenue curve meets the marginal cost curve at the point A, where the quantity is 100 units and marginal revenue is equal to $15. The profit-maximizing output for the monopoly is therefore 100 units.

What price will the monopolist charge? The monopolist will charge the highest price at which it can sell 100 units. We can read this price from the demand curve. When the quantity is 100 units, the price on the demand curve is $30. Therefore the monopolist's profit maximizing combination of quantity and price is 100 units sold at a price of $30. At this price-quanity combination, its revenue is $30 \times 100 =$3,000$ and its costs are $15 \times 100 =$1,500$. Therefore its maximum possible profit is $3,000-$1,500= $1,500.

Figure 7.4: Marginal Revenue, Price, and Marginal Cost

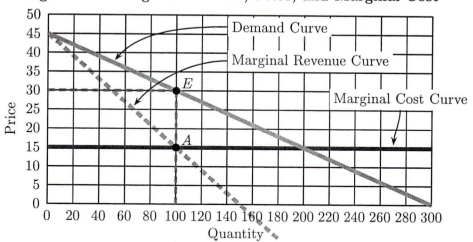

We suggest that you work through the following exercise to solidify your understanding of the way that a monopoly chooses quantity and price.

Exercise: MightySoft Plays Hardball[9]

Bill Barriers, president of MightySoft Inc, is marketing a new software product called DoorStops. According to his market researchers, the demand for DoorStops is given by the equation

$$P = \$100 - \frac{1}{1000}Q$$

where P is the price per copy of DoorStops and Q is the number of copies sold. MightySoft has spent \$1,000,000 on developing the product and \$500,000 on advertising it. In addition to these fixed costs, it has a variable cost of \$10 per unit sold. Therefore, if it sells Q copies of DoorStops, MightySoft's total costs will be $C(Q) = \$1,500,000 + \$10Q$. At all levels of output its marginal cost is \$10.

Exercise 7.9   The demand equation implies that the demand curve must be a straight line. To draw this line, all one needs to do is to find two points on the line and connect them. According to the demand

---

[9]Answers to these questions are found on page 211.

equation, if $Q = 0$ then $P = $ \$_____, and if $Q = 100{,}000$ then

$P = $ \$_____. Draw the demand curve for DoorStops in Figure 7.5.

Exercise 7.10 On Figure 7.5, draw and label the marginal cost curve and the marginal revenue curve for DoorStops. **Hint:** Proposition 7.4 tells you how to find the equation for the marginal revenue curve.

Figure 7.5: The DoorStop Monopoly

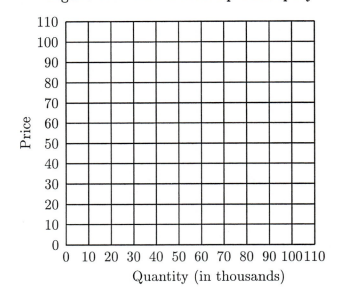

Exercise 7.11 On Figure 7.5, label the intersection of the marginal revenue curve and the marginal cost curve with the letter A. Draw a vertical dotted line from A to the horizontal axis to find the profit-

maximizing quantity, which is _____.

Exercise 7.12 On Figure 7.5, extend the dotted vertical line through the point A up to the demand curve. Label the point where this line meets the demand curve B. Draw a horizontal dotted line from B to

the vertical axis. What price will MightySoft charge? \$_____.

Exercise 7.13 MightySoft's profit-maximizing total revenue is \$___

_____, its total cost is \$_____, and its profit is \$ _____.

Monopoly Pricing and Elasticity (Optional)

According to Proposition A.1 on page 415, if demand is inelastic, then price and revenue move in the same direction along the demand curve. This fact has an interesting implication for monopoly pricing. A profit-maximizing monopolist will never choose a price-quantity combination that falls in the *inelastic* portion of the demand curve. Why is this? Because if demand is inelastic at the current price, the firm will be able to increase its revenue by increasing its price and reducing its quantity. Not only does the firm's revenue increase, but since the quantity sold is reduced, the firm will have lower total costs. Since profits are the difference between revenue and costs, a price increase will increase the monopolist's profits on both accounts.

We know that a profit-maximizing monopolist will charge a price that is higher than its marginal cost. If we know the monopolist's price elasticity of demand, we can find out *how much* higher price will be than marginal cost. Since a profit-maximizing monopolist sets marginal revenue equal to marginal cost, the difference between price and marginal cost will be the same as the difference between price and marginal revenue. As we see from Equation 7.1, the difference between price and marginal revenue is equal to the price cut needed to sell an extra unit times the number of units sold. Therefore the difference between price and marginal cost is also equal to the loss in revenue from the price cut needed to to sell an extra unit. If demand is very elastic, a firm will not have to reduce its price by very much to sell an extra unit. If demand is very inelastic, the firm will have to reduce its price a lot in order to sell one more unit. Therefore it is not surprising to learn that the difference between marginal revenue and price is greater as demand is more inelastic. When demand is elastic,[10] the exact relation between marginal cost and price for a profit-maximizing monopolist can be shown to be as follows:

$$\text{Price} \times \left(1 + \frac{1}{E_d}\right) = \text{Marginal Cost} \tag{7.2}$$

From Equation 7.2 we see that the more inelastic is demand, the greater will be the difference between price and marginal cost. This fact has an interesting implication for monopolists that practice third-degree price discrimination by charging different prices in two different markets. In this case, the monopolist will have the same marginal cost for each market, and he will choose prices that satisfy Equation 7.2 for each market. He will

---

[10] As we have already remarked, a monopolist with non-negative marginal cost will never choose to sell a quantity that is on the inelastic portion of its demand curve.

therefore charge a higher price in the market that has the more inelastic demand.

Food For Thought

Many of the pricing policies of real-world businesses that seem quite puzzling at first glance are understandable if you think about price discrimination.

■   Why do you suppose it is that a round-trip airplane ticket between two major American cities can cost $300 if you stay over a Saturday night and $1500 if you do not? Can you think of a reason why it is in the airlines' interest to insist that the name on your ticket matches your photo ID when you board the plane?

■   Why do grocery stores issue discount coupons instead of just reducing their prices?

■   Why do movie theaters, sporting events, and museums offer reduced rates to senior citizens and to children.

■   We know that university administrators would like you to believe that they give scholarships to low-income students because they are concerned about equality of opportunity. Can you think of any other reason why they might do this?

■   Federal Express offers two kinds of overnight delivery. There is *priority overnight*, which is guaranteed to reach its destination by 10:30 am the next day, and *standard overnight*, which is guaranteed to be delivered by 3 pm the next day. Priority overnight costs about 20% more than standard overnight. Federal Express will often make *two* delivery trips to the same office, in the same day, to avoid delivering standard overnight packages before 10:30. How can you explain this behavior?

■   The IBM LaserPrinter Series E was identical to the standard IBM Laser Printer, except for its lower price and slower printing speed. The reason for the speed difference was that IBM installed an extra chip in the Series E that inserted wait states to slow down the printer. Why do you suppose that IBM did this?

■   The *Journal of Public Economics*, a scholarly journal published by North Holland Publishing Company, offers subscriptions to individuals for $180 per year and to libraries for $1331 per year. How would you explain this price difference?

■ Why do you think that paperback editions of books do not appear until several months after the hardback was published? Do you think that the price difference between the hardback and paperback edition is greater than, equal to, or smaller than the difference in production costs?

Answers to Warm-up Exercises

W 7.1: 0; **W 7.2**: 40, $1000, $200, $800; **W 7.3**: 50, $750, $250, $500; **W 7.4**: 60, $600, $300, $300; **W 7.5**: $25, 40; **W 7.6**: 12, $300, $60, $240; **W 7.7**: 30, $450, $150, $300; **W 7.8**: 36, $360, $180, $180; **W 7.9**: $15, 30; **W 7.10**: $15, 30; **W 7.11**: 5, $15, $50; **W 7.12**: $25, $12 \times \$25 - 12 \times \$5 = \$240$; **W 7.13**: $15, $12 \times \$15 - 12 \times \$5 = \$120$; **W 7.14**: $360, The best uniform price is $15, which yields profits of $300—thus price discrimination allows the monopolist to increase its profits by $60.

Answers to Exercises

Ex. 7.1: Redheads; 0, 0, 0; 1, 18, 13; 1, 16, 11; 1, 14, 9; 2, 24, 14; 3 , 30, 15; 3, 24, 9; 4, 12, −8; Others: 1, 20, 15; 1, 18, 13; 2, 32, 22; 3, 42, 27; 3, 36, 21; 3, 30, 15; 4, 32, 12; 4, 12, −8; **Ex. 7.2**: $10, $14; **Ex. 7.3**: $15, $27, $42; **Ex. 7.4**: 1, 20, 15; 2, 36, 26; 3, 48, 33; 4, 56, 36; 5, 60, 35; 6, 60, 30; 7, 56, 21; 8, 24, −16; **Ex. 7.5**: $14, $36; **Ex. 7.6**: $6 higher; **Ex. 7.7**: The redhead with Buyer Value $3 and the non-redhead with Buyer Value $8 will go unshorn; **Ex. 7.8**: Three redheads and one other person will stay shaggy; **Ex. 7.9**: $100, $0; **Ex. 7.11**: 45,000; **Ex. 7.12**: $55; **Ex. 7.13**: $2,475,000, $1,500,000 + (\$10 \times 45,000) = \$1,950,000$; $2,475,000$-$1,950,000=$525,000$.

Lab Notes for Experiment 7

Distribution of Demanders

Your instructor will post the information on the distribution of types and Buyer Values that you need in order to complete Tables 7.5 and 7.6.

Table 7.5: Distribution of Demander Types: Sessions 2 and 3

Buyer Value	Number of Demanders
$21	
$16	
$11	

Table 7.6: Distribution of Demander Types: Session 4

Type and Buyer Value	Number of Demanders
Nonstudent with B. V. $21	
Nonstudent with B. V. $16	
Nonstudent with B. V. $11	
Student with B. V. $21	
Student with B. V. $16	
Student with B. V. $11	

Sales, Revenue, and Distribution of Buyer Values

You instructor will post the information needed to complete Tables 7.7-7.12.

In Table 7.7 record the quota assigned to each firm by the cartel, the number of units that it sold, and its total revenue in Session 2.

Table 7.7: Sales and Revenue in Session 2

Firm ID	Firm's Quota	Number of Units Sold	Firm's Total Revenue

In Table 7.8 record the number of demanders with each Buyer Value who *actually bought* tickets in this Session 2. (This should not be confused with the distribution of Buyer Values of all the demanders who participated in the experiment.)

Table 7.8: Buyers in Session 2

Buyer Value	Number of Buyers
$21	
$16	
$11	

In Table 7.9 record the quota assigned to each firm by the cartel, the number of units that it sold, and its total revenue in Session 3.

Table 7.9: Sales and Revenue in Session 3

Firm ID	Firm's Quota	Number of Units Sold	Firm's Total Revenue

In Table 7.10 record the number of demanders with each Buyer Value who *actually bought* tickets in Session 3.

Table 7.10: Buyers in Session 3

Buyer Value	Number of Buyers
$21	
$16	
$11	

In Table 7.11 record, for each firm, the quotas that the cartel assigned for sales to students and non-students, the number of units sold to students and non-students, and the total revenue from sales to students and to non-students.

Table 7.11: Prices and Sales for Students and Nonstudents

Firm ID	Student Quota	Non-student Quota	Units Sold to Students	Units Sold to Non-Students	Revenue from Students	Revenue from Non-Students

In Table 7.12 record the numbers of demanders with each Buyer Value who *actually bought* tickets in Session 4.

Table 7.12: Buyers in Session 4

Buyer Value	Number of Buyers
$21	
$16	
$11	

Homework for Experiment 7

Problem 7.1 Use the information in Tables 7.7 and 7.8 to complete Table 7.13, which summarizes the experimental results in Session 2.

Table 7.13: Experimental Outcomes: Session 2

Mean Price	
Total Number of Units Sold	
Total Profits of All Firms	
Total Consumers' Surplus	
Sum of Firms' Profits and Consumers' Surplus	

Hints:

- The mean price can be found by dividing the total revenue of all firms by the total number of units that they sold.

- Recall that the cost of each unit produced is \$5. Total profits of all firms is equal to the total revenue of all firms minus total costs.

- Total Consumers' Surplus is the sum of the Buyer Values of everyone who bought a ticket minus the total amount of money that buyers paid for tickets. You can find the sum of the Buyer Values of those who bought tickets from Table 7.8. The total amount that consumers paid for tickets is equal to the total revenue of firms.

Problem 7.2 Suppose that the industry operated competitively without any cartel agreement. The answers that you provide here will help you to draw the competitive supply curve. Recall that each firm can produce up to 100 units at a cost of $5 per unit.

Part a) At prices below $5, how many units will firms supply?   _____

At prices above $5, how many units will firms want to supply?   _____

Part b) On Figure 7.6, use red ink to draw the vertical segment of the competitive supply curve corresponding to prices below $5. The graph is not wide enough to show the vertical segment of the supply curve corresponding to prices above $5, so you don't need to show this part. At a price of exactly $5, each firm is indifferent between supplying any number of tickets between 0 and 100. Therefore you can complete the (visible part of) the supply curve by drawing a horizontal line across the graph at a height of $5.

Part c) Use the information from Table 7.5 of your lab notes to draw the demand curve during Sessions 2 and 3 for airline tickets on Figure 7.6.

Figure 7.6: Competitive Supply and Demand

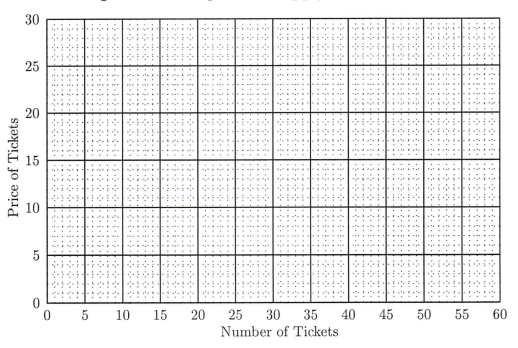

Problem 7.3 From the supply and demand curves that you drew in Figure 7.6, you can find the price and quantity that would be predicted by competitive equilibrium theory for the market in Sessions 2 and 3. You can also calculate firms' profits and consumers' surplus in competitive equilibrium. Make these calculations to complete Table 7.14.

Table 7.14: Competitive Predictions

Mean Price	
Total Number of Units Sold	
Total Profits of All Firms	
Total Consumers' Surplus	
Sum of Firms' Profits and Consumers' Surplus	

Problem 7.4 Complete Table 7.15 to show the prices, quantities and profits that would be predicted for the market in Sessions 2 and 3 if there were only one firm and it charged the profit-maximizing, monopoly price. Assume that a demander will buy only if the price is at least $1 below his Buyer Value.

Table 7.15: Monopoly Predictions

Mean Price	
Total Number of Units Sold	
Total Profits of All Firms	
Total Consumers' Surplus	
Sum of Firms' Profits and Consumers' Surplus	

Problem 7.5   Table 7.13 shows the actual prices, quantities and profits that were observed in Session 2.   Table 7.14 shows the predictions that competitive equilibrium theory makes and Table 7.15 shows the predictions that monopoly theory makes for these outcomes. Which of the two theories comes closer to predicting the results of Session 2? _____

Problem 7.6 Use the information in Tables 7.9 and 7.10 to complete Table 7.16, which summarizes the *observed* results of Session 3.

Table 7.16: Experimental Outcomes: Session 3

Mean Price	
Total Number of Units Sold	
Total Profits of All Firms	
Total Consumers' Surplus	
Sum of Firms' Profits and Consumers' Surplus	

Problem 7.7   Table 7.16 shows the actual prices, quantities and profits that were observed in Session 3. Table 7.14 shows the predictions that competitive equilibrium theory makes and Table 7.15 shows the predictions that monopoly theory makes for these outcomes. Which of the two theories came closer to predicting the actual results of Session 3? _____

Problem 7.8   Use the information in Tables 7.11 and 7.12 to complete Table 7.17, which summarizes the *observed* results of Session 4.

Problem 7.9 In both Sessions 2 and 4, the cartel agreements were enforced by the market manager. In Session 2, the monopolist had to charge the same price to everyone. In Session 4, it could price-discriminate between students and non-students. Use Tables 7.13 and 7.17 to answer the following:

Part a) In which session did firms make larger profits?   _____

Part b) In which session was total consumers' surplus larger?   _____

Table 7.17: Experimental Outcomes: Session 4

Mean Price	
Total Number of Units Sold	
Total Profits of All Firms	
Total Consumers' Surplus	
Sum of Firms' Profits and Consumers' Surplus	

Part c) In which session was the sum of firms' profits and consumers' sur-

plus larger? _____

Problem 7.10 We defined the **market efficiency** to be the actual total profits of all market participants expressed as a percentage of the maximum possible profits that could be achieved for all participants in the market (see page 22). Also recall that for a market like this one, the competitive equilibrium outcome maximizes the sum of the profits of all participants.

Part a) Using the information in Tables 7.13 and 7.14, calculate the market

efficiency of the *experimental outcome* in Session 2. _____

Part b) Using the information in Tables 7.15 and 7.14, calculate the market efficiency of the *theoretically predicted outcome* for a profit-maximizing

monopoly in Session 2. _____

Part IV

Firms and Technology

Experiment 8

Entry and Exit

The Ins and Outs of the Restaurant Business

Have you ever wondered what it would be like to open a restaurant? In this experiment, even if your cooking is so bad that your dog won't eat it, and even if you are too surly to wait tables, you will have your chance.

Restaurants, like most other businesses, have some costs that are the same no matter how many units they sell and some costs that depend on the number of units sold. The former are known as **fixed costs** or equivalently as **overhead costs**, and the latter are known as **variable costs**. A firm's **total cost** is the sum of its fixed costs plus its total variable costs.

Examples of fixed costs for a restaurant include the cost of renting the building in which it locates, the cost of kitchen equipment, booths and tables, the cost of advertising, and the cost of employing a chef. A restaurant will have to pay these costs regardless of how many meals it sells. In contrast, the cost of the ingredients used in meals will vary with the number of meals sold, and thus is a variable cost.

In the real world anyone is free to open a restaurant, but it clearly wouldn't be profitable for everyone to do so. If very few people open restaurants, demand for meals at most restaurants will be high and profits will be high, but if too many people open restaurants, then demand at each restaurant will be lower and competition will cause at least some of them to lose money. In this experiment, we study the way that competitive forces determine the number of restaurants that open.

Instructions

In this market, anybody who wants to open a restaurant can do so. The restaurants are small (intimate, as they say in the restaurant guides). If you open a restaurant you can serve up to four customers. Restaurant operators must pay a *fixed cost* of $20 no matter how many customers they get. In addition to its fixed costs, each restaurant has a *variable cost* of $5 per customer. A restaurant's *total cost* is the sum of its $20 fixed cost plus the total of its variable costs for all the meals it sells.

In this experiment, a restaurant will have a total cost of $20 if it sells no meals, $25 if it sells one meal, $30 if it sells two meals, $35 if it sells three meals, and $40 if it sells four meals. We can describe a restaurant's total cost by a **total cost function** $C(n)$ as follows: for n customers, where n is between 0 and 4, total cost is $C(n) = \$20 + 5n$.

Everyone in the class is a potential customer for any of the restaurants. Everyone gets a Personal Information Sheet with his or her Buyer Value for each market session. If you choose to buy a meal, the market manager will pay you your Buyer Value, so that your profit ("consumer's surplus") from buying a meal will be your Buyer Value *minus* the price you pay for the meal. If you own a restaurant, you can still buy a meal either in your own restaurant or in somebody else's. Of course, if you buy a meal in your own restaurant you will be counted as one of your four customers and the variable cost of your own meal will be $5, like anyone else's.

Stage 1–To Open or Not to Open a Restaurant?

Each round of each session has two stages. In the first stage, everyone must decide whether to open a restaurant. Before anyone has to make a decision, the market manager will give you a rough idea of the distribution of Buyer Values by asking for a show of hands for each possible Buyer Value. The market manager will then publicly ask class members, in succession, whether each intends to open a restaurant. When it is your turn to decide, you will know how many people are already committed to opening restaurants. If you choose to open a restaurant you will be charged $20 in overhead cost, no matter how many meals you sell, and you will be given a customer list that has spaces for four names, since you have a "seating capacity" of four customers. If you decide not to open a restaurant, you will have no overhead cost and will not be allowed to sell meals.

Stage 2–Posting Prices and Selling Meals

In the second stage of any round, restaurant operators post prices at which they are willing to sell meals to any buyer (until they fill up their restaurants). These posted prices should be clearly visible to buyers and to other sellers. If it is convenient, each restaurant will be assigned a location next to the blackboard, where its owner can post a price. Customers can either choose a restaurant and buy a meal at its currently posted price or wait for the posted prices to change. Firms can change their posted prices at any time. When a customer buys a meal at a restaurant, the owner must record the price that the customer paid for the meal and the customer's identification number and Buyer Value.

Later Rounds of Trading in Session 1

At the end of the first round of trading the market manager will report the profits of each restaurant. The market manager may also choose to present the market demand curve on the blackboard. After this information has been made available, another round of trading begins.

In all rounds of trading in the first session, customers' Buyer Values are the same as in the first round. In each new round, class members are given another chance to decide whether or not to enter the restaurant industry. The market manager proceeds exactly as in the first round, asking class members whether they intend to open a restaurant. Those who choose to open a restaurant are charged $20 in overhead cost, and those who choose not to open a restaurant have no overhead cost and are not allowed to sell meals. In the second stage of each round, prices are posted and purchases made, just as they were in the first round. At the end of the round, results are reported to the class.

Session 2–Introducing a Sales Tax

In Session 2, the distribution of Buyer Values is the same as in the first session, though Buyer Values of individuals may be different. As in the first session, the market manager asks class members in turn, whether they want to open a restaurant. Overhead cost remains at $20. In this session the government initiates a sales tax of $3 per meal sold, which increases each restaurant's total variable cost to $8 per meal (the original $5 plus the $3 tax). Thus a restaurant that serves n meals will have a total cost, including the sales tax, of $C(n) = \$20 + 8n$. In all other respects the market procedures are as in Session 1.

Warm-up Exercise

In order to prepare for this experiment, please answer these warm-up questions before you come to class.[1]

W 8.1   You have opened a restaurant and find that you can sell up to 4 meals at a price of $15 per meal, but that at any higher price you would be unable to sell any meals. In order to maximize your profit (or minimize your losses), how many meals should you sell? __4__ What would be your total profit (or loss)? $ __20__

W 8.2   You have opened a restaurant and find that you can sell up to 4 meals at a price of $7 per meal, but that at any higher price you would be unable to sell any meals. In order to maximize your profit (or minimize your losses), how many meals should you sell? __4__ What would be your total profit (or loss)? $ __-12__

W 8.3   You have opened a restaurant and find that you can sell up to 4 meals at a price of $3 per meal, but that at any higher price you would be unable to sell any meals. In order to maximize your profit (or minimize your losses), how many meals should you sell? __0__ What would be your profit (or loss)? $ __-20__

W 8.4   If you have already opened a restaurant, what is the lowest price at which you will be willing to sell meals? $ __5__

W 8.5   Let P be the average price at which you expect to sell meals, and suppose that you believe you will be able to sell 4 meals at this price. What is the smallest value of P such that you would be willing to enter the industry? $ __10__

   In Session 2, Buyer Values are the same as in Session 1, and hence the demand curve remains the same as before. All firms have to pay a sales tax of $3 for each meal sold.

W 8.6   In Session 2, is the sales tax a variable cost or a fixed cost for a restaurant? __Variable cost__

---

[1]Answers will be found on page 237.

W 8.7 In Session 2, including the sales tax, a restaurant has variable costs of $ __8__ and fixed costs of $ __20__ .

W 8.8 In Session 2, if you have already opened a restaurant, what is the lowest price at which you would be willing to sell meals? $ __8__

What Do You Expect to See?

■ Do you think that most restaurants will make money in the first round of Session 1? __NO__

■ How do you think that the results of the first round will affect the number of restaurants that open in the next round of Session 1?

__It will decrease__

■ Do you think that most restaurants will make money in the last round of Session 1? __Yes__

Discussion of Experiment 8

Realism and the Restaurant Experiment

Though the imaginary restaurants in our experiment are smaller and less complicated than real restaurants, the experiment does illustrate some important features of actual markets, both in retail business and in manufacturing industries.

Features of the experimental restaurant market that mirror actual markets include the following:

- Free Entry into the Industry. In our experiment anybody is permitted to open a restaurant and all potential entrants face the same cost structure. This situation corresponds closely to the environment faced by most small businesses.

- Short-Run and Long-Run Decision-Making. Actual firms are able to change some of their business decisions quickly as they obtain new information. Other decisions involve long-term commitments, and firms can only change them slowly. For example, a restaurant can quickly decide to order more meat or vegetables from the wholesalers. It can also change the number of hours its employees work, and it can hire or lay off employees on short notice. By contrast, it can only change the size of the restaurant, or go in and out of business, over a longer period of time. The period during which firms have time to change some, but not all, of their business decisions is called the **short run**. The period of time in which all of a firm's business decisions can be changed is called the **long run**. In our experiment, restaurants can change pricing and output decisions during the course of a round (the short run), but they accept their overhead costs at the beginning of a round and cannot go out of business and drop these costs until the next round.

- Limited Capacity. In our experiment the restaurants are limited to four customers. In the short run, real firms are restricted in their capacity by the size of their physical plant and by other design features. Often in the real world, capacity limits are more flexible than the limits in our experiment. A firm may be able to produce more output than its plant is designed for, but this will typically increase costs per unit of output and may lower quality. For service firms, like restaurants, retail stores, ski resorts, or medical clinics, accepting more customers than the plant is designed to accommodate increases congestion and makes the environment less pleasant for customers.

- Fixed Costs. In our experiment any firm entering the industry must pay a fixed cost that is independent of the amount of output it produces. This is the cost of fixed inputs such as the rental of a building, heating, and lighting, which have to be paid so long as a firm stays in business, no matter how many units the firm produces or sells. When overhead costs are nonrecoverable, they are known as **sunk costs**. In our experiment a restaurant owner has to pay a fixed cost of $20 to open a restaurant. This cost is a sunk cost, since even if the restaurant shuts down, its owner cannot reclaim the $20. In the real world sunk costs often include advertising, the purchase of specialized buildings and equipment, and specialized training for workers.

- Variable Costs. In our experiment, firms have variable costs of $5 per meal sold. These costs correspond to the cost of inputs such as raw materials and labor, which vary with the amount of output produced.

The Short Run and the Long Run

The Short Run

In the short run a firm has to pay the same amount of fixed costs, no matter how much it produces, and there is not time for new firms to enter the industry. The **short-run industry supply curve** is the industry supply curve obtained when fixed costs cannot be changed, and the number of firms in the industry is also unchanged. Sometimes, after a firm has invested in fixed inputs, it finds that demand for its output is not as great as it had expected when it made the investment. It may be that the firm can find no way to recover all of its fixed costs. Nevertheless, if the firm finds that for some positive output its revenue exceeds its *variable* costs, it should minimize losses by continuing production for the short run.

The **short-run equilibrium** for a competitive industry occurs at the price and quantity at which the short-run supply curve meets the demand curve. At this point, the variable cost of producing an extra unit is equal to the price.

The Long Run

An industry is in **long-run competitive equilibrium** if it is in short-run equilibrium, and if in addition, no firms that are in the industry want to exit and no firms that are not in the industry want to enter. An industry that is in short-run equilibrium will not be in long-run equilibrium if some firms are making losses. If firms are not making enough revenue to cover both variable and fixed costs, then in the long run some will go out of business as their leases expire and their equipment wears out. An industry that is in short-run equilibrium with firms making very high profits will also not be in long-run equilibrium. If firms are making more than enough to cover both their variable and fixed costs, new firms will be attracted into the industry. Thus, for an industry to be in long-run equilibrium, firms that are in business must not be losing money, and no new firm can make money by joining the industry.

If all of this sounds a little confusing, you will probably find that things are cleared up by looking at an example.

Short- and Long-Run Equilibrium: An Example

Suppose that there are 32 demanders in the market and the distribution of their Buyer Values is given in Table 8.1.

Table 8.1: Distribution of Customer Types

Buyer Value	Number of Buyers
24	8
18	8
12	8
8	8

As in the experiment, each restaurant that opens must pay an overhead cost of $20, each has a capacity of four customers, and each has variable costs of $5 per meal served. The short-run supply curve is determined in Stage 1 by decisions of market participants about whether or not to open restaurants. Since firms are able to enter or leave the industry after each round, the short run lasts for only one round.

Short-Run Equilibrium with Excess Capacity and Losses

Suppose that in the first round, seven people decide to open restaurants. In the short run, all of the restaurants that enter the industry must pay overhead costs no matter how many meals they sell. Since there is nothing a restaurant can do to alter its fixed costs in the short run, it should ignore these costs in deciding how much to supply. The only costs that affect supply in the short run are the variable costs.

Figure 8.1: Short Run with Excess Capacity

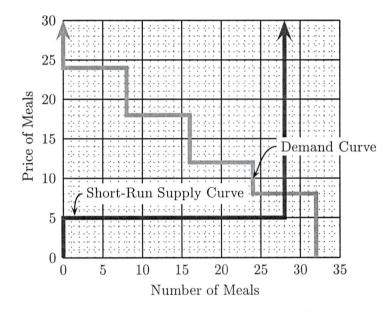

The short-run supply and demand curves are drawn in Figure 8.1. At any price above \$5, the revenue from selling a meal is greater than the variable cost of serving it. Therefore at prices above \$5, every restaurant will want to sell four meals. At a price of exactly \$5, restaurants are indifferent between selling and not selling; and at a price below \$5, restaurants are unwilling to sell any meals. Since seven restaurants have opened, 28 meals are offered at any price above \$5. From Figure 8.1, we see that the short-run equilibrium price is \$8 a meal and the number of meals sold is 28. At a price of \$8, each firm's revenue ($8 \times 4 = \$32$) exceeds its variable costs ($5 \times 4 = \$20$) by \$12, so it is earning \$12 toward covering its overhead costs.

Although the firm should consider only variable costs when deciding how much to produce, we must remember that when we calculate the firm's profit we have to subtract total costs, including fixed costs, from revenue. When fixed costs are $20 and variable cost is $5 per unit, the total cost of producing 4 meals is $20 + ($5 \times 4) = $40. Total cost ($40) exceeds total revenue ($32) by $8, so at this short-run equilibrium each firm in the industry loses $8. Although each restaurant owner regrets her decision to open, selling four meals at $8 each is the best she can do. If she didn't sell any meals at all, her revenue would be $0 and her variable costs would also be $0, but since she still has to pay $20 in fixed costs, she would suffer a loss of $20, which is worse than losing $8.

We would not expect seven restaurants to continue to lose money through many rounds of the experiment. In the long run, enough restaurants would go out of the business so that the survivors would not operate at a loss.

Short-Run Equilibrium with "Short Capacity" and Profits

Suppose that in Stage 1, five people decide to open restaurants. When there are five open restaurants, at any price above $5 a total of 20 meals will be offered by these five restaurants. The short-run supply curve is as shown in Figure 8.2.

Figure 8.2: Short-Run Supply and Demand for Meals

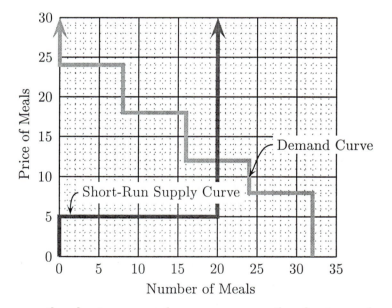

In this case, the short-run supply curve crosses the short-run demand curve at a point where the price is $12 and 20 meals are sold. Total revenue of each restaurant is $4 \times $12 = $48. Total costs of each restaurant are

$20 + (4 \times \$5) = \$40$. Restaurant revenue more than covers both variable and fixed costs, allowing each restaurant to make profits of $8.

In the long run, these profits are likely to attract additional entrants to the industry. As we will show, there is room for one more person to open a restaurant and make a profit (or at least not lose money). Therefore this short-run equilibrium is also not a long-run equilibrium.

A Long-Run Equilibrium

Suppose that six firms enter the industry. Then at any price higher than $5 the quantity supplied is 24. The resulting supply curve is shown in Figure 8.3. The supply and demand curves coincide on the interval where the quantity is 24 and the price ranges from $8 to $12.

Figure 8.3: Long-Run Equilibrium

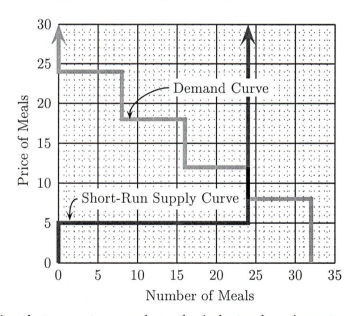

We claim that an outcome where the industry has six restaurants and the price is anywhere between $10 and $12 is a long-run equilibrium. At a price of $10, restaurants have revenue of $10 \times 4 = \$40$ and total costs of $20 + (\$5 \times 4) = \$40$. Therefore their profits are $0. At any price below $10, firms would make too little money per meal to cover their total costs. At prices higher than $12, firms could not sell enough meals to break even. At prices between $10 and $12, every restaurant makes a profit or at least breaks even, so none of them will go out of business. You have already seen that if a seventh restaurant were to open, all restaurants would lose money, so no new entrants will be lured by potential profits.[2]

We could have found a long-run equilibrium price and quantity without going to the trouble of drawing all of these short-run supply and demand curves, by using the following reasoning. In long-run equilibrium firms must not be losing money. Therefore the price must be at least as great as the **average cost of production**. A firm's average cost of production is its cost per unit of output including both variable and fixed costs. To calculate a firm's average cost, divide its total costs by the number of units of output that it produces.

In long-run equilibrium, all firms must be operating in such a way as to minimize their average cost. In this example, a restaurant minimizes its average cost by operating at full capacity and selling 4 meals. When a restaurant sells 4 meals, it has total costs of $20 + (\$5 \times 4) = \$40$. Its average costs are $10, and so the long-run equilibrium price must be at least $10. If the price is exactly $10, then none of the people who opened restaurants has any reason to drop out and none of the people who did not open restaurants would profit from entering the industry. Therefore $10, which is the average cost per unit of output when restaurants operate at full capacity, is a long-run equilibrium price. We see from the demand curve that at a price of $10, 24 meals would be sold. Since each restaurant has a capacity of 4 customers, it takes 6 restaurants to serve 24 meals, and so there will be 6 restaurants in long-run equilibrium.

Food for Thought

■ If you wanted to open an additional coffee house in a college town, how would you decide whether it is likely to make money?

■ Suppose that the largest employer in a small industrial city decides to close its local plant and the total number of people employed in the city decreases drastically. What would you expect to be the *immediate* effect on the number of customers in each restaurant, and on the profitability of each restaurant?

---

[2] Some economists would argue that the only long-run equilibrium price is the zero-profit price of $10, since any price greater than $10 would lure other firms into the industry. But, if a seventh firm entered the industry, each firm would still need to sell all four meals to make a profit, and so together firms would sell more than twenty meals. For demanders to buy more than 20 meals, the price would have to drop to $8, which would drive the revenue of all firms below their total costs, and cause all entrants to lose money.

■ Suppose that in the small industrial city discussed above, after two or three years, employment does not recover to its previous levels. What would you expect to happen to the number of restaurants that are in business? What would you expect to happen to the number of customers in each restaurant that stays open?

Answers to Warm-up Exercises

W 8.1: 4, $20; **W 8.2**: 4, loss of $12; **W 8.3**: 0, loss of $20; **W 8.4**: $5; **W 8.5**: $10; **W 8.6**: It's a variable cost; **W 8.7**: $8, $20; **W 8.8**: $8.

Lab Notes for Experiment 8

Recording Market Fundamentals

In Table 8.2 record the distribution of Buyer Values as posted by your instructor.

Table 8.2: Distribution of Demander Types

Buyer Value	Number of Buyers
24	
18	
12	
8	

Recording Transactions, Prices, and Profits

To complete Tables 8.3 and 8.4, you will need to calculate total revenues and total costs for each restaurant. The total revenue of a restaurant is the sum of the prices that it receives for all the meals that it sells. According to the instructions for this experiment, a restaurant's total costs will be \$_____

if it sells 4 meals, \$_____ if it sells 3 meals, \$_____ if it sells 2 meals,

\$_____ if it sells 1 meal, and \$_____ if it sells no meals.

In Table 8.3 record the price received for each meal sold by each restaurant in the first round of Session 1. Then calculate total revenue, total costs, and profits of each restaurant in this round.

Table 8.3: Restaurants' Sales–Session 1, Round 1

Restaurant Owner's ID	Prices Paid by Restaurant Customers			Total Revenue	Total Cost	Profit

■ In the *first* round of Session 1, the number of firms making a profit was

_____, and the number of firms taking a loss was _____.

In Table 8.4 record the price received for each meal sold by each restaurant in the *last* round of Session 1. Then calculate total revenue, total cost, and profits of each restaurant in this round.

Table 8.4: Restaurants' Sales–Session 1, Last Round

Restaurant Owner's ID	Prices Paid by Restaurant Customers				Total Revenue	Total Cost	Profit

■   In the *last* round of Session 1 the number of firms making a profit was

_____, and the number of firms taking a loss was _____.

In Table 8.5 record the price received for each meal sold by each restaurant in the *first* round of Session 2. Then calculate total revenue, total cost, and profits of each restaurant in this round. *Be sure to include the $3 sales tax in your calculation of a restaurant's total cost.*

Table 8.5: Restaurants' Sales–Session 2, Round 1

Restaurant Owner's ID	Prices Paid by Restaurant Customers			Total Revenue	Total Cost	Profit

■ In the first round of Session 2, the number of firms making a profit was _____, and the number of firms taking a loss was _____.

In Table 8.6 record the price received for each meal sold by each restaurant in the *last* round o Session 2. Then calculate total revenue, total cost, and profits of each restaurant in this round. *Be sure to include the $3 sales tax in your calculation of a restaurant's total cost.*

Table 8.6: Restaurants' Sales–Session 2, Last Round

Restaurant Owner's ID	Prices Paid by Restaurant Customers				Total Revenue	Total Cost	Profit

■ In the last round of Session 2, the number of firms making a profit was

_____, and the number of firms taking a loss was _____.

Experiment 9

Network Externalities

Having your own telephone isn't of much use if your friends don't have a phone. What good is a fax machine if the people you want to send stuff to don't have a fax? Being able to send and receive e-mail is valuable only if the people with whom you want to correspond have e-mail. The World Wide Web becomes far more useful as more people use it.

The technology for the fax machine was developed by inventors in Scotland and in Italy about 150 years ago. As recently as 1980, fax machines were still rare. Suddenly in the mid-1980's the demand for fax machines exploded, and today they are commonplace. The first session introduces the idea of network externalities and explores the workings of a market for a good that becomes more valuable to everyone as more people purchase it.

How did Microsoft come to dominate the market for computer operating systems at the expense of Apple? What became of WordStar, Visicalc, and Lotus 1-2-3? How did Bill Gates get so rich? The second and third sessions of this experiment feature fierce battles for market supremacy between competing computer operating systems, in an environment where the strong are likely to devour the weak.

Instructions

Session 1: A Network of Picture Phones

In Session 1 you will participate in a market for Picture Phones. These are telephones that send and receive pictures of the conversing parties. You can talk on a Picture Phone with someone only if both of you have Picture Phones. Your Buyer Value for a Picture Phone therefore depends on the number of other people who also have these phones.

Your *Initial Value* for a Picture Phone is given on your Personal Information Sheet. (About 1/6 of the people in the room have each of the possible initial values running from 1 to 6.) Your Buyer Value will depend both on your Initial Value and on the total number of phones sold, according to the formula:

$$\text{Buyer Value} = \text{Initial Value} \times \text{Network Externality Factor},$$

where the *Network Externality Factor* depends on the total number of demanders who buy a Picture Phone. Your instructor will post a table showing exactly how the Network Externality Factor is determined by the number of purchases.

In each round of this session the market manager will post a fixed price for Picture Phones. If you want to buy a Picture Phone at the posted price, you should register your ID number on the manager's Sales Record Sheet. Once you have purchased a phone, you will be asked to move to a designated area of the room, so that others can see how many people have bought phones so far. Your Buyer Value will be determined by the total number of people who bought Picture Phones during the round. Your profit (or loss) will be your Buyer Value minus the price you paid.

Session 2: Competing Standards in Computers

In this session there will be three sellers of computer operating systems. Demanders must decide which operating system, if any, to buy. Buyers will have network externalities only with people who buy the same operating system. People with different operating systems are not able to exchange files and other information as cheaply and easily as those with the same operating system. Your instructor will post a table showing the way that Buyer Values for each operating system are related to the number of persons who purchase the product.

Buyers' Profit Information

When you first buy an operating system, you have to pay not only the price charged by the seller but also a learning cost of $15. (As you may know from experience, learning to use a new operating system is time-consuming and costly.) In subsequent rounds, you must either buy an updated version of your current system from the seller who sold it to you or switch to another system. If you update the operating system that you had in the previous round, you won't have to pay the learning cost. But if you change operating systems from one round to another, you will have to pay the $15 learning cost as well as the price charged by the supplier. To find your profits, subtract the sum of the price you pay for the operating system and your learning cost (if any) from your Buyer Value.

Sellers' Profit Information

Sellers of operating systems have a marginal cost of $5 for each unit they sell. When they first open for business, they must pay a fixed cost of $75. At the end of each round, sellers will have the option of going out of business. After the first round, for each round that they remain in business, sellers must pay an additional fixed cost of $50 (for advertising and promotion) regardless of how many units they sell.

In any round, if a seller's market share falls below 1/6, she will have to declare bankruptcy. (The market manager, acting as a banker, reserves the right to force bankruptcy on firms that he deems to be in financial trouble.) Firms that have been declared bankrupt must leave the market. With bankruptcy comes limited liability. Firms that have been declared bankrupt will lose at most $50 from their misadventure. At the end of the last round of play, those sellers who are still in business will each receive an additional payment of $15 for each customer that they sold to in the final round. (This payment represents the value to the seller of an installed customer base.)

Sellers can vary their prices or offer discounts as they wish throughout this session. Sellers are allowed to sell at less than marginal cost or even to bribe buyers to use their operating system by selling at a negative price. At the beginning of each new round, each seller can decide whether to drop out or continue into the next round.

Session 3: Can New and Better Break in?

Will Windows' stranglehold on the computer operating system market ever be broken by Linux, Rhapsody, Be, or some hopeful monster, yet unborn?

In this session, a new operating system appears. The new system is better than any of the old systems in the sense that if it had the same number of customers as the old systems, all demanders' Buyer Values would be 50% higher.

The firm with the largest customer base in the last round of Session 2 will also be allowed to sell in Session 3. Customers who stay with the old firm will not have to pay the learning cost. Learning the new system is more costly than learning one of the old systems. Any customer who switches operating systems will have to pay a $20 learning cost as well as the price charged by the seller.

Warm-up Exercise

Warm-up for Session 1

The Network Externality Factors in the Picture Phone industry are given in Table 9.1.[1]

Table 9.1: Network Externality Factors

If Number of Phones Sold Is in Range	Network Externality Factor Is
1–8	1
9–16	2
17–24	3
25–32	4
33–40	5
41–48	6

W 9.1 If Picture Phones sell for $20 and 35 people buy Picture Phones, the Network Externality Factor is _____. If you buy a Picture Phone and your Initial Value is $6, your profit (loss) will be $ _____, if your Initial Value is 4 it will be $ _____, and if your Initial Value is 2 it will be

$ _____.

W 9.2 If Picture Phones sell for $5 and 48 people buy Picture Phones, the Network Externality Factor is _____. If you buy a Picture Phone and your Initial Value is $6, your profit (loss) will be $_____, if your Initial Value is 4 it will be $ _____, and if your Initial Value is 2 it will be $ _____.

---

[1]Answers to these exercises are found on 271.

Warm-up for Session 2

The Buyer Values of all demanders for an operating system depend on the number who buy that type of system according to the schedule reported in Table 9.2. In the first round of trading, there are three firms, A, B, and C, producing three competing operating systems, OS A, OS B, and OS C. Suppose that in Round 1, OS A sells 25 units, OS B sells 10 units, and OS C sells 15 units.

Table 9.2: Buyer Values of OS

If Number of Users of OS Type Is in Range	Buyer Value Is
1–8	$10
9–16	$20
17–24	$30
25–32	$40
33–40	$50
41–48	$60

W 9.3 What is the Buyer Value of OS A to a demander? $ _____ What is the Buyer Value of OS B to a demander? $ _____ What is the Buyer Value of OS C to a demander? $ _____

W 9.4 In Round 1, if a demander buys OS A for $15, what is the demander's profit or loss on this round? $ _____

W 9.5 In Round 2, suppose that a demander who bought OS B in Round 1 faces a price of $15 for the upgraded version of OS B and a price of $15 for OS A. If the demander buys the OS B upgrade, his profits are $ _____ .

What are his profits if he switches to OS A? $ _____ (Remember to take learning costs into account.)

W 9.6 In Round 1, Firm A's total costs are $ _____ and Firm B's total costs are $ _____ .

Warm-up for Session 3

In the last round of Session 2, Firm A had 48 customers and Firms B and C had dropped out of the market. Firm A remains in the market in Session 3, and Firm D enters the market with a new, technically superior, operating system. Suppose that the relation between Buyer Values and market share is as given in Table 9.3

Table 9.3: Buyer Values of OS

If Number of Users of OS Type Is in Range	Buyer Value of Old Technology Is	Buyer Value of New Technology Is
1–8	$10	$15
9–16	$20	$30
17–24	$30	$45
25–32	$40	$60
33–40	$50	$75
41–48	$60	$90

W 9.7 If in Round 1 of Session 3, Firm D's new operating system attracts 10 customers away from Firm A (which previously sold 48 units) what will be the Buyer Value of Firm D's operating system? $ _____ What will be the Buyer Value of Firm A's operating system? $ _____

W 9.8 If in Round 1, Firm D's new operating system attracts 20 customers away from Firm A, what will be the Buyer Value of Firm D's operating system? $ _____ What will be the Buyer Value of Firm A's operating system? $ _____

W 9.9 Suppose that buyers believe that in Round 1, Firm D's new operating system will attract 20 customers away from Firm A, and suppose that Firm A charges $40 for the current upgrade of its operating system. What will buyers expect their profits to be if they stay with Firm A? $ _____ Given these expectations, what price should Firm D charge if it wants buyers to expect to make $1 more profit in this round by switching to OS D than by staying with OS A? $ _____

Discussion of Experiment 9

Network Externalities

A product is said to exhibit **network externalities** if its Buyer Value for those who consume it is higher, the greater the number of other consumers who also consume the product.

Send-and-Receive Technologies

Some of the most striking instances of network externalities occur with products that aid communications. The value to you of a device that sends and receives messages will be larger, the greater the number of people who can receive your messages and send messages to you. For this reason, communications devices like the telegraph, telephone, fax machine, and computers connected to the internet all exhibit strong network externalities. Each of these technologies enjoyed a period of explosive growth as the value of being connected to the network increased at the same time that the network grew.

Dramatic innovations in send-and-receive technologies are not unique to the 19th and 20th centuries. Knowing how to read and write is of little value if there isn't much to read, and if few others can read the things that you write. For many centuries, literacy was confined to a very small elite. With Gutenberg's invention of the printing press in 1457, the cost of reproducing the printed word was greatly reduced, but the cost of learning to read remained high, in terms of time and effort. In many countries it was recognized that teaching people to read and write confers benefits not only on those who are taught, but also on all others who can communicate with them by the written word. As a result, many governments began to offer free public education. As literacy spreads, the ability to read and write becomes more important, and in many countries, literacy has become nearly universal. In contrast, even today there are societies where few people learn to read and write, and where the incentives to become literate remain small.

Shared Infrastructure

Another source of network externalities is the development of shared support facilities, which are known as **infrastructure**. If only a few people own high-definition television sets, they will not be of much use because broadcasting companies will not produce many television shows in that format. If you have an Apple Macintosh computer, you hope that more people will buy Macintoshes so that software developers will write for the Mac. If only a few people in your country have automobiles, then it is difficult to find gasoline stations, repair shops, and good roads. As more people acquire automobiles, the shared infrastructure grows and owning an automobile becomes more attractive. Sony's Beta system for showing videos lost out to the VHS system as the number of VHS users increased and the number of movies available for VHS exceeded the number available for the Beta system. Consumers' willingness to pay for CD players increased drastically as more CD players were sold, because a large installed base of CD players induced record companies to record more music on CDs.

Network Externalities and the Demand Curve

We have seen that the demand curve is a powerful tool for studying markets without network externalities. Will this tool also work when there are network externalities? The answer is yes, but constructing a demand curve is a little more subtle.

Before we draw a demand curve with network externalities, let us take a second look at the demand curve for the familiar case where there are no network externalities. In previous experiments, we have drawn this demand curve by finding the quantities that are demanded at each possible price. Sometimes it is more useful to work in the other direction. That is, instead of finding the *quantity* demanded at each *price*, we find the highest *price* at which each *quantity* will be demanded.

In the case where each demander can buy up to one unit of the good, finding the highest price at which q units will be demanded is straightforward. To sell q units you will need to find q buyers, each of whom has a Buyer Value that is at least as high as the price you are asking. So how high can you set your price and still find q buyers? If you set your price equal to the qth highest Buyer Value in the market, then there will be q buyers who are willing to buy at that price. Moreover, if you try to raise the price any higher, the qth buyer will no longer want to buy, and you will not be able to sell all q units. But this tells us what we want to know. The highest price at which q units will be demanded is the qth highest Buyer Value. If we define a function $P(\cdot)$ such that $P(q)$ is the qth highest Buyer Value, then it will always be the case that q units will be demanded at the price $P(q)$. Economists sometimes call this function the **inverse demand function**.

The No-Regrets Demand Curve with Network Externalities

When we draw a demand curve for a good with network externalities, it is convenient to do so by finding the price(s) at which each quantity will be demanded, much as we did in the discussion of the previous paragraph. For each quantity q, let us define $P(q)$ to be the qth highest Buyer Value *when exactly q units are sold.* The phrase in italics is needed because when there are network externalities, each demander's Buyer Value depends on the total number of units that are sold. It is useful to think of $P(q)$ as defining a "no-regrets" demand curve. Suppose that at the price $p = P(q)$, the q demanders with the largest Buyer Values all buy the good and the remaining demanders with lower Buyer Values do not buy it. In this case, no demander will have regrets about his decision to buy or not buy. Since the lowest Buyer Value of the q *buyers* is $P(q)$, each of them has a Buyer Value that is at least as high as the price. Therefore none of the q buyers will regret buying at price $P(q)$. The remaining *demanders that did not buy* all have Buyer Values that are no larger than $P(q)$, and therefore none of them would make a profit by buying given that the total number of items sold is q. It follows that at the price $P(q)$ none of these demanders will regret their decision not to buy.[2]

To fix our ideas, let us work with an example. Consider a group of 100 companies that interact occasionally with each other. They are given an opportunity to join a video conferencing network. The value to each firm of joining the network is proportional to the total number of firms that join. We will number the firms $1, 2, \ldots, 100$, where Firm q is the qth largest of these firms. Larger firms find it more valuable to belong to the network than smaller firms. Firm q's Buyer Value is equal to $\$(100 - q)$ times the total number of firms that are in the network. If k firms join the network, Firm q's Buyer Value will be $\$(100 - q)k$. If Firm q expects exactly q firms to join the network, its Buyer Value will be $\$(100 - q)q = \$100q - q^2$. Since Firm q always has the qth highest Buyer Value, and since its Buyer Value when exactly q firms join the network is $\$100q - q^2$, it follows that $P(q) = \$100q - q^2$. In Figure 9.1 we have drawn the graph of the no-regrets demand function, $P(q) = \$100q - q^2$, for q ranging from 0 to 100.

---

[2]The careful reader will notice that if one of the demanders that is currently not buying decides to buy (and the others continue to buy) then the number of buyers would become $q + 1$, so that the demander with the $q + 1$st highest Buyer Value may find it profitable to buy. The function $P(q)$, as we have defined it, is the no-regrets demand curve that applies either when demanders are too unimaginative to notice that if they buy they will increase the total number of users by one, or when there are so many buyers that a single additional buyer has a negligible effect on the Buyer Value of any one individual.

Figure 9.1: A No-Regrets Demand Curve

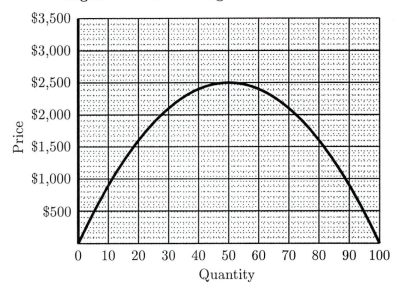

In addition to the parabola $P(q) = \$100q - q^2$, the no-regrets demand curve includes a vertical line segment extending upward from the origin. This line segment is included because if firms believe that the number of firms in the network will be zero, then every firm's Buyer Value will be 0 and no firms will want to join the network.

Equilibrium with Network Externalities

Now that we have drawn a demand curve, we can add a supply curve and find competitive equilibrium. Let us assume that the cost of adding each additional firm to the network is $2,100. Then the supply curve for connections to the network is a horizontal line segment running across the graph at a height of $2,100, as shown in Figure 9.2.

The supply curve crosses the demand curve at three points, which we have labeled B, C, and D, corresponding to outcomes in which the number of firms connected to the network is 0, 30, and 70. Each of these outcomes is an equilibrium quantity when the cost of joining the network is $2,100. If everyone believes that no firms will join the network, then nobody will want to join; if everybody believes that exactly 30 firms will join the network, then exactly 30 firms will want to join; and if everybody believes that exactly 70 firms will join the network, then exactly 70 firms will want to join.

Figure 9.2: Network Supply and Demand

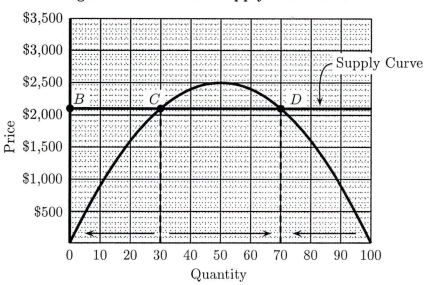

Stable and Unstable Equilibria

When a market has more than one equilibrium, it is often useful to investigate the **dynamics** of that market. The dynamics of any economic system describes the movement of the variables in that system over time when it is out of equilibrium. By studying the dynamics, we can often determine whether an equilibrium is likely to persist, even if the market is subject to small shocks and surprises. A **stable equilibrium** is an equilibrium such that after small movements away from equilibrium the system will return to (or very close to) the equilibrium. An **unstable equilibrium** is an equilibrium such that after very small movements away from equilibrum, the system will move even further away. A useful way to think about the difference between stable and unstable equilibrium is this: If you set a bowl on the floor and drop a marble into the bowl, the marble will roll to the bottom. If you jiggle the bowl, the marble will temporarily move away from the bottom but will soon return to its original position. This is an example of a stable equilibrium. If you invert the bowl and (carefully) set the marble on top of the bowl, the marble will stay there. But now if you jiggle the bowl, the marble will roll onto the floor and will not return to the top of the bowl. This is an example of an unstable equilibrium.

The dynamic issue that concerns us is whether the number of firms in the network will increase or decrease if it starts out at some arbitary quantity q. Let us assume that firms will leave the network if they are losing money and that firms will join the network if, given the current number of members, they could make a profit by joining. Suppose that the initial number of members is q. If $P(q)$ <\$2,100, then Firm q, which has a Buyer Value of $P(q)$, is paying a higher price than its Buyer Value, so it will leave the network, causing q to decrease. If we look at Figure 9.2 we see that $P(q)$ <\$2,100 when $0 < q < 30$ and when $70 < q \leq 100$. Therefore if q is in either of these ranges, q will decrease over time. In Figure 9.2, we have drawn leftward-pointing arrows just above the horizontal axis to show that q will decrease whenever it is in these regions.

Looking at Figure 9.2, we see that $P(30)$ =\$2,100 and $P(31)$ >\$2,100. Therefore if Firms 1 through 30 initially belong to the network, they will all be willing to stay. Then, since $P(31)$ >\$2,100, Firm 31 would make a profit by joining the network, which would now have 31 members. We see from the graph that $P(32)$ >\$2,100 and so if the network attracts 31 members, Firm 32 will join. Since $P(q) \geq$ \$2,100 for all q ranging from 30 to 70, if the network gets larger than 30, it will grow until it has 70 members. In Figure 9.2, we have drawn a rightward-pointing arrow just above the horizontal axis to show that q will increase whenever it is between 30 and 70.

We can now see which of the equilibria are stable and which are unstable by looking at the arrows in Figure 9.2. If the initial quantity q is smaller than 30, the arrow points to the left and the quantity will decrease over time until it reaches 0. If the initial quantity is between 30 and 70, the arrow points to the right and the quantity will increase over time until it reaches 70. If the initial quantity is between 70 and 100, the arrow points to the left and the quantity will decrease over time until it reaches 70. Therefore the equilibrium in which 0 firms join the network and the equilibrium in which 70 firms join are both stable.

The equilibrium with 30 firms, on the other hand, is unstable. A small change in either direction will move q further away from 30. Suppose that initially, Firms 1 through 30 belong to the network. If by some accident one firm drops out of the network, then at least one of the remaining 29 firms will find it unprofitable to belong and will leave. But when this happens, the Buyer Values of the remaining firms will fall once again and another firm will leave, and so on until the network has no remaining members.[3] If, on the other hand, Firm 31 decides to join Firms 1 through 30 in the network, then not only will Firm 31 make a profit, but Firm 32 can make a profit by

---

[3]Group health insurance plans occasionally fail in this way, as healthy people drop out of the plan. Such a collapse is known in the insurance industry as a "death spiral."

joining Firms 1 through 31, and so on, until the network has 70 members.

Of the two stable equilibria, the high-level equilibrium has greater total profits. The equilibrium with no firms in the network results in zero profits for everyone, while in the 70-firm equilibrium, Firms 1 through 69 all make positive profits and the other firms make zero profits. Clearly Firms 1 through 69 would prefer the high-level equilibrium if they could reach it. Suppose that the network starts out at the equilbrium with no members. If Firms 1 through 70 all believed that the others will join, then it would be profitable for each of them to join.[4] When we study the dynamics, we see something very interesting. To get to the high-level equilibrium from the zero equilibrium, it would not be necessary for all 70 firms to agree in advance to join. All that would be needed is to achieve a **critical mass** of 31 members. That is, the number needed to get just beyond the unstable equilibrium at 30. If Firm 31 joins, then it will be profitable for Firm 32 to join. At this point, the dominoes begin to fall. Firm 33 will be attracted by the other 32 members, and then 34, and so it goes all the way up to 70.

If your experience in the second round of Session 1 was typical, your class was able to coordinate sufficiently to reach critical mass. If this happened you probably saw a good deal of hesitation and discussion until a critical number of students bought Picture Phones, and then you saw a great rush of purchases once critical mass was reached. In large markets, where information about what others are doing is not as good as it was in your classroom, this coordination is harder to achieve. Sellers of network goods may try to reach critical mass by offering special promotions in which early purchasers get price discounts and by advertising that is intended to convince potential buyers that there are many other users of their product.

An Example with Gaps Between Buyer Values

For classroom experiments it is convenient to have a relatively small number of types of demanders. When there are a small number of types, we have a slightly more complicated demand curve with steps corresponding to gaps between the Buyer Values of one type and the next. It will be helpful to work out an example that is similar to the market for Picture Phones in Session 1.

In this example, there are 5 types of demanders and 6 demanders of each type. Demanders of Type 1 have Initial Values of 1, demanders of Type 2 have Initial Values of 2, and so on up to Type 5. The Buyer Value

---

[4]Firm 70 would be just indifferent.

of each demander is equal to his Initial Value multiplied by a "Network
Externality Factor" that depends on the total number of units sold. Table
9.4 specifies the way that Network Externality Factors are determined by
the total number of units sold.

Table 9.4: Network Externality Factors

If Number of Units Sold Is in Range	Network Externality Factor Is
1–6	1
7–12	2
13–18	3
19–24	4
25–30	5

For this market, a no-regrets demand curve is drawn in Figure 9.3. To
construct this curve, we first graph $P(q)$, which is the qth highest Buyer
Value when the number of units sold is q. We complete the demand curve
by drawing vertical lines to fill in the gaps.[5]

If q is any number from 1 to 6, the Network Externality Factor is 1. Since
there are 6 demanders of each type, the demander with the qth highest Buyer
Value must be a Type 5 with an Initial Value of $5. Since $P(q)$ is equal to
the Initial Value of a Type 5 times the Network Externality Factor, it follows
that $P(q) = \$5 \times 1 = \$5$ for all q from 1 to 6. If we assume that buyers can
buy fractional units, then we can "fill in the line" so that the graph of $P(q)$
includes the horizontal line segment running from $(0, 5)$ to $(6, 5)$.

If q is any number from 7 to 12, the Network Externality Factor is 2.
For q in this range, the demander with the qth highest Buyer Value must
be a Type 4, with Initial Value 4. Therefore for q ranging from 7 to 12,
$P(q) = \$4 \times 2 = \$8$. Assuming, again, that demanders can buy fractional
units, the graph of $P(q)$ includes the horizontal line segment running from
$(6, 8)$ to $(12, 8)$. Similar reasoning will show that for q in the range from 13 to
18, $P(q) = \$3 \times 3 = \$9$; for q in the range from 19 to 24, $P(q) = \$2 \times 4 = \$8$;
and for q in the range from 25 to 30, $P(q) = \$1 \times 5 = \$5$. This explains the
5 horizontal line segments on the demand curve.

---

[5]We have drawn the vertical lines for the "upward" jumps as dashed lines, because
they are not actually on the no-regrets demand curve. Drawing the no-regrets demand
curves for these intervals is a little tricky, but we don't really need to explore these "funny
bits" of the curve, since they are never stable equilibria.

Figure 9.3: A Network Demand Curve

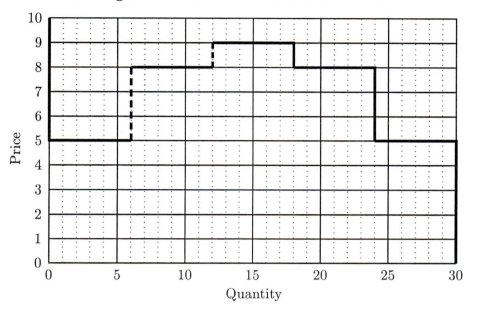

We also need to show that the solid vertical line segments drawn in Figure 9.3 really belong on the demand curve. If the price is greater than $5 and nobody buys the product, then the Network Externality Factor is 1 and the highest Buyer Value is only $5, so that nobody will want to buy the good. Therefore the demand curve includes the vertical line segment that extends upward from $(0,5)$. Next let us show that the vertical line segment from $(30,0)$ to $(30,5)$ belongs to the demand curve. If the quantity is 30, the Network Externality Factor is 5, which implies that the lowest Buyer Value (that of the Type 1s) is $5 = \$1 \times 5$. Therefore at any price below $5, all 30 demanders will make a profit by buying the product, and hence the demand curve should include all points at which the quantity is 30 and the price is less than 5. The vertical line segment running from $(24,5)$ to $(24,8)$ also belongs to the demand curve. If $q = 24$, then the Network Externality Factor is 4, and therefore at prices between $5 and $8, the 24 demanders of Types 2, 3, 4, and 5 would want to buy since their Buyer Values are at least $2 \times 4 = \$8$. At these prices with $q = 24$, demanders of Type 1 are not willing to pay more than $5. Therefore, if the price is between $5 and $8, and the 24 demanders of Types 2-5 buy the product, each of them will make a profit while the 6 Type 1s will not want to buy. Finally we show that the vertical line segment running from $(18,8)$ to $(18,9)$ belongs to the demand curve. If $q = 18$ the Network Externality Factor is 3. At prices between $8 and \$9, the 18 demanders of Types 5, 4, and 3 will all want to buy since their Buyer Values are at least \$3 × 3 = \$9. At these prices the Type 2s and Type 1s will not want to buy. Thus we have shown that each of the solid vertical line segments in Figure 9.3 belongs to the demand curve.

In the following exercise, you should determine the equilibrium quantities by finding the intersection of a horizontal supply curve with the solid portions of the demand curve in Figure 9.3.

Exercise: Finding Equilibrium

Exercise 9.1 Suppose that the cost of production is \$9.50 so that the supply curve is a horizontal line at a height of \$9.50. Draw this supply curve on Figure 9.3. What is the equilibrium number of Picture

Phones sold? ———

Exercise 9.2 Suppose that the supply curve is horizontal at a price of \$8.50. Draw the supply curve on Figure 9.3. There are two stable

equilibrium quantities, ——— and ——— .

Exercise 9.3 Suppose that the supply curve is horizontal at a price of \$7.00. Draw the supply curve on Figure 9.3. There are two stable

equilibrium quantities, ——— and ——— .

Exercise 9.4 Suppose that the supply curve is horizontal at a price of \$4.00. Draw the supply curve on Figure 9.3. What is the equilibrium

number of Picture Phones sold? ———

Exercise 9.5 Suppose that the supply curve is horizontal at a price of \$7.00 and that initially 8 demanders buy Picture Phones. With this

quantity what is the Network Externality Factor? ——— Would you expect the number of phones sold to increase or decrease over time?

——————— Which of the two equilibria is the quantity likely to reach

if others see that 8 people have bought Picture Phones? ———

Exercise 9.6 Suppose that the supply curve is horizontal at a price of \$7.00 and that initially only 2 demanders buy Picture Phones. With

this quantity what is the Network Externality Factor? ——— Given this Network Externality Factor, how many demanders would find it

profitable to buy Picture Phones? _____ If demanders will not buy
Picture Phones unless they can make a profit by doing so given the

current number of buyers, will more demanders buy? _____

A Brief History of the Fax Machine

The principle of the fax machine was patented in 1843 by Alexander Bain, a Scottish inventor. An Italian abbot, Giovanni Caselli, built a working version of Bain's fax machine in 1856, which he called the pantelegraph. In 1865 Caselli established a fax system between Paris and several other French cities. Despite its promise, fax technology fell into disuse after a few years, being crowded out by the more primitive electric telegraph, which had gotten started just a few years earlier. At the turn of the century, further advances were made with the fax technology as newspapers began to use this method to send copies of photographs between cities. In the 1920s millions of dollars were spent on developing the fax and it was expected to become a common household appliance, but again it flopped. In the 1970s demand for fax machines began to grow in Japan, because Japanese, with its large number of letters is difficult to typeset.

Figure 9.4: Number of Fax Machines Shipped (in 1,000s)

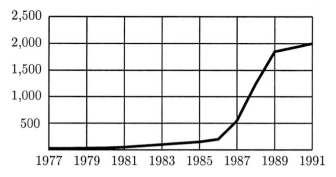

Figure 9.4 shows the growth of sales of fax machines in the United States.[6] In 1970 there were fewer than 50,000 fax machines in existence. In the early 1980s the number of fax machines began to grow slowly. In the

---

[6]Figures 9.4 and 9.5 are taken from Chapter 34 of Varian [11].

late 1980s, sales of fax machines suddenly accelerated, reaching more than 2 million per year in 1991.

What caused this explosion of demand? Technical advances in the early 1980s drastically reduced the production cost of fax machines. When production costs decrease, the supply curve shifts downward. In any market we expect that a downward shift in the supply curve will result in lower prices and increased sales. Figure 9.5 shows the sharp fall in the price of fax machines that took place in the early 1980's. Between 1982 and 1984

Figure 9.5: Price of Fax Machines

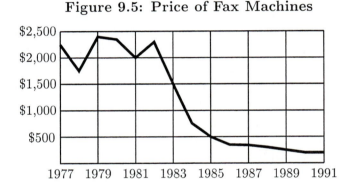

the price fell from more than $2,000 to less than $1,000, and by 1987 it had fallen to about $200. The increase in sales resulting from a fall in price is especially strong because of network externalities. The Buyer Values of those who have not yet purchased a fax machine rise as the number of units sold increases. The combination of rising Buyer Values and falling prices leads to dramatic increases in the number of units purchased.

You are likely to have observed a similar sequence of events in Session 1 of your classroom experiment. In the first round of the session, the price was high, and although there may have been some initial sales, Picture Phones did not catch on and those who did buy them lost money. In later rounds, as the price fell, you probably saw that a few brave souls with high Initial Values entered the market. Seeing these entrants, others with slightly lower Initial Values found it profitable to buy. And finally, as the number of entrants grew it became profitable for almost everyone to buy a Picture Phone. You were observing network externalities in action.

Competing Standards with Network Externalities

Two or more incompatible technologies that are in competition for the same demanders are said to be **competing standards**. Where there are competing standards and also network externalities, it is often the case that a demander's Buyer Value for a particular version of the product (a standard) depends more strongly on the number of other consumers who share the *same standard* than it does on the total number of consumers using other standards. Externalities of this type are said to be **standard-specific network externalities**.

Examples of Competing Standards

The market for computer operating systems is one of the most conspicuous examples of competing standards with standard-specific network externalities. If you want to share files or software with someone, or if you are looking for someone to give you good advice, it is convenient if you both use the same operating system. For these reasons, an operating system will be more useful to you the more widely it is used. Perhaps an even more important source of network externalities arises from shared infrastructure in the form of software written for each operating system. Software developers will write more software for those operating systems that are more widely used. Demanders are willing to pay more for an operating system if there is a lot of software available for it.

Today, the great majority of personal computers use the Microsoft Windows operating system. The Apple Macintosh system is much less popular, but still has some market share. Techies often prefer one or another brand of the Unix system to Windows. In the not-so-distant past, most computers used the DOS system, while other systems like NextStep and IBM's OS2 were considered possible contenders. If you look in computer magazines, you will see a good deal of discussion of possible alternative systems for the future, such as Linux (a version of Unix), Be, and Rhapsody. These future systems enjoy technical advantages over Windows, but lack the network externalities that arise from a large user base.

Within the computer industry, there are many examples of competing standards in software products. With software such as word processors or spreadsheets, it is valuable to be able to share files and knowledge with others who use the same product. The markets for these products, as well as for many other kinds of software, began with a relatively large number of competing standards that were at least partially incompatible. As use of the product became more widespread, one of these standards came to dominate the market. For example, the first computer spreadsheet introduced was called Visicalc. Several competing products appeared, including Lotus 1-2-3, Quattro, and Microsoft Excel. Lotus overcame Visicalc's early lead to emerge temporarily as the market leader, but was not able to maintain this lead and was overtaken by the current leader, Excel, which now has by far the largest market share. In the early days of word processing, there were many competing word processors, and sharing files between them was awkward at best. The first word processor to achieve wide distribution was WordStar, which was released in 1978. Sales of WordStar rose rapidly from $2 million in 1980 to $70 million in 1984. In the mid-1980s, several competing products were introduced, including WordPerfect, Volkswriter, Final Word, XyWriter, and Microsoft Word. WordStar failed to keep up with technical and marketing innovations and lost market share, while WordPerfect and Word gained ascendancy. In recent years, bundled "Office Suites," which contain both a spreadsheet and a word processor (as well as some other office software) have come to dominate the market. Currently, Microsoft Office, which includes both Excel and Word, has a dominant market share.[7]

Competing standards are by no means confined to new, high-technology industries. In many parts of the country in the 1960s it was difficult for owners of Japanese cars to find parts and experienced mechanics to repair their cars. As the number of Toyotas and Hondas sold in the United States increased dramatically, parts and repairs became readily available and consequently ownership of Toyotas and Hondas became more attractive. In the period from 1887-1892, an intense battle of competing standards was fought in the emerging electric power industry between a group founded by Thomas Edison (later to become General Electric) and the Westinghouse power company.[8] The Edison group used a direct current (DC) system and Westinghouse used alternating current (AC). Appliances that worked with one system would not work with the other. Edison had an early lead, but eventually with the help of technical improvements in alternating current technology, the Westinghouse technology prevailed. Ultimately, a converter was invented that enabled the DC power stations to be integrated into the AC power grid.

An even older example of competing standards is to be found in the

---

[7]In 1996, Microsoft claimed to have a 75% market share of this market. Its rival, Lotus, claimed to have a market share of 26.3%.

[8]An entertaining discussion of this battle can be found in Shapiro and Varian [9].

history of languages. If you want to communicate with someone, it is certainly helpful to speak the same language. The children of immigrants to the United States found it more useful to speak English than their parents' native tongues because this enabled them to communicate with more people. Regional languages and dialects in many parts of Europe have all but disappeared as mobility increased and people found it advantageous to communicate with a broader population. The development of English as the most-commonly-spoken second language in the world is a result not of the intrinsic merits of the English language, but simply a consequence of the network externality of being able to communicate with the large number of people in all parts of the world who use English as a first or second language.

Network Externalities, Lock-in, and Innovation

We will focus attention on three forces that play an essential role in the development of industries with competing standards:

- The presence of standard-specific network externalities

- Lock-in effects

- Rapid technical improvement

If you have a Macintosh computer and you want to switch to a Windows system, you will have to learn a whole new set of commands and conventions. You will find that your old software doesn't work on your new computer, so you will also have to replace your software. If you want to switch word processors, you need to learn new keyboard commands. If you have a tape deck for playing records and you want to switch to a CD player, you will have to replace your record collection. If you run an airline and you want to replace your fleet of Boeing airplanes with planes made by Airbus, you will have to retrain your crew to fly the new planes and your mechnics to work on them. If you grew up in Turkey and want to live in Germany, you will probably have to learn German.

We say that there is **lock-in** when it is costly to switch from one competing standard to another. The customers who are currently using a product are known as the product's **installed customer base**. As we discovered in a previous experiment, in the long run in industries like the restaurant industry where there is free entry and no lock-in, firms' profits are likely to be driven to zero. In industries with competing standards and lock-in effects, the pressure from potential entrants is less severe. The presence of lock-in gives an advantage to a firm with a large installed customer base because its current users are not likely to switch products unless the advantages of the alternative product exceed the cost of switching.

We have found two reasons to expect that a dominant firm with a large installed customer base will be able to keep its customers even if it charges higher prices than its competitors. First, there are standard-specific network externalities, which means that demanders have higher Buyer Values for the dominant firm simply because of its large customer base. In addition to these network externalities, because of switching costs, its current customers are willing to maintain and upgrade the product that they are currently using even if it is somewhat more expensive than competing products.

Both of these forces suggest that a firm that takes an early lead in an industry with network externalities and lock-in should be able to increase its lead and ultimately drive out its competitors. Yet when we look at the history of such industries, we see that the early leaders do not always win the dominant market share. Apple Computer had an early lead both in hardware and in operating systems, but it is now a relatively minor player. WordStar was the first commercially successful word processer and is now defunct. WordPerfect gained the leading market share and then lost it to Word. Visicalc, the first spreadsheet, was crowded out by Lotus, which in turn has lost most of its share to Excel. Why were these early leaders unable to take advantage of network externalities and lock-in to achieve market dominance? Perhaps the main threat to an entrenched firm is technological innovation. If innovators can produce a new standard that is much better than that offered by the currently dominant firm, they may be able to persuade users to switch, despite the costs. A second threat arises when the challengers realize that a large installed customer base is a valuable asset—an asset worth paying for. In order to gain this asset, challengers may be willing to bear large early losses in order to break into the market. Since the prize is large, they are willing to spend a lot of money on research and advertising, and are willing to discount their product aggressively in order to attract customers away from the dominant firm.

In classroom experiments, sellers who gain the largest market share in Round 1, and thus generate the highest Buyer Values, are eager to capitalize on their advantage, and often increase their prices in Round 2. At the same time, the sellers with low market shares realize the importance of gaining market share, and often charge very low prices (especially to new customers).[9] As a result, the firm that has the largest market share in the first round often loses its share by the end of the second or third round.

---

[9]Occasionally they offer their product for free or even bribe customers to accept it.

Further Reading

The economics of network externalities is a relatively new area, but one in which some very interesting work is being done. As far as we know, the most accessible and thorough textbook discussion available is Chapter 34 of *Intermediate Microeconomics* by Hal Varian [11]. If you are tired of textbooks and want to read a more lively discussion with lots of real-world examples, we strongly recommend *Information Rules* by Varian and his coauthor Carl Shapiro [9]. If you guessed that there must be a good internet site devoted to network externalities, you guessed right. The place to look is Nicholas Economides' Internet Site for Network Economics, which is located at http://raven.stern.nyu.edu/networks/site.html.

Answers to Warm-up Exercises

W 9.1: 5, $(6 \times 5) - \$20 = \$10$, $(4 \times 5) - \$20 = \$0$, $(2 \times 5) - \$20 = -\$10$; **W 9.2**: 6, $(6 \times 6) - \$5 = \$31$, $(4 \times 6) - \$5 = \$19$, $(2 \times 6) - \$5 = \$7$; **W 9.3**: \$40, \$20, \$20; **W 9.4**: $\$40 - \$15 - \$15 = \$10$; **W 9.5**: $\$20 - \$15 = \$5$, $\$40 - \$15 - \$15 = \$10$; **W 9.6**: $\$75 + (5 \times 25) = \$200$, $\$75 + (5 \times 10) = \$125$; **W 9.7**: \$30, \$50; **W 9.8**: \$45, \$40; **W 9.9**: \$0, \$24.

Answers to Exercises

Ex. 9.1: 0; **Ex. 9.2**: 0, 18; **Ex. 9.3**: 0, 24; **Ex. 9.4**: 30; **Ex. 9.5**: 2, increase, 24 units; **Ex. 9.6**: 1, 0, No.

Lab Notes for Experiment 9

Market Data for Session 1

Your instructor will post a table showing how network externality factors in Session 1 are related to the number of units sold. Record this information by completing the first column of Table 9.5.

Table 9.5: Network Externality Factors: Session 1

If Number of Units Sold Is in Range	Network Externality Factor Is
	1
	2
	3
	4
	5
	6

In Table 9.6, record the price of Picture Phones, the number of Picture Phones sold, and the Network Externality Factor in each round.

Table 9.6: Prices in Session 1

Round Number	1	2	3	4
Price of Picture Phones				
Number of Phones Sold				
Network Externality Factor				

Your instructor will post the number of demanders with each possible Buyer Value who participated in Session 1. Record this information in Table 9.7.

Table 9.7: Distribution of Initial Values

Initial Value	Number of Demanders
1	
2	
3	
4	
5	
6	

Your instructor will also post the number of demanders with each Initial Value *who bought Picture Phones* in each round of Session 1. Record this information in Table 9.8.

Table 9.8: Buyers by Initial Value

Initial Value	Number of Buyers			
	Round 1	Round 2	Round 3	Round 4
1				
2				
3				
4				
5				
6				

Use the information posted by your instructor to complete Tables 9.9, 9.10, and 9.11 for Session 2, and Tables 9.12 and 9.13 for Session 3. For each firm and for each round, enter the total number of units sold by the firm, the highest and lowest prices that it received for units sold, and its total revenue.

Table 9.9: Firm A in Session 2

Round	Units Sold	Highest Price	Lowest Price	Total Revenue
1				
2				
3				
4				

Table 9.10: Firm B in Session 2

Round	Units Sold	Highest Price	Lowest Price	Total Revenue
1				
2				
3				
4				

Table 9.11: Firm C in Session 2

Round	Units Sold	Highest Price	Lowest Price	Total Revenue
1				
2				
3				
4				

Table 9.12: Old Firm in Session 3

Round	Units Sold	Highest Price	Lowest Price	Total Revenue
1				
2				
3				
4				

Table 9.13: New Firm in Session 3

Round	Units Sold	Highest Price	Lowest Price	Total Revenue
1				
2				
3				
4				

Homework for Experiment 9

Problem 9.1 We defined $P(q)$ to be the qth highest Buyer Value when the number of buyers is q. (See page 257.) For Session 1, $P(q)$ will be equal to the qth highest Initial Value times the Network Externality Factor when q units are sold. For each q, you can use Table 9.7 to determine the qth highest Initial Value, and you can use Table 9.5 to find the Network Externality Factor when q units are sold. In this experiment, there are 6 ranges of quantities such that $P(q)$ is constant over each range. Complete Table 9.14 to show $P(q)$ for each of these ranges.

Table 9.14: Table for P(q)

Quantity Range	$P(q)$ in this Range
1 to _____	$6
_____ to _____	$10
_____ to _____	
_____ to _____	
_____ to _____	
_____ to _____	

Problem 9.2 In Figure 9.6, graph the no-regrets demand curve for Session 1. **Hint:** You can use the information in Table 9.14 to graph $P(q)$. Add a vertical line segment corresponding to zero sales at each price above $6 and draw vertical line segments to fill in the jumps between the horizontal line segments in your graph of $P(q)$. See the discussion on page 261, where we drew a curve for a similar case.

Figure 9.6: No-Regrets Demand Curve: Session 1

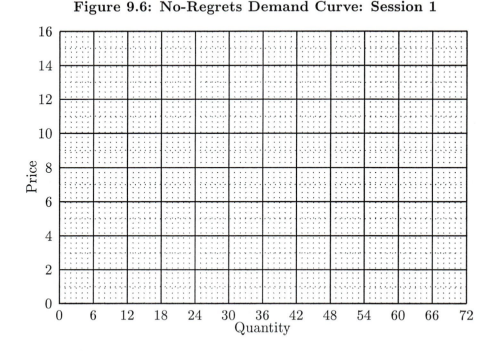

Problem 9.3 On Figure 9.6, draw a horizontal supply curve at a price of $15. What is the equilibrium quantity at this price? _____

Problem 9.4 In Round 1 of Session 1, the price was $15.

How many Picture Phones were sold in this round? _____

How many of the buyers made positive profits? _____

How many of the buyers took losses? _____
If there had been a second round where the price was still $15, how many

Picture Phones do you think would have been sold? _____

Problem 9.5 On Figure 9.6, draw a horizontal supply curve at a price of $11. What are the two stable equilibrium quantities when the supply curve

is horizontal at $11? _____

Problem 9.6 In Round 2 of Session 1, the price was $11.

How many picture phones were sold in this round?   _____
Which of the two equilibrium quantities was closer to the outcome of the

experiment?   _____

How many of the buyers made positive profits?   _____

How many of the buyers made losses?   _____

Problem 9.7   On Figure 9.6, draw a horizontal supply curve at a price of
$9. What are the two stable equilibrium quantities when the supply curve

is horizontal at $9?   _____
Calculate the total amount of profits that buyers would make in the equi-

librium with the higher quantity. $ _____
Suppose that initially the market was stuck at a low-level equilibrium where
nobody would buy a Picture Phone at a price of $9 and the government
offered to sell Picture Phones for $5 to the first k buyers, where k is the
number of demanders with Buyer Value $6. What do you think would hap-

pen to the total number of Picture Phones sold?   _____

Problem 9.8   (Answer this question only if your class ran Round 3 of Session 1, with a price of $9.)

How many picture phones were sold in Round 3?   _____
Which of the two equilibrium quantities was closer to the outcome of the

experiment?   _____

Problem 9.9   Complete Table 9.15 to show the number of units sold,
revenue, costs, and profits of each firm in each round of Session 2. You can
find the number of units sold and total revenue in Tables 9.9, 9.10, and 9.11.
The way to calculate the firm's costs is explained on page 251. The firm's
profits are its revenue minus its costs.

Problem 9.10   Complete Table 9.16 to show total profits or loss of each
of the three firms over all of the rounds of Session 2. For firms that do not
go bankrupt, total profits are equal to the sum of the profits made in each
round plus $15 for each unit sold in the final round. Firms that go bankrupt
will have losses equal to the smaller of their actual losses and $50.

Table 9.15: Sales, Revenue, and Profits: Session 2

	Round 1	Round 2	Round 3	Round 4
Firm A Sales				
Firm A Revenue				
Firm A Costs				
Firm A Profits				
Firm B Sales				
Firm B Revenue				
Firm B Costs				
Firm B Profits				
Firm C Sales				
Firm C Revenue				
Firm C Costs				
Firm C Profits				

Table 9.16: Total Profits or Losses: Session 2

Firm	Total Profit (Loss)
A	
B	
C	

Problem 9.11 In the last round of Session 2, what fraction of all sales was

made by the largest firm? _____

Did the firm with the largest share in the first round have the largest share

in the last round? _____

Did the firm with the largest share make the greatest total profits? _____
Describe any particularly interesting or successful marketing devices used
by firms in this session.

_____

_____

_____

Problem 9.12 Complete Table 9.17 to show the number of units sold,
revenue, costs, and profits of each firm in each round of Session 3.

Table 9.17: Sales, Revenue, and Profits: Session 3

	Round 1	Round 2	Round 3	Round 4
Old Firm Sales				
Old Firm Revenue				
Old Firm Costs				
Old Firm Profits				
New Firm Sales				
New Firm Revenue				
New Firm Costs				
New Firm Profits				

Problem 9.13 Complete Table 9.18 to show total profits or loss of each of
the two firms over all rounds of Session 3. For firms that do not go bankrupt,
total profits are equal to the sum of the profits made in each round plus $15

for each unit sold in the final round. Firms that go bankrupt will have losses equal to the smaller of their actual losses and $50.

Table 9.18: Total Profits or Losses: Session 3

Firm	Total Profit (Loss)
Old	
New	

Problem 9.14 Did the firm with the new technology win the largest market

share?   _____

Did the firm with the new technology make a profit?   _____
Describe any particularly interesting or successful marketing devices used by firms in this session.

_____

_____

_____

Problem 9.15 Try to think of examples where it seems possible that existing technologies remain in place due to network externalities and lock-in, despite the existence of technically superior alternatives.

_____

_____

_____

Experiment 10

Measuring Productivity

Paper Airplane Factories

In this experiment you will make and fly paper airplanes.[1] You will produce the airplanes in a work group, or **firm.** There will be a series of experiments in which we measure the effect on output of variations in the number of workers in the firm. The experiment also illustrates the notions of gains from specialization of labor, congestion at a work site, and learning-by-doing in production processes.

There will be no money or grade rewards for performance in this experiment (but lots of glory, if you like glory).

Instructions

Each firm has fixed inputs, consisting of one worktable, one red pen, and one company truck (a manila folder used to transport unfolded sheets of paper). From session to session we will vary the amount of labor used. Firms will be allowed to use as many sheets of paper as they like, but the amount of fixed inputs will remain unchanged.

Your instructor will inform you of the number of workers per firm in each session. A "quality control inspector" (not a member of the firm) will be appointed to observe the output of each firm and count the number of finished airplanes it produces. Each firm gets four minutes to discuss its organizational plans; then production begins. Firms will be given three minutes in which to produce as many finished airplanes as possible. Members of the

---

[1]This experiment was originally developed by Janet Gerson of the University of Michigan. We are grateful to her for sharing her experience.

most productive firm will be warmly congratulated. The market manager will then calculate the average output of each of the firms in the session and write the results on the blackboard.

Product Specifications

A finished paper airplane must be built according to the following specifications. (Your instructor may choose to add additional requirements.)

- Take an ordinary sheet of paper and tear it once vertically and once horizontally, to make four small sheets of equal size. Planes will be made from these small sheets.

- Each plane must be folded in the way described on the attached instructions.

- The words "Econ Glider" must be written on the underside of each wing, using the company pen. No other pen can be used for this purpose.

- When the above steps are completed, the plane must be given a test flight in the designated test-flight area.

- After testing, the plane must be put in a wastebasket designated as the shipping container.

Production Rules

All airplanes that a firm produces must be folded on the firm's worktable. Each sheet of paper used to make an airplane must be obtained from the Stock Clerk by one of the workers, using the company truck. The company truck holds only one sheet of paper at a time. The quality-control inspector will count an airplane as finished only if it is produced according to the above specifications, test-flown, and placed in the shipping container. "Goods-in-process" that are not finished at the end of three minutes do not count at all.

Discussion of Experiment 10

Diminishing Returns

Think about any firm that you like, a restaurant, a manufacturing plant, a university. Imagine that you are trying to increase the output of this firm by adding more workers without changing the size of the physical plant. Adding a few more workers beyond those currently employed is likely to increase the firm's output. With more waiters and more kitchen and cleaning help, the restaurant can serve people faster and serve more elaborate meals. With more workers, it may be possible to speed up a manufacturing process and produce more output in a given amount of time. With more professors, a university can offer more classes and give students more attention. But as you continue to add labor without increasing the size of the plant, the *extra* output gained from an additional worker will eventually diminish. The waiters in the restaurant will start to trip over each other, the cooks will annoy each other, and it will get more and more difficult to pack additional customers into the restaurant's dining room. Similar problems arise if you continue to add workers to a factory without a corresponding expansion of the factory floor, or if you continue to add professors to a university without increasing classroom and office capacity.

Observations like these are so nearly universal that economists have given this effect a name: **the Law of Diminishing Returns.**[3] The law of diminishing returns can be stated as follows:

> As a firm successively adds more units of a single variable input while holding constant the amount of other inputs, the extra output that results from an additional unit of the input eventually diminishes as the amount of the variable input increases.

The qualification "eventually" is needed to give this law any claim to generality. For example, the extra output added by a second worker may be greater than the output of a single worker, and this may also be true for a third, fourth, or fifth worker. But the Law of Diminishing Returns asserts that at some point, the extra output gained from an extra worker starts to decline and continues to decline as more workers are added.

---

[3] As we will see from its definition, it would be more accurate to call this the Law of *Eventually* Diminishing Returns.

Think about your favorite restaurant. How many meals could it serve per day if only one person came to work and had to act as food preparer, cook, server, and dishwasher. If a second person showed up at work, the two of them could start to specialize on tasks and could probably serve *more than* twice as many meals in a day. The appearance of a third worker might add even more output than did the second. Or think about tasks like moving a piano, cutting down a tree with a two-man saw, or building a car on an assembly line. In each case, we would expect that the extra output gained per extra worker might increase as the first few workers are added, but eventually as the number of workers using the same equipment gets large, the extra output resulting from adding an extra worker would decrease.

The law of diminishing returns applies not only to labor, but to any other input as well. If a restaurant increases the size and convenience of its kitchen and its dining area without increasing the size of its staff, it will probably be able to produce a few more meals per day, but additional increases in the size of its plant without additions to its labor force are likely to lead to ever diminishing additions to its output. The same principle applies to a manufacturing plant or a university.

Inputs and Output

Typically a firm will use **labor**, **land**, **capital goods**, and **raw materials** as inputs into its production process. A firm's capital goods are the durable assets that it uses in production. These often include structures, tools, machinery, and any other physical inputs that are not used up by the process of production. A firm's raw materials are the materials used up in production. In this experiment a firm's capital goods include its workspace, company pen, and company truck. The raw materials are sheets of paper made into airplanes. In this experiment, the amount of capital goods is held constant as the amount of labor and raw materials used is varied.

A firm's **production function** specifies the maximum amount of output that the firm can produce as a function of the amount of each input that it uses. If we hold the quantities of all other inputs constant and simply vary the quantity of labor that the firm uses, then the amount of output is a function of the single variable, labor input. A firm's **average product of labor** is equal to the total output divided by the total number of workers employed by the firm. A firm's **marginal product** of labor is defined to be the extra output that is produced from adding an extra unit of labor.

For example, suppose that (holding constant the amount of other inputs) a firm can produce 10 units of output with one worker, 16 units of output with two workers, and 18 units of output with three workers. We can write the production function as $Q = f(L)$, where Q is the quantity of output and L is the number of workers. Then $f(1) = 10$, $f(2) = 16$, and $f(3) = 18$. The average product of labor is 10 units with one worker, 8 units with two workers, and 6 units with three workers. The marginal product of the first worker is 10 units, the marginal product of the second worker is 6 units, and the marginal product of the third worker is 2 units.

In our experiment we hold constant the firm's capital goods and vary the amount of labor from one session to the next.[4] When we measure the relationship between labor input and total output, we are observing points on the production function. Instead of increasing the size of the group by one worker at a time, in our experimental design we increase the number of workers by more than one as we move from one session to the next.[5] Because we proceed by increments greater than one, we have to adapt the standard definition of marginal productivity. By definition, marginal productivity is the extra output that a firm with a given number of workers gets from adding one more worker (of average skill). Here we observe the extra output that we get by adding a certain number of workers. We will estimate the marginal product of a single worker by dividing the extra output from the additional workers by the number of additional workers. For example, if a group with 15 workers produces 45 airplanes, and a group with 20 workers produces 55 airplanes, then the additional 5 workers increase output by 10 units. Our measure of the marginal product per additional worker when there are 15 workers is therefore $(55 - 45)/5 = 2$.

Food for Thought

Here are some issues that you may want to think about and discuss in order to deepen your understanding of the organization of firms.

■ Estimate the total amount of output that one firm could produce using the same plant and equipment that all of our firms had, but with an additional 200 workers? 500 workers?

---

[4]We also allow the laborers to use as much of the raw material, paper, as they need to make the planes.

[5]Adding workers in larger increments averages out variations due to differences in workers' skill levels, and also makes it possible to complete our experiment in a reasonable amount of time.

■   Give some examples of the division of labor and the specialization of tasks that you observed during the experiment.

■   You were given only a short time for organizing the work groups and practicing. What do you think would have happened to productivity if these groups continued to work together for several sessions of three minutes?

■   Did someone in your firm become a leader, or firm manager? If someone did, was this helpful? If not, would stronger leadership have helped?

■   You may have noticed some variation in the skill levels of the workers. In an industry where firm managers get to pick workers, the best workers might be hired first. How would this affect marginal productivity as more workers are added?

■   In the later rounds of airplane building, people will have more experience than they had in the earlier rounds. How could this effect lead to misleading results? How might you improve the experimental design so as to better separate such "learning-by-doing" effects from the effects of firm size on output?

Lab Notes for Experiment 10

Recording the Outputs of Firms

Your instructor will post the information that you need to complete the first three rows of Table 10.1. For each session, Total Output per Firm is equal to the Combined Output of All Firms divided by the Number of Firms. Average Product of Labor is equal to the Total Output per Firm divided by the Number of Workers per Firm.

Table 10.1: Output in Each Session

	Session Number				
	1	2	3	4	5
Number of Workers per Firm					
Number of Firms					
Combined Output of All Firms					
Total Output per Firm					
Average Product of Labor					

Experiment 11

Comparative Advantage and Trade

Two Island Economies

If you get a World Atlas, and stare very carefully with a high-quality magnifying glass, you may be able to spot the outline of Ricardo Island, a speck in the mid-Atlantic. Ricardo Island is divided between two countries, Richland, on the north end of the island, and Poorland, on the south. Poorland has twice as many people as Richland.

Inhabitants of Ricardo Island produce and consume only two goods, bread and fish. Every islander insists on consuming bread and fish in fixed proportions—in sandwiches that are made with one fish and one loaf of bread. The number of sandwiches that an islander can make is equal to the *minimum* of the number of fish and the number of loaves of bread that he or she acquires. The payoff to an islander will be one dollar for each sandwich that he or she can make at the end of each session. For example, if an islander has 7 fish and 4 loaves of bread at the end of trading, she can make just 4 sandwiches (4 is the minimum of 4 and 7) and her payoff is $4.

Everyone who lives on the island has 20 hours of labor time that can be divided between producing fish and producing bread. In Richland, it takes a person 1 hour to produce a fish and 1.5 hours to produce a loaf of bread. In Poorland, life is harder. It takes 3 hours to produce a fish and 2 hours to produce a loaf of bread.

Session 1–Economies Without Trade

In Session 1 of this experiment, there is no trade, either within or between countries. Individuals can make sandwiches only with the bread and fish that they themselves have produced. As a participant in the experiment, you will be asked to choose an allocation of your 20 hours of time between producing fish and producing bread.

You should prepare for this session by working out the best strategy for inhabitants of each country before you come to class.

Session 2–Free Trade Between Countries

In Session 2, it is possible for anyone to make trades with anyone else in either country.

In this session you must decide how to allocate your 20 hours of time between producing fish and bread. Before you decide what to produce, you may want to look around for possible trading partners and discuss the terms at which you would trade. When you have decided on your time allocation, the market manager will give you fish and/or bread tickets that represent the number of fish and loaves of bread that you produced. To simplify trading, the market manager will not give you tickets for fractional units of bread or fish, but will round *down* to the next smaller whole number.

After you have received your fish and bread tickets, you can make trades with anyone living in either country. To make a trade, simply exchange tickets with someone who is willing to make a deal with you. Trade in fractional tickets is not allowed, but fractional "prices" can be achieved by, for example, trading 2 fish for 1 loaf of bread, or 2 fish for 3 loaves of bread.

When you have completed trading, compute your payoff, which is the minimum of the number of fish and the number of loaves of bread that you have at the end of trading. When trading has ceased, the market manager will survey the group to determine whether there is anyone who still has extra fish that are not matched by loaves of bread, or extra loaves of bread that are not matched by fish.

If time is available, there will be a second round of Session 2. Tickets acquired in the first round are of no use in the second round and should be discarded. Once again, you must decide how to allocate time between producing fish and producing bread, and when you receive your tickets you can trade them with anyone willing to trade. When you have finished trading, calculate your payoff for this round.

Warm-up Exercise

In order to prepare for this experiment, please answer these warm-up questions before you come to class.[1]

W 11.1 If you live in Richland, how many hours would it take you to produce 6 loaves of bread and 11 fish?_____ If you live in Poorland, how many hours would it take you to produce 3 loaves of bread and 4 fish?

_____

W 11.2 Write an equation that states that the number of hours required for a Richlander to produce B loaves of bread and F fish is equal to 20.

_____

W 11.3 Since your payoff is the minimum of B and F, it is wasteful to produce more bread than fish or more fish than bread. If you are a Richlander and cannot make any trades, then in order to get the largest possible payoff, you should choose B and F to satisfy the two simultaneous equations: $B = F$ and $1.5B + F = 20$. To get the highest possible payoff, a Richlander who cannot make any trades should produce _____ loaves of bread and _____ fish.

W 11.4 Write an equation that states that the number of hours required for a Poorlander to produce B loaves of bread and F fish is equal to 20.

_____

W 11.5 To get the highest possible payoff, a Poorlander who cannot make any trades should produce _____ loaves of bread and _____ fish.

---

[1] Answers to these exercises can be found on page 314.

What Do You Expect to See?

■   The inhabitants of Poorland are less productive in producing both goods than the inhabitants of Richland. Can they possibly gain anything by trading with Richlanders?

_____

■   Do you think that if there is free trade with Richland, Poorlanders will be made even poorer?

_____

■   Do you think that the citizens of Richland are likely to be harmed by trading with the low-wage country, Poorland?

_____

Discussion of Experiment 11

"It is the maxim of every prudent master of a family, never to attempt to make at home what it will cost him more to make than to buy.... What is prudence in the conduct of every private family, can scarce be folly in that of a great kingdom. If a foreign country can supply us with a commodity cheaper than we ourselves can make it, better to buy it of them with some part of the produce of our own industry, employed in a way in which we have some advantage.... By means of glasses, hotbeds and hotwalls, very good grapes can be raised in Scotland, and very good wine can be made of them at about thirty times the expense for which equally good can be bought from foreign countries. Would it be a reasonable law to prohibit the importation of all foreign wines merely to encourage the making of claret and burgundy in Scotland?" (Adam Smith, *The Wealth of Nations*, Book IV, Chap. II).

The Free-Trade Debate

In his elegant, eighteenth-century prose, Adam Smith, the founder of modern economics, explained the principle whereby individuals or nations with differing abilities can gain by specialization and trade. This idea has been a centerpiece of economic thinking ever since. Indeed, the design for this experimental market is borrowed from an example in a book published in 1817 by the English economist David Ricardo, *Principles of Political Economy and Taxation*. Ricardo called his two countries England and Portugal, and his commodities were wine and cloth.[2]

Adam Smith and David Ricardo were active participants in a national debate over English trade policy. Smith and Ricardo favored elimination of existing high tariffs on the importation of grain to England. Their arguments did not prevail during their lifetimes. However, in 1846, the British government repealed the Corn Laws, and over the next few years removed

---

[2]Ricardo's contemporary, Robert Torrens, observed that in Ricardo's example, international trade would be mutually beneficial even if one of the two countries were better at producing *both* goods.

most of England's tariffs on imported goods. This enabled England to specialize in manufactured goods and to import cheap food from abroad.

Most present-day economists favor free international trade, for essentially the same reason that Smith and Ricardo proposed. They believe that free trade allows citizens in all trading countries to benefit from specialization according to comparative advantage. If you read the newspapers or listen to political debates, you will be aware that the economists' way of thinking about these matters has not won universal agreement. One of several semi-popular books espousing a contrary view is *The New Protectionism*, by Tim Lang and Colin Hines [7], which advocates restricting global free trade in favor of greater "regional self-sufficiency."

> "Trade liberalization hopes to bring more trade, yet more international trade brings more of the problems the world needs less of: threats to the environment, uneven spread of unemployment, and widening gaps between rich and poor, both within societies and between societies." (page 3)

> "Thus, the basic thesis of free trade is that instead of being self-sufficient, each one should specialize and produce what it is best at and can produce most cheaply, i.e. the things in which it has a 'comparative advantage' ... This theory runs into difficulty where one country can produce products more cheaply than others, and has no incentive to trade, or where a country has little or no comparative advantage in anything." (page 21)

Of course, our experimental trading economy, which was designed to illustrate the principle of comparative advantage, is far simpler than any modern economy. While this experiment suggests a strong, mutually beneficial force exerted by free international trade, it is certainly possible that the simplifications made cause us to overlook harmful side effects of trade. A large literature in economics is devoted to more general and realistic approaches to the question of the benefits and costs of international trade.

Absolute and Comparative Advantage

In our experiment, it takes a Richlander 1 hour to produce a fish and 1.5 hours to produce a loaf of bread, and it takes a Poorlander 3 hours to produce a fish and 2 hours to produce a loaf of bread. A Richlander can produce more of either good in 1 hour than can a Poorlander. In 1 hour, a

Richlander can produce 3 times as many fish and $1\frac{1}{3}$ times as many loaves of bread as a Poorlander. Although in absolute terms, Richlanders are better at producing both goods, in *relative* terms their advantage over Poorland in producing fish is greater than their advantage in producing bread. It is useful to define some terms to help us express these differences in a clearcut way.

A person's **productivity** in producing a good is the number of units that he or she can produce per unit of time. Person 1 is said to have an **absolute advantage** over Person 2 in the production of a good if she has higher productivity than Person 2 in producing that good. In an economy with two goods, A and B, Person 1 is said to have a **comparative advantage** in the production of Good A, if the *ratio* of her productivity in producing Good A to her productivity in producing Good B is greater than the *ratio* of Person 2's productivity in producing Good A to his productivity in producing Good B. If Person 1 has a comparative advantage in producing Good A, then it follows from simple algebra that Person 2 has a comparative advantage in producing Good B. Thus we see that even if one person has an *absolute* advantage over another in all goods, it is impossible for one person to have a *comparative* advantage over another in all goods.

Example:

> In our experiment, the productivity of a Poorlander in producing fish is 1/3 and in producing bread is 1/2. The productivity of a Richlander is 1 in producing fish and $1/1.5 = 2/3$ in producing bread. Richlanders, therefore, have an absolute advantage in the production of both fish and bread. The ratio of a Richlander's productivity in producing *fish* to her productivity in producing *bread* is $1/(2/3) = 3/2$. The ratio of a Poorlander's productivity in producing *fish* to his productivity in producing *bread* is $(1/3)/(1/2) = 2/3$. Since $3/2 > 2/3$, we see that a Richlander has a comparative advantage over a Poorlander in producing fish. The ratio of a Richlander's productivity in producing *bread* to her productivity in producing *fish* is $(2/3)/1 = 2/3$. The ratio of a Poorlander's productivity in producing *bread* to his productivity in producing *fish* is $(1/2)/(1/3) = 3/2$. Since $2/3 < 3/2$, we see that a Poorlander has a comparative advantage over a Richlander in producing bread.

Production Possibilities and Trade

The set of all output combinations that a person or group can produce is known as the **production possibility set** for that person or group. The set of all output combinations that can be produced without wasting anything is called the **production possibility frontier**. We will show how to draw production possibility sets and production possibility frontiers by looking at an example that is similar to the trading environment in our experiment.

Individuals' Production Possibility Sets

The production possibility set for a single Richlander consists of all possible combinations of fish and bread that she can produce in 20 hours. It takes her 1 hour to produce a fish and 1.5 hours to produce a loaf of bread. The amount of time required to produce F fish and B loaves of bread is therefore $F + 1.5B$ hours. In 20 hours, she could produce any combination of F fish and B loaves of bread such that $F + 1.5B = 20$. This equation specifies a Richlander's production possibility frontier. If a Richlander can also waste some output (either by working inefficiently or by working less than full time), the production possibility set includes every output combination such that $F + 1.5B \leq 20$.

Figure 11.1: A Richlander's PPS

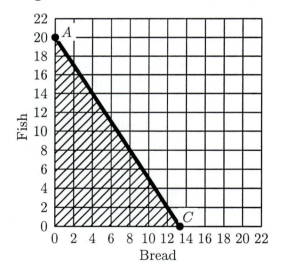

In Figure 11.1 we graph a Richlander's production possibility set and production possibility frontier. The production possibility frontier consists of all of the points satisfying $F + 1.5B = 20$, which is the equation for a straight line. To graph a straight line, you only need to find two points on the line and connect them with a straightedge. One point on this line is found where a Richlander spends all of her time fishing. In this case she will have 20 fish and 0 loaves of bread. This is the point labeled A in Figure 11.1.

Another point on this line, which we label C, is found where she spends all of her time producing bread. In this case she will produce $20/1.5 = 13.33$ loaves of bread and 0 fish. The dark line connecting the points A and C is a Richlander's production possibility frontier. A Richlander's production possibility *set* consists of all nonnegative quantities of fish, F, and bread, B, such that $F + 1.5B \leq 20$. This set is the shaded triangle in Figure 11.1.

Each Poorlander has 20 hours to allocate between producing fish and bread, and it takes him 3 hours to produce a fish and 2 hours to produce a loaf of bread. We have shown you how to draw a Richlander's production possibility set, now it is your turn to draw a Poorlander's production possibility set.

Exercise: A Poorlander's Possibilities[3]

Figure 11.2: A Poorlander's PPS

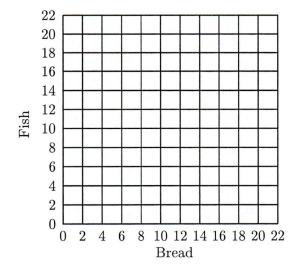

Exercise 11.1
a) If a Poorlander spends all 20 hours producing fish and produces no

bread, how many fish can he produce? _____
b) If a Poorlander spends all 20 hours producing bread and produces

no fish, how many loaves of bread can he produce? _____

---

[3] Answers can be found on page 314.

Exercise 11.2 The equation that determines a Poorlander's production possibility frontier is   _____

Exercise 11.3 Draw and label the production possibility frontier for a Poorlander on Figure 11.2, and shade in the production possibility set.

National Production Possibility Sets Without Trade

A national production possibility set shows all the combinations of total outputs that can possibly be produced with the resources available in a country without engaging in trade.[4] The national production possibility set is obtained by "adding up the outputs" of all individuals in the country.

Suppose that Richland has 10 residents and Poorland has 20 residents. The national production possibility set for Richland is like the individual production possibility set of a Richlander simply scaled up by a factor of 10. Figure 11.3 shows the production possibility set for the country of Richland. Similarly, the national production possibility frontier for Poorland, which has 20 residents, is like the individual production possibility set for a Poorlander scaled up by a factor of 20. (See Figure 11.4.)

Figure 11.3: Richland's National PPS

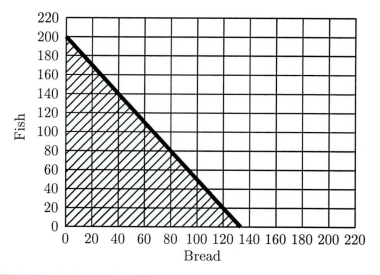

---

[4]Trade economists like to call this set the production possibility set in *autarky*.

Figure 11.4: Poorland's National PPS

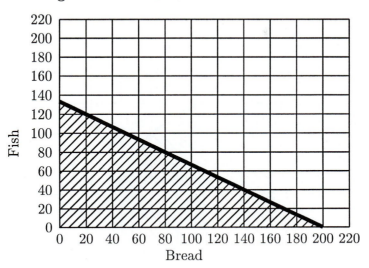

International Production Possibility Set

The **international production possibility set** for two or more countries depicts all of the possible combinations of total outputs that could be produced in these countries when people are allowed to trade freely across countries.

Here we will construct the international production possibility set for the two countries on Ricardo Island. First, let us find the greatest amount of fish that could be produced in the two countries if everyone in both countries specialized in fish and produced no bread. Each Richlander could produce $20/1 = 20$ fish and each Poorlander could produce $20/3 = 6.66$ fish. Since there are 10 Richlanders and 20 Poorlanders, total output of fish would be $(10 \times 20) + (20 \times 6.66) = 333.3$. The point $(0, 333.3)$ on the international production possibility frontier is labeled C on Figure 11.5.

Next, let us find the greatest amount of bread that could be produced if everyone in both countries produced only bread. Each Richlander could produce $20/1.5 = 13.33$ loaves of bread and each Poorlander could produce $20/2 = 10$ loaves of bread. Since there are 10 Richlanders and 20 Poorlanders, the total amount of bread will be $(10 \times 13.33) + (20 \times 10) = 333.3$. Therefore the point $(333.3, 0)$ is on the international production possibility frontier. We have marked and labeled this point as A on Figure 11.5.

Now let us find output combinations where some of each good is produced. If everyone specializes according to comparative advantage, then

Figure 11.5: An International PPS

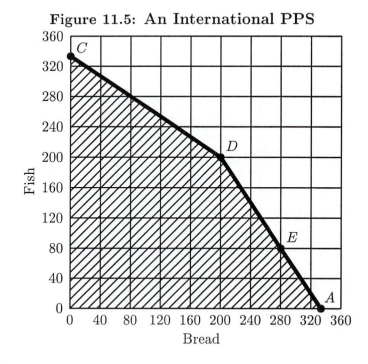

Richlanders will spend all their time producing fish and Poorlanders will spend all of their time producing bread. Each Richlander would produce 20 fish and no bread, and each Poorlander would produce 10 loaves of bread and no fish. Since there are 10 Richlanders and 20 Poorlanders, total production of fish would be $10 \times 20 = 200$ and total production of bread would be $20 \times 10 = 200$. Thus the point $(200, 200)$ is also a possible output combination. We label this point D.

Output combinations along the line segment DA can be produced if all Poorlanders specialize in bread and if Richlanders divide their time between producing fish and bread. For example, suppose that Poorlanders produced only bread and that Richlanders spend 8 hours producing fish and 12 hours producing bread. Each of the 10 Richlanders would then produce 8 fish and 8 loaves of bread. Richlanders' total output of fish and bread would be $10 \times 8 = 80$ units of each. Poorlanders would produce a total of 200 loaves of bread and no fish. The total output of bread in the two countries would be $200 + 80 = 280$, and the total output of fish would be 80. The point $(280, 80)$ lies on the line segment DA and is labeled E. Similarly, outputs along the line segment CD can be achieved by having Richlanders specialize in fish, and having Poorlanders divide their time between producing fish and bread.

The international production possibility frontier for the two countries on Ricardo Island is the broken line CDA. Assuming that it is always possible to waste any amount of either good, the international production possibility set is the shaded area consisting of all the points on or below CDA.

Two Exercises on Comparative Advantage

The first of these exercises explores comparative advantage and the patterns of trade in competitive equilibrium for two trading countries.

Exercise: North and South Potato[5]

The small countries of North and South Potato each have 100 workers. Workers in each country work 50 hours per week and can spend their time producing either food or clothing. It takes a North Potato worker 20 hours to produce a unit of food and 5 hours to produce a unit of clothing. It takes a South Potato worker 40 hours to produce a unit of food and 5 hours to produce a unit of clothing. People in each country consume food and clothing only in fixed proportions, one unit of food per unit of clothing.

Exercise 11.4 If no trade is allowed and people in North Potato consume only the goods that they produce themselves, then each week,

each person in North Potato will consume _____units of food and

_____units of clothing.

Exercise 11.5 Which of the two countries has a comparative advan-

tage in the production of food?_____
Which has a comparative advantage in the production of clothing?

_____

Exercise 11.6 If the countries each specialize according to compara-

tive advantage, then North Potato will specialize in _____ and

it will produce _____ units of this good per week. South Potato will

----

[5]Answers are found on Page 314.

specialize in _____ and it will produce _____ units of this good per week.

Exercise 11.7   On Figure 11.6, draw the international production possibility frontier for North and South Potato.

Figure 11.6: Potato Possibility Set

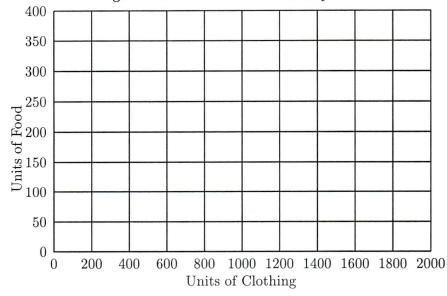

Exercise 11.8   If there is free international trade between North and

South Potato, then in competitive equilibrium, approximately _____

units of food and _____ units of clothing will be produced in total. **Hint:** In competitive equilibrium with free trade, the total output will be on the international production possibility frontier. It will also be the case that the total amount of food consumed is equal to the total amount of clothing consumed. Draw a line on Figure 11.6 showing the points where the amount of food equals the amount of clothing. The point where this line intersects the international production possibility frontier shows the competitive equilibrium quantities.

Exercise 11.9   In competitive equilibrium with free international

trade, the country of _____ will produce both food and clothing

and the country of _____ will produce only one good. **Hint:**

Which country needs to specialize in order for equal amounts of food and clothing to be produced in the most efficient way?

The international production possibility frontier shows possible outputs if countries specialize according to comparative advantage. In the following exercise, we explore the possible combinations of outputs if the countries specialize incorrectly.

Exercise: Production on Bozo Island[6]

Times are tough on Bozo Island. Like Ricardo Island, it has two countries, Richland with 10 residents and Poorland with 20 residents. Productivities of Richlanders and Poorlanders are the same as on Ricardo Island. The governments of both countries on Bozo Island are controlled by lawmakers whose rhetorical skills exceed their economic understanding. Richland's lawmakers are determined to protect the *bread* industry from competition with "cheap foreign labor." Poorland's lawmakers have decided to protect the *fish* industry from "unfair foreign competition." For this purpose, the two countries have passed some rather curious laws, known as the Bozo Protection Laws or BPLs.

The Richland Bozo Protection Law reads as follows: Richlanders are allowed to produce fish only if *Poorlanders* do not produce any bread.

The Poorland Bozo Protection Law reads: Poorlanders are allowed to produce bread only if *Richlanders* do not produce any fish.

The effect of the Bozo Protection Laws is to make it illegal to specialize according to comparative advantage. If Richland specialized in fish and Poorland specialized in bread, then both countries' BPLs would be violated. If Richland specialized in fish and Poorland produced some of each good, then the Richland BPL would be violated, since Richlanders aren't allowed to produce fish unless Poorlanders are producing only fish. Similarly, if Poorland specialized in bread and Richland produced some of each good, the Poorland BPL would be violated.

So when are the BPL's *not* violated? If Richland specializes in bread and Poorland specializes in fish there is clearly no violation. Also, if Richland specializes in bread and Poorland produces some of each good, or if Poorland specializes in fish and Richland produces some of each good neither BPL is violated. Finally, there is no violation if both countries produce only fish or only bread.

---

[6]Answers can be found on page 314.

Exercise 11.10 If Richland specializes in bread and Poorland specializes in fish, the total amount of bread produced on Bozo Island will

be _____ and the total amount of fish produced will be _____. On Figure 11.5, mark the point that shows this output combination and label it it G.

Exercise 11.11 Suppose that everyone in Poorland specializes in fish and everyone in Richland produces 8 fish and 8 loaves of bread.

Then Poorland will produce _____ fish and no bread, while Richland

will produce _____ fish and _____ loaves of bread. Adding total

production in the two countries, we find that a total of _____ fish and

_____ loaves of bread are produced. Mark the point that designates this output combination on Figure 11.5 and label it H.

Exercise 11.12 On Figure 11.5, use red ink to draw the international production possibility frontier for Bozo Island, assuming that everyone abides by the Bozo Protection Laws. **Hint:** This production possibility frontier includes the points G and H that you found, as well as the points A and C.

Exercise 11.13 On Figure 11.5, shade in the area consisting of output combinations that are possible on Ricardo Island but not possible on Bozo Island, as long as the BPLs are obeyed.

Exercise 11.14 To make a fish sandwich, you need one fish and one loaf of bread. What is the largest total number of fish sandwiches that

can be made on Ricardo Island, where free trade prevails? _____ What is the largest number of fish sandwiches that can be made on

Bozo Island, where the Bozo Protection Laws are enforced? _____

Competitive Equilibrium with Free Trade

As in our earlier experiments, we can look for competitive equilibrium prices and quantities. Things are a little more complicated here for two reasons: (1) participants must decide both about what to produce and about what to consume, and (2) we have two prices to work with, the price of bread and the price of fish. We want to find prices that equalize supply and demand in both the fish and the bread markets.

We can think of each individual making two separate decisions. First, acting as a producer, she decides how to allocate her time between producing bread and fish. Her income is equal to the total value of the output she produces. Second, acting as a consumer, she uses the income that she earned from production to buy the combination of bread and fish that gives her as many sandwiches as she can possibly afford.

Let us investigate whether there is a competitive equilibrium in which the price of a fish is $1 and the price of a loaf of bread is also $1. It takes a Richlander 1 hour to produce a fish and 1.5 hours to produce a loaf of bread. Since it takes her longer to produce a loaf of bread than a fish, and since the price of bread is the same as the price of fish, she will maximize her income by spending all of her time producing fish. This means that a Richlander will produce 20 fish and earn an income of $20. It takes a Poorlander 3 hours to produce a fish and 2 hours to produce a loaf of bread, so he will maximize his income by spending all of his time producing 10 loaves of bread, in which case he earns an income of $10. Thus each of the 10 Richlanders will produce 20 fish and no bread, and each of the 20 Poorlanders will produce 10 loaves of bread and no fish. Therefore the total supply of fish is 200 fish and the total supply of bread is 200 loaves.

Now let us examine the demand for bread and fish at these prices. Every Richlander has an income of $20. Since the number of sandwiches she can make is the minimum of the number of fish and the number of loaves of bread that she acquires, she will spend her income on equal amounts of bread and fish. With $20, a Richlander can buy 10 fish and 10 loaves of bread and make 10 sandwiches. Each Poorlander has an income of $10. The best combination that a Poorlander can afford is 5 fish and 5 loaves of bread, which will make 5 sandwiches. Since there are 10 Richlanders and 20 Poorlanders, the total amount of fish demanded is $(10 \times 10) + (20 \times 5) = 200$, and the total amount of bread demanded is $(10 \times 10) + (20 \times 5) = 200$.

The bread and fish markets will be in competitive equilibrium if the quantity demanded is equal to the quantity supplied in both markets. As we have seen, at a price of $1 for fish and $1 for bread, 200 fish and 200 loaves will be produced. We also saw that at these prices, 200 fish and 200 loaves will be demanded. So at these prices, the quantity supplied equals the quantity demanded, both for bread and for fish. Therefore there is a competitive equilibrium where the prices are $1 per fish and $1 per loaf of bread.

Prices of $1 per unit for both goods are not the only prices at which there is a competitive equilibrium. Notice that demand and supply in this market depend only on the *ratio* of prices, and not on their absolute magnitudes. Thus at prices of $2 per unit for each good, there would also be a competitive equilibrium, with each Richlander and each Poorlander producing and consuming exactly the same amount of each good as at prices of $1 for each good.

In fact, it is possible to show that any prices p_f for fish and p_b for bread such that $2/3 < p_f/p_b < 3/2$, will be competitive equilibrium prices. To see this, note that at all such prices, Richlanders will specialize in fish and Poorlanders will specialize in bread, so that total supplies will still be 200 fish and 200 loaves of bread. A little more work will show that at any of these prices, 200 fish and 200 loaves of bread will be demanded.

Comparative Advantage and Gains from Trade

How is the free trade debate resolved in the case of Ricardo Island? Is free trade good for one country and not the other? Is it good for both countries? Is it bad for both countries?

The answer in the example that we have just completed is clear. Everyone in both countries gains from opening the borders to trade. As a result of trade, Richlanders are able to increase their consumption from 8 sandwiches to 10, and Poorlanders are able to increase their consumption from 4 sandwiches to 5.

How is this possible? With trade, the citizens of the two countries are able to specialize according to their comparative advantage. It takes a Richlander longer to make a loaf of bread than to catch a fish. It takes a Poorlander longer to catch a fish than to make a loaf of bread. If Richlanders specialize in catching fish and Poorlanders specialize in baking bread, then the total amount of both fish and bread that are produced on Ricardo Island will be larger than if Richlanders baked their own bread and Poorlanders caught their own fish. Since free trade makes it possible to increase total world production of both goods, it also makes it possible for both Richlanders and Poorlanders to be better off. To help you to grasp the logic behind this result, we will conclude our discussion with a fable.

The Tale of the Mad Inventor

For years, the inhabitants of Ricardo Island resisted trade between nations. Richlanders feared trade with their poorer neighbors, believing that "poverty is contagious." An eminent Richland industrialist-politician orated:

> "If we open our borders to trade, you will ask 'What's that sucking sound?' It will be the sound of Richland jobs being sucked away to Poorland."

Poorlanders were convinced that if they started to trade with Richland they would only be exploited. A popular Poorland politician maintained that

> "Free trade is all very well for countries that are equally productive, but free trade doesn't work for poor countries like ours because we can't produce *anything* as well as the rich countries."

One day, a wild-eyed inventor appeared before the elders of Richland and announced that he had devised a remarkable new technique for converting fish into bread. He proposed to open a factory in Richland. This factory would be able to convert a fish into a loaf of bread. He would buy fish from Richlanders at $1 per fish and sell bread to them for $1 per loaf.

The elders of Richland scratched their heads and went home to think about what this would mean. They concluded that the proposed factory was very good news for them. Since time immemorial, Richlanders have spent their time making 8 fish (8 hours) and 8 loaves of bread (12 hours), which they would then make into 8 sandwiches. If the inventor installed his factory, each of them could spend all 20 hours catching 20 fish, and then exchange 10 fish at the factory for 10 loaves of bread. Thus they could each have 10 sandwiches instead of 8.

Shortly after he met with the Richlanders, the same inventor appeared before the elders of Poorland and announced that he had discovered a method of converting bread into fish. He would build a factory in Poorland that could convert a loaf of bread into a fish. He would buy bread from Poorlanders at $1 per loaf and would sell fish to them for $1 each. The Poorlanders studied his proposal and were pleased with it. They realized that they could spend all 20 hours baking 10 loaves of bread and then exchange 5 loaves for 5 fish at the factory. This would allow them each to consume 5 sandwiches instead of the 4 that they had consumed in the past.

In both countries, the mad inventor built factories on the seacoast, with impressive chimneys and high wire fences. In both countries, people happily exchanged goods at the factory. All were able to consume more sandwiches than before. The inventor received the highest honors from the politicians of both countries.

As time went on, residents of both countries became curious about the factories. "How is it possible to take a loaf of bread and turn it into a fish?" asked Poorlanders. "Fish to bread—what about the smell?" inquired Richlanders. One night a group of curious Richlanders tunneled under the fence and entered the factory door. To their astonishment, they discovered that the factory entrance and its chimneys were just a Hollywood-like facade. Behind the facade, they found nothing more than a loading dock and a boat. At about the same time, a group of Poorlanders broke through their fence and found a similar setup.

How do you explain what the Mad Inventor was doing?

Food for Thought

■ On Ricardo Island, can two people who live in the same country make any trade that benefits both of them? Are mutual gains from trade possible between two people who live in different countries? Why are the answers to the previous two questions different from each other?

■ In the passage from *The New Protectionism* that was quoted previously, we found the following remark.

> "This theory [the theory of comparative advantage] runs into difficulty where one country can produce products more cheaply than others, and has no incentive to trade, or where a country has little or no comparative advantage in anything."

Do you agree?

Answers to Warm-up Exercises

W 11.1: 20 hours, 18 hours;   **W 11.2**: $1.5B + F = 20$;   **W 11.3**: 8, 8;   **W 11.4**: $3F + 2B = 20$;   **W 11.5**: 4, 4.

Answers to Exercises

Ex. 11.1: $20/3 = 6.66$, $20/2 = 10$; **Ex. 11.2**: $3F + 2B = 20$; **Ex. 11.3**: The PPF is a straight line, meeting the vertical axis at 6.66 and the horizontal axis at 10; **Ex. 11.4**: 2, 2; **Ex. 11.5**: North Potato, South Potato; **Ex. 11.6**: food, 250, clothing, 1,000; **Ex. 11.7**: The PPF is two line segments, one running from $(0, 375)$ to $(1000, 250)$ and one from $(1000, 250)$ to $(2000, 0)$; **Ex. 11.8**: 333, 333; **Ex. 11.9**: South Potato, North Potato; **Ex. 11.10**: 133.33, 133.33; **Ex. 11.11**: 133.33, 80, 80, 213.33, 80; **Ex. 11.12**: The PPF is two line segments, one running from $(0, 333.33)$ to $(133.33, 133.33)$ and one from $(133.33, 133.33)$ to $(333.33, 0)$; **Ex. 11.13**: This will be the diamond-shaped area between the PPF for Bozo Island and the PPF for Ricardo Island; **Ex. 11.14**: 200, 133.33.

Lab Notes for Experiment 11

Recording Market Outcomes

Your instructor will post the information that you need to complete Tables 11.1 and 11.2, which record production decisions and payoffs received by Richlanders and PoorLanders in the last round of Session 2.

Table 11.1: Output and Payoffs in Richland

Number of Students	Fish Output	Bread Output	Final Fish Holdings	Final Bread Holdings	Payoff
	20	0	10	10	$10
	8	8	8	8	$8

You are likely to find that most Richlanders chose to produce 20 fish and no bread, and were then able to trade 10 of their fish for 10 loaves of bread. These individuals will all get payoffs of $10. In the first column of the first row of Table 11.1, record the number of Richlanders in your experiment for whom this was the case. Some Richlanders probably chose to produce 8 fish and 8 loaves and made no trades. These Richlanders will all get payoffs of $8. In the first column of the second row of Table 11.1, record the number of Richlanders for whom this was the case. There may be a few Richlanders who made other production decisions and/or had different trading outcomes. Record their production, final holdings, and payoffs in the remaining rows. (Recall that a Richlander's payoff is the minimum of her final holdings of bread and of fish.)

You are likely to find that most Poorlanders chose to produce no fish and 10 units of bread, and were then able to trade 5 loaves of bread for 5 fish. In the first column of the first row of Table 11.2, record the number of Poorlanders in your experiment for whom this was the case. Some Poorlanders probably chose to produce 4 fish and 4 loaves, and made no trades. In the first column of the second row of Table 11.2, record the number of Poorlanders for whom this was the case. Record the production, final holdings, and payoffs of Poorlanders who made other production decisions and/or had different trading outcomes in the remaining rows.

Table 11.2: Output and Payoffs in Poorland

Number of Students	Fish Output	Bread Output	Final Fish Holdings	Final Bread Holdings	Payoff
	0	10	5	5	$5
	4	4	4	4	$4

Homework for Experiment 11

Problem 11.1

Part a) From the information in Tables 11.1 and 11.2, you will be able to calculate the average payoffs that Richlanders and Poorlanders received in Session 2 with free trade. Record this information in Table 11.3. Then calculate and record the largest payoffs that Richlanders and Poorlanders could receive if they did not trade.

Table 11.3: Payoffs with and without Trade

	Average Payoff with Free Trade	Maximum Payoff with No Trade
Richlanders		
Poorlanders		

Part b) Is free trade better or worse than no trade for citizens of Richland?

_____

Part c) Is free trade better or worse than no trade for citizens of Poorland?

_____

Problem 11.2 From the information in Tables 11.1 and 11.2, you will be able to calculate the total amounts of bread and fish produced and consumed in Richland and in Poorland. (The amount consumed is the amount that people have at the end of trading.) Record this information in Table 11.4.

Table 11.4: Production and Consumption

	Bread Produced	Bread Consumed	Fish Produced	Fish Consumed
Richland				
Poorland				

Problem 11.3

Part a) If a country consumes more of a good than it produces, then the difference between the quantity that it consumes and the quantity that it produces is its **imports**. If a country produces more of a good than it consumes, then the difference between its production and its consumption is its **exports**. Record the amount of goods exported or imported from each country in Table 11.5.

Table 11.5: Exports and Imports

	Bread Imported	Bread Exported	Fish Imported	Fish Exported
Richland				
Poorland				

Part b) If the bread-exporting country exported twice as much bread as the amount of fish it imported, we would say that the average price of a fish was 2 loaves of bread. More generally, the average price of fish relative to bread is given by the ratio of the number of loaves of bread exported to the number of fish imported by the country that exports bread and imports fish.

In this experiment, the average price of fish relative to bread was _____

Problem 11.4 In Session 2 of this experiment:

which country exports bread and imports fish?   _____

which country imports bread and exports fish?   _____

which country has a comparative advantage in fish?   _____

which country has a comparative advantage in bread?   _____

Problem 11.5   In Session 2 of this experiment: who can produce more

bread per hour, a Richlander or a Poorlander?   _____

which country exported bread and imported fish?   _____

Does this mean that free international trade is inefficient?   _____

Problem 11.6   In the Tale of the Mad Inventor, Richlanders were able to exchange as many fish as they liked for an equal number of loaves of bread at the factory. When this option is available, Richlanders can attain many consumption bundles that would be unavailable to them if they were not able to make such exchanges. For example, we observed that they could obtain 10 fish and 10 loaves of bread by producing 20 fish and trading 10 of them for 10 loaves of bread.

Figure 11.7: Trading with the Madman

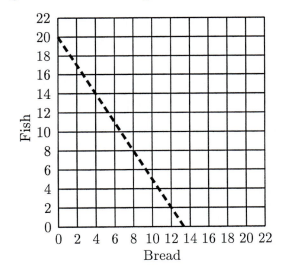

Part a) On Figure 11.7, we have drawn a dashed line to show the production possibility frontier for Richlanders when they make no trades. Now draw a solid line to show all of the combinations of fish and bread that

Richlanders could obtain by producing only fish and making trades with the mad inventor. Label this line AB.

Part b) Write an equation that describes all of the points on the line AB

that you have drawn.   _____

Part c) Suppose that instead of making their sandwiches with one fish and one loaf, Richlanders always make their sandwiches with one fish and two loaves of bread. What is the largest number of this kind of sandwich that a

Richlander could produce without making any trades?   _____
What is the largest number of this kind of sandwich that a Richlander could

make after trading with the mad inventor?   _____

Part V

Information, Auctions, and Bargaining

Experiment 12

Adverse Selection

A "Lemons" Market

If you have ever purchased a used car from a stranger, you probably have worried about whether she was telling you the whole truth about the car. Perhaps you thought: "The seller knows a lot more about her car than I do. If the car is any good, why does she want to sell it?"

Today's experiment simulates a used-car market. There are two kinds of used cars in the market, bad used cars (commonly known as "lemons") and good used cars. Used-car owners sell their cars to car dealers.[1] Dealers are unable to tell the difference between good cars and lemons.[2] Sellers, on the other hand, have lived with their cars and know very well whether their car is a lemon or not.

Instructions

Used Car Owners (Suppliers)

An owner's **reservation price** for an object is the smallest price that the owner would accept for the object. Thus if you are a used-car owner, you will want to keep your car unless you are offered at least your reservation price. You should be willing to sell to the person who makes you the highest offer that is greater than your reservation price.

---

[1] Although people usually associate car dealers with the role of sellers, in this experiment they function as buyers purchasing cars for resale.

[2] Some macho buyers may kick the tires and lift up the hood; they may even talk about fuel pumps and suspension systems, but this is all for show.

In this experiment, some used-car owners will have lemons and some will have good used cars. Understandably, owners of good used cars will have higher reservation prices for their cars than lemon owners. The owner of a good used car has a reservation price of $1600 for her car, and a lemon owner has a reservation price of $0. A used-car owner's profit from selling her car will be the price she receives for it minus her reservation price. If she doesn't sell her car, her profits are zero.

Used-Car Dealers (Buyers)

Some people are willing to pay more for used cars than these cars are worth to their current owners. In fact, there are a large number of people who are willing to pay $500 for a car that is known to be a lemon and $3500 for a car that is known to be good. These consumers are not directly represented by participants in the experiment, but their willingness-to-pay determines the Buyer Values of the dealers. Dealers will discover the quality of each car that they buy shortly after they buy it, and they are required by law to reveal this quality to consumers. Dealers can resell good used cars for $3500 and lemons for $500 each.

Session 1–Monopolistic Used-Car Dealers

This session consists of a thought experiment, in which you decide what price to offer for used cars. Before you come to class, read through these instructions and work the warm-up exercises. These will help you to decide on the most profitable actions to take in this session.

Imagine that you are the only used-car dealer in town. All used-car owners in your town must either sell their used cars to you or keep them. At the time you buy a used car, you cannot tell whether it is a good used car or a lemon. However, between the time you buy the car and the time you resell it, you will find out whether the car is a lemon or a good car. You will resell all of the cars that you buy. You can resell lemons for $500 and good cars for $3500.[3] Your profits are equal to the revenue you get from reselling cars minus the total amount of money you pay for cars. You must post a single price at which you are willing to purchase all used cars that are brought to you. Buyers will bring their cars to you if the price you post is higher than their reservation prices.

---

[3]In your town, used-car dealers (unlike the initial owners) are required by law to reveal the actual quality of their cars to their customers.

We consider two alternative situations. In Situation A, there are six good used cars and six lemons in your town. In Situation B, there are four good cars and eight lemons in your town. In this session you will be asked to submit your name or identification number, the price that you would offer for used cars in Situation A, and the price that you would offer for used cars in Situation B.

Session 2–A Competitive Used-Car Market

In this session, the used-car market is competitive and car buyers interact with sellers. Most class members are used-car owners (sellers). Half of the car owners have good used cars and half of them have lemons. Some class members are used-car dealers. If you are a dealer, you will be given some blackboard space on which you can post the price that you are willing to pay for used cars. You can change your posted price at any time. You can buy as many used cars as people are willing to sell to you. When you buy a car, you should record the seller's identification number on your Record of Purchases. At the time of the purchase, you will not know which cars are good and which are lemons.

At the end of trading, dealers will bring their Records of Purchases to the market manager. The market manager will calculate the average value of *all* used cars purchased by *all* dealers. If you are a dealer, the value to you of each used car that you buy will be equal to the average value of used cars purchased by *all* dealers. For example, suppose that all dealers combined purchased a total of 10 good used cars and 5 lemons. The average value of these cars is

$$\frac{(\$3500 \times 10) + (\$500 \times 5)}{15} = \$2500.$$

A dealer who bought 3 used cars will receive a total revenue of $\$2500 \times 3 = \$7500$. The dealer's profits are then $7500 *minus* the total amount she paid for the 3 cars that she bought.

Session 3–A Used-Car Market with More Bad Cars

Session 3 is conducted exactly like Session 2, except that in this session, only 1/3 of the used cars are good and 2/3 of the used cars are lemons.

Session 4–Quality Certification (Optional)

In this session, as in Session 3, 1/3 of the used cars are good and 2/3 are lemons. In this session, used-car owners who have good used cars are allowed to show their Personal Information Sheets to dealers to prove that they have good used cars. Used-car dealers can ask to see an owner's Personal Information Sheet before buying a used car and can offer different prices to a seller depending on whether or not she can prove that she has a good car. When a used-car owner sells a used car to the dealer, the dealer should record the price and the seller's identification number on the dealer's Record of Purchases. If the seller proves that her car is a good used car, the dealer should mark an asterisk next to the price.

In Session 4 (unlike in Session 3), a dealer's revenue is equal to the total value of the cars *that he actually purchased* rather than the average value of all cars purchased by all dealers.

Warm-up Exercise

W 12.1 [4] Suppose that in Session 1, you are a monopoly car dealer in a town where six used-car owners have good cars and six have lemons. What is the lowest price at which lemon-owners would sell their cars? _____

Would the owners of good cars sell their cars at this price? _____ What is your profit if you offer this price? _____

W 12.2 In Session 1, the lowest price at which *all* used-car owners will sell their cars is _____ . What is your profit if you offer this price? _____

W 12.3 In Session 1, if there are six good used cars and six lemons in town, what price should you offer for used cars in order to maximize your profits? _____

W 12.4 In Session 1, suppose that the used-car owners in your town have four good cars and eight lemons. What is the lowest price at which lemon-owners will sell their cars? _____ If you offer this price, your profit is _____ . What is the lowest price at which *all* used-car owners will sell their cars? _____ If you offer this price your profit is _____ .

W 12.5 In Session 1, if there are four good used cars and eight lemons in town, what price should you offer in order to maximize your profits? _____

---

[4] Answers to these exercises can be found on page 339.

Discussion of Experiment 12

Markets with Asymmetric Information

Our experimental used-car market is an example of a market with **asymmetric information.** Asymmetric information occurs when traders on one side of the market know things that traders on the other side of the market do not. At first blush, asymmetric information might not seem to be a serious problem for markets. Usually it would be cheap and easy for traders who know things that others don't know to pass this information on. The problem, as you may have guessed, given your experiences in real-world markets and in the experiment, is that traders who have detailed information may benefit from concealing or misrepresenting this information. Talk is cheap. If a buyer offers a higher price to those who say they have good cars than to those who say they have lemons, lemon owners will want to say they have good cars. In the design of all sessions except Session 4, there is nothing to prevent them from doing so.[5]

Adverse Selection

Asymmetric information often leads to a market problem that is known as **adverse selection.** Adverse selection occurs in a market when buyers or sellers would, on average, be better off trading with someone selected at random from the population than with those who volunteer to trade. A classic example of adverse selection occurs in used-car markets. As we saw in our experiment, it can happen that in equilibrium the used cars that come onto the market are not a random selection from the population of used cars but just the worst ones. When this happens, a used-car buyer who thinks that the used cars that are for sale are of average quality will be sadly mistaken.

The problem of adverse selection also applies to insurance markets. The customers that are most likely to want insurance are the people who face the highest risks, but these are the people that insurance companies would

---

[5]In real life, even if you don't value the truth for its own sake, lying to those you deal with regularly will hurt you. If your acquaintances catch you in a lie, they are likely to mistrust you in the future. In an arm's length business encounter with someone whom you are not likely to meet again (like a stranger to whom you sell a used car) this constraint on behavior is missing.

least like to have as customers. For example:

- The people who most want to buy collision insurance for their cars are those who drive a lot and are most likely to have accidents.

- The people who are most eager to buy health insurance are those who have reason to think that they are going to have an expensive illness.

- The people who are most likely to buy life insurance are those who have reason to believe that they are likely to die soon.

- The people who are most eager to buy annuities are those who have reason to believe that they will live for a long time. (An **annuity** is a promise to pay somebody a fixed amount every year until he or she dies.)

Insurance companies are well aware that their customers will, on average, be worse insurance risks than a randomly-selected member of the population. Accordingly, instead of basing their estimates of the risks they face on statistics for the population as a whole, they base them on statistics for *insured* people in previous years.

Moral Hazard

Another problem of asymmetric information, similar to adverse selection, is known in the insurance industry as **moral hazard**. Adverse selection occurs when your trading partners have less favorable *characteristics* than the population at large. Moral hazard occurs when the *actions* taken by your trading partners are less favorable for you than the actions of the average member of the population.

Examples of moral hazard include the following. People who have fire insurance will be less interested in preventing fires than those without fire insurance. People who have insurance against auto theft are likely to take fewer precautions against having their car stolen than people who do not have insurance. People with unemployment insurance may search less intensely for jobs. Workers whose performance is not monitored may shirk. Construction contractors whose work is not closely inspected may do shoddy work, the flaws of which do not become apparent until after they are paid.

With moral hazard, as with adverse selection, the problem is that people on one side of the market know something that the people on the other side do not. Moral hazard is sometimes called the case of **hidden action**. With moral hazard, one side of the market is not able to observe the actions taken by the people they deal with.

Where moral hazard is a problem, the market participant without information tries to monitor performance of the participant with information, and to make this performance part of the terms of the contract. Fire insurance companies have inspectors who observe precautions taken by their large industrial customers. Auto theft insurers may give discounts to customers who have anti-theft devices on their cars. Unemployment insurance runs out after a few weeks of unemployment. Firms try to monitor their workers' performance. People that hire contractors often hire inspectors to observe that construction proceeds according to specifications. Because monitoring is expensive, and usually imperfect, even with monitoring the problem of moral hazard remains a serious one.

Demand and Supply in a Lemons Market

Demand and supply analysis can help us to predict the outcome in a market where, as in our used-car experiment, there is adverse selection. Since suppliers know the quality of their own used cars, we can construct the supply curve in the same way that we drew supply curves for previous experiments. But drawing a demand curve requires more care.

At first glance, it may seem impossible to draw an appropriate demand curve for a lemons market. Demanders cannot observe the quality of a car before they buy it. The amount that a demander is willing to pay for a used car depends on the average quality of the used cars that are for sale. But, as we discovered in the experiment, the average quality of the used cars that owners are willing to sell depends on the price. So how can we draw a demand curve?

In order to determine equilibrium in a lemons market, we need to introduce a new idea, the idea of **self-confirming beliefs**. Self-confirming beliefs have the property that if people hold these beliefs and act on them, the consequences of their actions will be consistent with these beliefs. We illustrate the idea of self-confirming beliefs by considering two examples of lemons markets that are similar to the markets in our experiment.

Example 1

There are 25 potential used-car buyers, each of whom is willing to pay $1200 for a good used car and $400 for a lemon. Potential buyers want to buy at most one car. Before they purchase a used car, buyers are not able to tell whether it is a good used car or a lemon.

The current owners of good used cars have a reservation price of $700 for their cars, and the current owners of lemons have a reservation price of $200. In this market, there are 5 good used cars and 15 lemons. At prices below $200, all current used-car owners would want to keep their cars, so no used cars would be offered for sale. At prices between $200 and $700, the lemon owners would all want to sell their cars, but the good car owners would want to keep their cars. Therefore at prices in this range, 15 used cars would be offered for sale, all of which would be lemons. At prices above $700, all used-car owners would want to sell their used cars, and so all 20 used cars would be offered. We can draw the resulting supply curve for used cars on Figure 12.1.

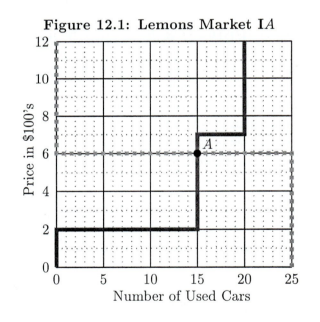

Figure 12.1: Lemons Market IA

Mistaken Optimism in Example 1

Suppose that all of the potential buyers believe that all 20 used cars, the 5 good cars as well as the 15 lemons, will be offered for sale. If this is the case, 1/4 of the used cars for sale will be good and 3/4 will be lemons. Therefore buying a used car is like buying a lottery ticket where you have a probability of 1/4 of winning $1200 (the Buyer Value of a good used car) and a probability of 3/4 of winning $400 (the Buyer Value of a lemon). We will assume that a buyer's willingness to pay for a lottery is the "expected value" of the lottery. The **expected value** of a lottery is equal to a weighted average of the possible amounts of payoff, where the weight placed on each possible payoff is the probability of receiving that payoff. In this example, the expected value of a used car is $\left(\frac{1}{4} \times \$1200\right) + \left(\frac{3}{4} \times \$400\right) = \$600$. This expected value is equal to the *average* value of used cars to buyers, if all used cars reach the market.

Now we can draw the demand curve for used cars, *given that buyers believe that all used cars will come onto the market*. At prices above $600, no demanders would want to buy a used car; at prices below $600, all 25 demanders would want to buy a used car; and at a price of exactly $600, all demanders would be indifferent between buying a used car or not. This means that the demand curve looks like the dashed line in Figure 12.1, with a horizontal segment at a height of $600. With these beliefs, the supply curve intersects the demand curve at the point A, where the price is $600 and the number of used cars supplied is 15. All of the used cars that are supplied will be lemons. (Since owners of good used cars have reservation prices of $700, they will not make their cars available for $600.)

But now we see that the optimistic belief that all 20 used cars would come to the market is *not* self-confirming. When demanders act on this belief, they discover that they are mistaken, since the only cars that came to market are the lemons. This mistaken belief is costly to the buyers since, although they paid $600 for used cars, they are sure to get only lemons, which are worth just $400. Demanders who started trading with the belief that all used cars would come to market would want to revise their views after this experience.

Pessimistic Self-confirming Beliefs in Example 1

Suppose that all demanders believe that the only used cars that will reach the market are lemons. Since a lemon is worth $400 to a buyer, when demanders believe this, the demand curve will look like the dashed line in Figure 12.2. When demanders hold these beliefs, the supply curve intersects the demand curve at the point B, where the price is $400 and the number of used cars supplied is 15. The 15 used cars that are supplied are all lemons, which confirms the pessimistic belief of demanders that all used cars that reach the market are lemons. Therefore, the belief that all used cars on the market are lemons is self-confirming. When demanders act on this belief, the market result is consistent with what they believe.

Figure 12.2: Lemons Market IB

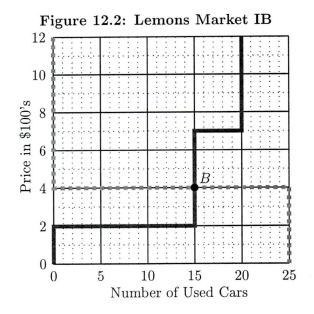

In Example 1, we discovered that the only self-confirming belief for demanders turns out to be that only lemons will reach the market.[6] In Example 2, a higher proportion of the used cars in the market are good, and consequently the optimistic belief that all used cars, including the good ones, will reach the market will be self-confirming.

Example 2

As in Example 1, there are 25 potential used-car buyers, each of whom is willing to pay $1200 for a good used car and $400 for a lemon. Also, as in Example 1, current owners of good used cars have a reservation price of $700 for their cars, and current owners of lemons have a reservation price of $200. Now, however, there are 10 good used cars and 10 lemons.

The supply curve for used cars is drawn on Figure 12.3. Using similar reasoning to that used in Example 1, we see that at prices between $200 and $700, only 10 used cars are supplied, all of which are lemons; while at prices above $700, 20 used cars will be supplied, 10 of which are good and 10 of which are lemons.

---

[6]As an exercise, you may want to show that the belief that the good car owners *and not the lemon owners* will sell their used cars is also not self-confirming.

Figure 12.3: Lemons Market II*A*

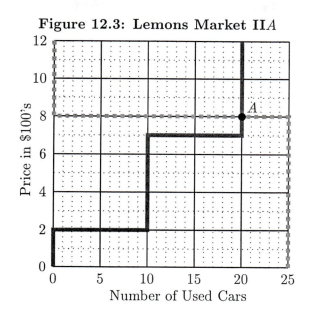

Optimistic, Self-confirming Beliefs in Example 2

As in the previous example, there are 25 used-car buyers, each of whom is willing to pay $1200 for a good used car and $400 for a lemon. Suppose that all buyers believe that all used cars, including the good ones, will be offered for sale. If this is the case, half of the used cars for sale will be good and half will be lemons. In this case, the expected value of a used car is $\left(\frac{1}{2} \times \$1200\right) + \left(\frac{1}{2} \times \$400\right) = \$800$. Therefore, if demanders believe that all used cars will come onto the market, each demander is willing to pay up to $800 for a used car. In this case, the demand curve is given by the dashed line in Figure 12.3, which includes a horizontal line segment at a height of $800.

Given these optimistic beliefs, the competitive equilibrium price is $800. Since $800 is greater than the $700 reservation price of good-car owners, all 20 used-car owners want to sell. Since when demanders act on this belief, their belief is confirmed by the market outcome, we say that the demanders' belief that all used cars will reach the market is self-confirming.

But this is not quite the end of the story. Remarkably, when half of the used cars are good and half are lemons, there are *two different* sets of self-confirming beliefs. The pessimistic belief that all used cars that reach the market are lemons also turns out to be self-confirming.

Pessimistic, Self-confirming Beliefs in Example 2

Suppose that all demanders believe that the only used cars that reach the market are lemons. Since a lemon is worth $400 to a buyer, the demand curve for demanders with this belief would look like the dashed line in Figure 12.4. With these beliefs, the supply curve intersects the demand curve at the point B, where the price is $400 and the number of used cars supplied is 10. At a price of $400, the 10 used cars that are supplied are all lemons, Thus the demanders' pessimistic belief that all used cars that reach the market are lemons is self-confirming.

Figure 12.4: Lemons Market IIB

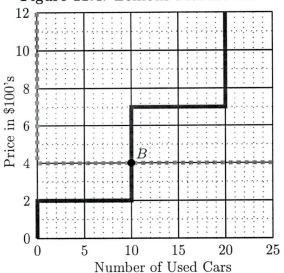

In Example 2, we found that in a used car market, there can be two very different outcomes, each of which is an equilibrium with self-confirming beliefs. In the next exercise, we explore a similar effect in the labor market.

Exercise: Capable Workers and Klutzes[7]

In some industries it is very difficult to monitor the performance of individual workers. In others it is quite easy. Let us consider an industry in which monitoring is difficult. There are two kinds of workers:

---

[7]Answers to this exercise can be found on page 339.

some are "capables" and some are "klutzes." Half of all workers in the labor force are capables and half are klutzes. A capable will produce $1200 of output per week for his employer. A klutz will produce only $400 of output per week. Capables and klutzes look and talk just the same. Capables know they are capable and klutzes know that they are klutzes. But if you ask, everybody will claim to be capable. Both capables and klutzes have the option of taking a job in another industry where performance can be closely monitored. In the other industry, capable workers could earn $700 per week and klutzes could earn only $200 per week.

Exercise 12.1 In the industry where monitoring is difficult, suppose that a firm has the pessimistic belief that the only workers it can hire are klutzes. What is the highest wage that this firm would be willing

to pay per week to hire a worker? $ _____

Exercise 12.2 If the firm offers this wage, what kind of workers will it attract? Explain your answer.

_____

_____

Exercise 12.3 In the industry where monitoring is difficult, suppose that another firm believes that half of its workers will be capables and half will be klutzes. Given this belief, what is the highest wage that

this firm would be willing to pay per week to hire a worker? $ _____

Exercise 12.4 If the firm offers this wage, are its beliefs about the quality of its workers likely to be confirmed? Explain your answer.

_____

_____

_____

Lessons from Lemons

The Private and Social Value of Certification

When there is asymmetric information about product quality, it is often possible, at some cost, to get a credible expert to certify the quality of an item. Typically, the initial owners of high-quality items will be willing to pay to have their quality certified. The "social gain" from certification, however, is not always the same as the private gain. The certification of high-quality items will not only increase the price that sellers of high-quality items receive, but it will also reduce the price that sellers of lower quality items receive. Thus total profits may either increase or decrease with the introduction of costly certification. We illustrate these two possible outcomes by revisiting Examples 1 and 2 from pages 329 and 332.

In Example 1 we found that in the only equilibrium with self-confirming beliefs, the price of used cars was $400 and the only used cars that were offered for sale were lemons. This happens even though buyers would be willing to pay up to $1200 for used cars that they knew to be good and current owners of good used cars would be willing to sell them for $700. The problem is that the current owners of good cars have no way to convince the buyers that their cars are good. Suppose that a new mechanic arrives in town. This mechanic places a high value on his reputation and is known to be scrupulously honest. For a cost of $100, the mechanic will check a car thoroughly and will certify good cars as good and lemons as lemons. A good-car owner who has her car certified could sell it for $1200. Since the inspection costs $100 and her reservation price is $700, she would make a profit of $400 by doing so. With the arrival of the mechanic, there is a new equilibrium. All good-car owners have their cars certified and sell them for $1200. They each make $400 more in profits than before the mechanic arrived. Lemon owners will not spend $100 to get their cars certified as lemons. They continue to sell their cars without certification, for a price of $400, to buyers who know that they are getting lemons. In this example, the introduction of the certification process increased the profits of good-car owners and had no effect on the profits of lemon owners. Total profits of all car owners are increased by the arrival of the mechanic.

Now consider the equilibrium with optimistic self-confirming beliefs that we found in Example 2. There are equal numbers of good cars and lemons in the hands of the original owners. There is an equilibrium in which the price of cars is $800 and all of the used cars are offered for sale. Now suppose that the mechanic moves to this town and offers to certify cars for $100. If the owner of a good car takes it to the mechanic and pays $100, the car will be certified as good and sell for $1200. Since uncertified cars are worth $800, she will increase her profits by $300 if she takes her car to the mechanic. There will be a new equilibrium in which all good car owners take their cars to the mechanic, have them certified, and sell them for $1200. Lemon owners will not have their cars certified. Buyers know that uncertified cars are lemons and will buy them for $400. Lemon owners are unhappy about the new situation, since before the mechanic arrived they were able to sell their cars for $800. What about total profits of lemon owners and good car owners? Before the mechanic arrived, everyone was getting $800 for a used car. After the mechanic arrived, the 10 good car owners each got an extra $400 for their cars, but the 10 lemon owners each got $400 less for their cars. Thus the total revenue received by car owners did not change. But the owners of good cars each had to pay $100 for certification, so the profits of each good-car owner increased by only $300 while the profit of each lemon owner decreased by $400. Total profits of all car owners are lower after the mechanic arrives.

Remarks on Multiple Equilibria

In Example 2 and in the story of "klutzes and capables," we found that two very different sets of beliefs about the nature of the economic environment can each be self-confirming if people act on these beliefs. The possibility of multiple, self-confirming equilibria is fairly common in economic models, and especially in models with asymmetric information.

The possibility of multiple equilibria is frustrating to economists, because it means that we cannot always make sharp predictions with the theory. On the other hand, these examples teach us an important lesson. Once we see that different sets of beliefs can lead to dramatically different outcomes, each of which is self-confirming, we begin to understand how it is that strikingly different economic outcomes, accompanied by different systems of beliefs about economic and social matters, can survive over long periods of time in different parts of the world.

When President Franklin Delano Roosevelt took office in 1933, in the depths of the Great Depression and in the midst of a banking crisis, he gave eloquent expression to this view in his Inaugural Address:

> "So first of all, let me assert my firm belief that the only thing we have to fear is fear itself—nameless, unreasoning, unjustified terror which paralyzes needed effort to convert retreat into advance."

In the more pedestrian language of this chapter, we could paraphrase Roosevelt's remarks as follows: "The economic ills of the Great Depression are the result of the economy falling into an equilibrium of pessimistic, self-confirming beliefs. If people regain confidence in the economy, it can reach a different equilibrium in which optimistic beliefs are self-confirming."

Food for Thought

■ Suppose that a company offers "grade insurance" that works as follows. For each course in which you get a grade below a C, the company pays you $500. Before offering the insurance policy for sale, the company looks over the transcripts of university students and finds that, on average, 10% of all grades given are below a C. Explain why the insurance company would be incorrect in assuming that it would only have to pay claims on about 10% of its policies. Explain how adverse selection and moral hazard would each affect this market.

■ It is common practice for a buyer who is thinking of buying a used car from a stranger to take the car to a mechanic and have it evaluated. If more than one potential buyer considers the car, these buyers don't share the information, but each of them takes it to a mechanic and each pays for a new evaluation. It appears that money could be saved if the *seller* would have the car evaluated and then make this evaluation available to all potential buyers. Why do you think this doesn't happen more often?

■ Many firms pay for insurance coverage for all of their employees. Typically, this coverage is compulsory. That is, the firm will not let you opt out of the coverage. Insurance companies often sell group rate insurance at a lower price to firms that have compulsory coverage than either to individuals or to firms where coverage is voluntary. How do you explain this?

■ Suppose that researchers discover a new medical test such that persons who fail this test are far more likely to have an expensive illness over the course of the next year than those who pass the test. An insurance company discovers that it would cost only half as much to insure those who have passed the test as to insure those who have failed it. This company plans to sell health insurance to persons who have taken and passed the test at half the price that it charges to others. Can you make a case for why a government might choose to make it illegal for insurance companies to do this? Suppose that insurance companies begin to offer insurance at one rate to those who have passed the test and at twice this rate to those who have failed it. If you had the choice of either (a) taking the test and then buying insurance at the rate that applies to you given the result of the test or (b) never taking the test and being insured at the rates that applied before the test was invented, which option would you choose?

Answers to Warm-up Exercises

W 12.1: $1, No, $(6 \times \$500) - (6 \times \$1) = \$2994$; **W 12.2**: $1601, $(6 \times \$500) + (6 \times \$3500) - (12 \times \$1601) = \$4788$; **W 12.3**: $1601; **W 12.4**: $1, $(8 \times \$500) - (8 \times \$1) = \$3992$, $1601, $(4 \times \$3500) + (8 \times \$500) - (12 \times \$1601) = -\$1212$; **W 12.5**: $1.

Answers to Exercise

Ex. 12.1: $400; **Ex. 12.2**: Klutzes only. Capables can earn $700 elsewhere. Klutzes can earn only $200 elsewhere; **Ex. 12.3**: $800; **Ex. 12.4**: At a wage of $800, capables and klutzes will all want to work for the firm. Since half of the workforce is capable, if it picks applicants at random, the firm can expect on average to get about equal numbers of each. So its beliefs will be, at least approximately, confirmed.

Lab Notes for Experiment 12

Recording Sales Information

In Table 12.1, record the number of good cars and lemons that were in the hands of the original owners at the beginning of Sessions 2–4.

Table 12.1: Distribution of Car Types

	Session 2	Session 3	Session 4
Number of Good Car Owners			
Number of Lemon Owners			

In Table 12.2, record the number of good cars and of lemons that were *sold* by their original owners in Sessions 2–4. In the last row, calculate the average value *to buyers* of the used cars that were sold in each session.

Table 12.2: Types of Cars Sold

	Session 2	Session 3	Session 4
Number of Good Cars Sold			
Number of Lemons Sold			
Average Value of All Cars Sold			

Complete Tables 12.3 and 12.4. In the first two columns record each dealer's ID number and the number of cars that he purchased. The Dealer's Total Cost is equal to the total amount that he paid for the cars he purchased. The Dealer's Total Revenue is the number of cars that he purchased times the Average Value of Cars Sold in the Session, which can be found in the last row of Table 12.2. A Dealer's Profits are equal to his Total Revenue minus his Total Cost.

Table 12.3: Purchases and Profits: Session 2

Dealer's ID	Number of Cars Bought by Dealer	Dealer's Total Cost	Dealer's Total Revenue	Dealer's Profits

Table 12.4: Purchases and Profits: Session 3

Dealer's ID	Number of Cars Bought by Dealer	Dealer's Total Cost	Dealer's Total Revenue	Dealer's Profits

In Table 12.5, record the total amount of money that each dealer spent on good cars and on lemons, and the number of good cars and lemons that each dealer bought. Then calculate the total value (to the dealer) of the cars purchased, and subtract each dealer's total expenditure to find Dealer's Profits.

Hint: Recall that dealers value each good used car at $3500 and each lemon at $500.

Table 12.5: Purchases and Profits: Session 4

Dealer's ID	Expenditures		Number of		Value of Dealer's Purchases	Dealer's Profit
	Good Cars	Lem-ons	Good Cars	Lem-ons		

Homework for Experiment 12

Problem 12.1

Part a) In Session 2, the original owners have _____ good used cars and

_____ lemons.

Part b) Owners of lemons are willing to sell their cars at any price above
$0. Owners of good used cars are willing to sell their cars at any price
above $1600. The number of used cars that will be offered for sale at prices

between $0 and $1600 is _____, and at prices above $1600 is _____

Part c) In Figure 12.5, draw the supply curve for used cars in Session 2.

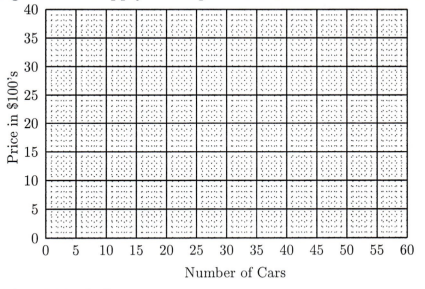

Figure 12.5: Supply and Optimistic Demand: Session 2

Problem 12.2 In Session 2:

Part a) What fraction of the used cars held by original owners are good

and what fraction are lemons?   _____

Part b) What is the average value to dealers of the used cars that are in

the hands of the original owners? $ _____

Hint: Since a good used car is worth $3500 and a lemon is worth $500 to dealers, the average value is the fraction of used cars that are good times $3500 plus the fraction of used cars that are lemons times $500.

Problem 12.3   Suppose that there are several potential buyers for used cars and that there is no limit to the number of cars that any of them can buy. If all buyers believe that used cars on average are worth V, then the demand curve for used cars will include a horizontal line running all the way across the graph at a height of V. Suppose that car buyers have the *optimistic* belief that all of the original owners of used cars will sell their cars.

Part a) With this optimistic belief, what is the value to a dealer of the

average used car that is offered for sale? $ _____

Part b) On Figure 12.5, draw the demand curve for used cars, assuming that all buyers have this optimistic belief.

Part c) Given this optimistic belief, at what price does the number of used

cars supplied equal the number demanded? $ _____

Part d) At this price, which types of used cars are sold?   _____

Part e) Is this outcome consistent with the demanders' belief that all own-

ers of used cars will sell them?   _____

Part f) Is the belief that all used-car owners will sell their used cars a self-

confirming belief?   _____

Problem 12.4   Suppose that in Session 2, car dealers have the *pessimistic* belief that only the lemon owners will sell their cars.

Part a) Then the expected value of a used car to a dealer is the price he

can get for a lemon, which is $ _____

Part b) On Figure 12.6, draw the supply and demand curves that apply if used-car dealers all believe that original owners will sell only lemons.

Part c) Given these pessimistic beliefs, at what price does the number of

used cars supplied equal the number demanded? $ _____

Figure 12.6: Supply and Pessimistic Demand: Session 2

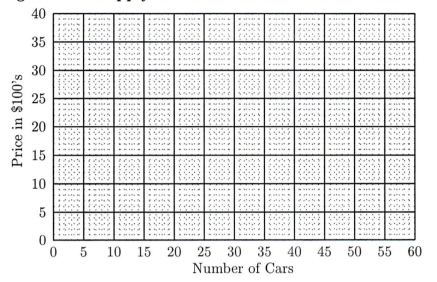

Part d) At this price, which types of used cars are sold?   _____
Part e) Is this consistent with the demanders' belief that only the lemon

owners will sell their cars?   _____
Part f) Is the belief that only the lemon owners will sell their used cars a

self-confirming belief?   _____

Problem 12.5 In the last round of Session 2, the average price at which

cars actually sold was $ _____
Was this price closer to the competitive equilibrium price with optimistic

self-confirming beliefs or pessimistic self-confirming beliefs?   _____
Hint To calculate the average price, sum the dealers' total costs in Table
12.3 and divide by the total number of cars purchased.

Problem 12.6 In Session 3:

Part a) The original owners have _____ good used cars and _____
lemons.
Part b) The number of used cars that will be offered for sale at prices

between $0 and $1600 is _____, and at prices above $1600 is   _____

Part c) In Figure 12.7, draw the supply curve for used cars in Session 3.

Figure 12.7: Supply and Optimistic Demand: Session 3

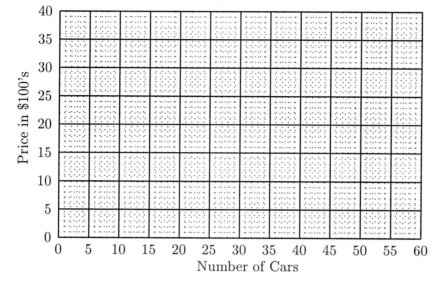

Problem 12.7 In Session 3:
Part a) What fraction of the used cars held by original owners are good

and what fraction are lemons?   _____

Part b) What is the average value to dealers of the used cars that are in

the hands of the original owners? $ _____

Problem 12.8 In Session 3, suppose that car buyers have the *optimistic* belief that all of the original owners of used cars will sell their cars.

Part a) How much is the average used car worth to dealers? $ _____
Part b) On Figure 12.7, draw the demand curve for used cars, assuming that all buyers have this optimistic belief.
Part c) Given these optimistic beliefs, at what price does the number of

used cars supplied equal the number demanded? $ _____

Part d) At this price, which types of used cars are sold?   _____
Part e) Is this outcome consistent with the demanders' belief that all own-

ers of used cars will sell them?   _____

Part f) Is the belief that all used-car owners will sell their cars a self-confirming belief?   ———

Problem 12.9 In Session 3, suppose that car dealers have the *pessimistic* belief that the only cars that suppliers will sell are lemons.

Part a) The expected value of a used car to a dealer is the price he can get for a lemon, which is $ ———

Part b) On Figure 12.8, draw the supply and demand curves that apply if used-car dealers all believe that original owners will only sell lemons.

Part c) Given these beliefs, at what price does the number of used cars supplied equal the number demanded? $ ———

Part d) At this price, which types of used cars are sold?   ———

Part e) Is this consistent with the demanders' belief that only the lemon-owners will sell their cars?   ———

Part f) Is the belief that only lemon-owners will sell their used cars a self-confirming belief?   ———

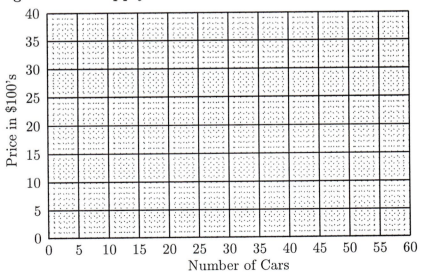

Figure 12.8: Supply and Pessimistic Demand: Session 3

Problem 12.10 In the last round of Session 3, the average price at which

cars actually sold was $ _____
Was this price closer to the competitive prediction for optimistic self-confirming

beliefs, pessimistic self-confirming beliefs, or to neither?   _____

Problem 12.11 In Session 4, every used-car owner has a certificate stating
whether the car is a good used car or a lemon. What is the most a dealer
would be willing to pay for a car from somebody who showed a good car

certificate? $ _____
What is the most a dealer would be willing to pay for a car from somebody

who showed a lemon certificate? $ _____
If you were a dealer, what is the most you would be willing to pay to a seller

who refused to show you a certificate? $ _____

Problem 12.12
Part a) In Figure 12.9, draw the demand and supply curves for used cars
that are certified to be good in Session 4, and in Figure 12.10 draw the
demand and supply curves for used cars that are certified to be lemons.

Figure 12.9: Certified Good Cars: Session 4

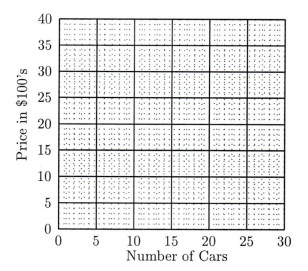

Figure 12.10: Certified Lemons: Session 4

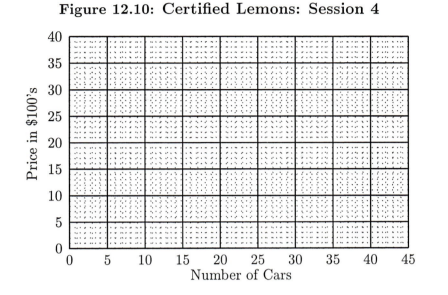

Problem 12.13 In Session 4:
Part a) What is the competitive equilibrium price for used cars that are

certified to be good? $ _____
Part b) What was the average price actually paid in the experimental mar-

ket for used cars that were certified to be good? $ _____
Part c) What is the competitive equilibrium price for used cars that are

certified to be lemons? $ _____
Part d) What was the average price actually paid in the experimental mar-

ket for used cars that were certified to be lemons? $ _____

Problem 12.14 The only difference between Sessions 3 and 4 was that in
Session 4, owners of good used cars could prove to buyers that their cars
were good.
Part a) Complete Table 12.6 to show how total profits of used-car sellers
and buyers were affected by this difference.
Hints: The total amount of profits made by all market participants is equal
to the total value to the buyers of the cars they purchased minus the total of
the reservation prices of the car owners who sold their cars. You can find the
numbers of lemons and good cars sold in Table 12.2. Since good-car owners
have a reservation price of $1600 and lemon owners have a reservation price

of \$0, you can use this information to calculate the Sum of Reservation Prices of Sellers. You can also calculate the total Value to Buyers of Cars Purchased since a good used car is worth \$3500 to a buyer and a lemon is worth \$500 to a buyer.

Table 12.6: Profits in Sessions 3 and 4

	Session 3	Session 4
Number of Lemons Sold		
Number of Good Cars Sold		
Sum of Reservation Prices of Sellers		
Value to Buyers of Cars Purchased		
Total Profits of All Market Participants		

Part b) Allowing good-car owners to prove that they had good cars caused

total profits of all market participants to (increase? decrease?) _____

from Session 3 to Session 4 by   \$_____

Experiment 13

Auctions

The wind is blowing briskly and the clouds gather overhead as you park your car along the road near the hand-lettered sign, **AUCTION TODAY**, and walk to the old farmhouse at the end of the driveway.

You have come to the auction intending to buy some antique furniture for your new house. You shoulder your way through the crowd and examine several items that seem likely to be of interest.

A few minutes later, the auctioneer arrives. He announces: "There is more than one way to skin a cat and there's more than one way to sell a houseful of jun..., er, antiques. Today we are going to use four different kinds of auctions."

Four Kinds of Auctions

An English Auction

The auctioneer walks over to a small chest of drawers and says, "Just to get warmed up, we will sell this little beauty in an ordinary auction, the kind that experts call an **English auction**."

In an English auction, the auctioneer first solicits an opening bid from somebody in the group. Then he asks if anyone has a higher bid. Anyone who wants to bid should call out a new price that is *at least* $1 higher than the previous high bid, or should give the auctioneer a nod when the auctioneer requests a bid. (In order to move things along more quickly, the auctioneer may try to solicit larger jumps in the bidding when it appears that the current bid is likely to be well below the final sales price.) The bidding continues until all bidders but one have dropped out. The highest bidder gets the object being sold for a price equal to the final bid.

In this auction, different people will have different Buyer Values for the chest of drawers. Your Buyer Value is the number consisting of the last two digits of your social security number. For example, if your social security number is 362-58-5283, your Buyer Value is $83. Your profit, if you are the high bidder, is your Buyer Value minus the price that you bid. Everyone else in the group will get zero profits in this session.

In order to allow several people to participate actively in the auction, we will divide the class into a few groups and run separate English auctions in each group. When each group completes its auction, the auctioneer will record the top bid and calculate the winning bidder's profits. The auctioneer will also survey each group to determine the two highest Buyer Values in the group.

A Dutch Auction

Having sold the chest of drawers, the auctioneer moves on to the next item for sale, a family portrait in a gilded frame, and says, "This masterpiece will go to the lucky person who makes the highest bid in a **Dutch auction**."

In a Dutch auction, the auctioneer starts with a price that he knows is higher than anyone's Buyer Value and lowers the price gradually until some buyer signals. The first buyer to signal gets the object at the price the auctioneer called just before the signal was made. In English-speaking countries, often the auctioneer counts downward until someone shouts "Mine!" Accordingly, the Dutch auction scheme is sometimes called "mineing."

Your Buyer Value for the family portrait is found by subtracting the last two digits of your social security number from 100. For example, if your social security number is 362-58-5283, your Buyer Value is $(100-83) = \$17$.

As before, the class will be divided into groups. The auctioneer will sell a family portrait with gilded frame to each group by means of a Dutch Auction. The auctioneer will count backwards from 100 until someone calls "Mine." The first person who calls "Mine" will get the family portrait for the last price counted out by the auctioneer. This bidder's profit will be her Buyer Value minus the price she paid. Everyone else in her group will get zero profits. When each group completes its auction, the auctioneer will record the winning bid and calculate the winning bidder's profits. The auctioneer will then survey the group to determine the two highest Buyer Values in the group.

A Sealed-bid, First-price Auction

The auctioneer next moves to an old bedstead. "This family heirloom can be yours. The owners are willing to let it go to the winner of a **sealed-bid, first-price auction**."

In a sealed-bid, first-price auction, bidders write their bids for the object and their names or identification numbers on slips of paper, and deliver them to the auctioneer. The auctioneer examines the bids and sells the object to the highest bidder at the price that he or she bid. Ties can be settled in various ways. In some auction markets, a coin is tossed. In some markets, the sale is awarded to the bidder standing closest to the auctioneer. We will use the method commonly used in Japan to settle ties, which is to play a game of stone-paper-scissors (*Jan Ken Pon* to the Japanese).

Your Buyer Value for the antique bedstead is given by the fourth-from-last and third-from-last digits of your social security number. For example, if your social security number is 362-58-5283, your Buyer Value will be $52. You will need to write your bid, Buyer Value, and identification number on a sheet of paper and hand the paper to the auctioneer.

The auctioneer will randomly divide the bid sheets into a few separate piles, representing different groups of buyers. From each group, the largest bid will be selected and a bedstead will be sold to the highest bidder at the highest bidder's bid price. For each group, the market manager will record the bids and Buyer Values of the top two bidders, the profits made by the highest bidder, and the two highest Buyer Values in the group.

A Sealed-bid, Second-price Auction

The auctioneer now moves along to admire a hand-painted chamberpot. "I am going to sell this elegant gem by means of a **sealed-bid, second-price auction**."

As in a sealed-bid, first-price auction, bidders write their bids for the object and their names or identification numbers on slips of paper, and deliver them to the auctioneer. The auctioneer opens the bids and sells the object to the highest bidder, but at the *price bid by the second-highest bidder*. If there is a tie for top bid, the winner of a game of stone-paper-scissors between the two tying bidders gets the object at the price at which the top bidders tied.

Your Buyer Value for the chamberpot is given by subtracting the number made up of the fourth-from-last and third-from-last digits of your social security number from 100. For example, if your social security number is

362-58-5283, your Buyer Value will be $(100 − 52) = 48. Once again, you will write your bid, Buyer Value, and identification number on a sheet of paper and hand the paper to the auctioneer. The top bidder in each group will make profits equal to his or her Buyer Value minus the *second-highest* bid in that group. Everyone else earns zero profits.

The auctioneer will randomly divide the bid sheets into a few piles, representing different groups of buyers. From each group, the highest and second-highest bid will be selected, and a chamberpot will be sold to the highest bidder at the *second-highest* bid price. For each group, the auctioneer will record the bids and Buyer Values of the top two bidders, the profits made by the highest bidder, and the two highest Buyer Values in the group.

Warm-up Exercise

To prepare for this experiment, please work through these exercises before coming to class.[1]

W 13.1 An object is sold by English auction, your Buyer Value is $85, and the other participants have Buyer Values of $40, $50, and $60. How much

would you expect to have to pay in order to get the object? $ _____

W 13.2 In a Dutch auction, would it ever be profitable to say "Mine!"

when the price is higher than your Buyer Value? _____

W 13.3 Would it ever be profitable to say "Mine!" when the price is equal

to your Buyer Value? _____

W 13.4 Suppose that in a Dutch auction, the auctioneer has reached a price that is lower than your Buyer Value. What is the advantage of waiting for him to count still lower and what is the risk if you do so?

_____

_____

W 13.5 In a sealed-bid, first-price auction, would it ever be profitable to

submit a bid that is higher than your Buyer Value? _____ Would it ever

be profitable to submit a bid that is equal to your Buyer Value? _____

---

[1]Answers are found on page 367.

The following questions concern bidding in a sealed-bid, second price auction.

In a sealed-bid, second price auction, you get the object only if you are the top bidder. The amount that you pay is equal to the bid made by the second-highest bidder. If you are not the top bidder, your profits for are zero.

W 13.6 Your Buyer Value is $10 and the highest bid made by anyone else is $8. How much profit will you earn if you bid $7? $ _____ If you bid $9?

$ _____ If you bid $10? $ _____ If you bid $11? $ _____ If you bid

$13? $ _____

W 13.7 Your Buyer Value is $10 and the highest bid made by anyone else is $10.50. How much profit will you earn if you bid $7? $ _____ If you bid

$9? $ _____ If you bid $10? $ _____ If you bid $11? $ _____ If you

bid $13? $ _____

What Do You Expect to See?

■ If Buyer Values are the same in both cases, which do you think will raise more money for the seller, an English auction or a sealed-bid, second-price

auction? _____

■ If Buyer Values are the same in both cases, which do you think will raise more money for the seller, a Dutch auction or a sealed-bid, first-price

auction? _____

■ Do you think the best bid for you to make in a sealed-bid, first-price auction should be higher than, lower than, or the same as the price at which you would say "Mine!" in the Dutch auction if nobody has yet done so?

_____

Discussion of Experiment 13

Auctions in the Real World

Although most of us are more accustomed to buying goods either from merchants who post prices on a take-it-or-leave-it basis or in bilateral negotiations with the seller, there are many interesting examples of goods that are sold by auction. The four types of auctions that we conducted during this experiment are only a few of the many auction types found round the world. A fascinating description of the variety of types of auctions used in traditional and modern societies is found in *Auctions and Auctioneering* by Ralph Cassady, Jr. [1]. Among the auction types that are recorded by Cassady are the following:

- The Japanese (Simultaneous Bidding) Auction. Bidders use hand signals to indicate their bids. All bids are made at approximately the same time, though it takes several seconds for all bidders to get their signals up and for the auctioneer to read them. The auctioneer finds the highest signaled bid and sells to the highest bidder at his bid price. These auctions have the advantage of taking place very quickly. Of course bidders have to be good at signaling and the auctioneer must be able to read the signals quickly.

- Handshake Auction. According to Cassady, "Buyers are seated in a semi-circle, each in turn having an opportunity to clasp the hand of the auctioneer and register his bid. Under cover of a piece of cloth, the bidder indicates the amount he is offering by pressing a certain number of the auctioneer's fingers at the moment that he announces a monetary unit, first 'tens', then 'rupees', then 'anas'." The auctioneer remembers the largest bid and announces the winner, but does not publicly announce the price bid by the winner. This method was used in fish markets in Karachi, Pakistan, and is reputed to have been used in China in ancient times. Cassady reports that in Karachi, in 1959, the handshake auction was replaced by the English auction.

- Whispered-Bid Auction. According to Cassady, "The auctioneer announces that the goods are up for sale, and would-be buyers approach him and whisper offers in his ear." Whispered-bid auctions are found in fish markets in Singapore, Manila, Venice, and Chioggia.

- Audible-Bid Rotation Auction. The bid passes in rotation according to a pre-specified order. When it comes to his turn, a bidder may either make a bid that exceeds the previous high bid or say "I pass." The bidding continues around in rotation until all bidders but one have said "I pass."

- Silent Auction. The seller displays the object, along with a slip of paper that states the minimum acceptable bid and the minimum increment by which bidders can increase the bid over the previous highest bid. Would-be buyers can enter their name, address, and a bid. New bids as entered must exceed the highest previous bid by at least the minimum increment. When a specified time deadline is reached, the object is sold to the highest bidder at the high bidder's bid price.

- Candle Auction. There are several variants of this kind of auction, which is essentially an English auction with a time limit. A particularly colorful version is known as a "Cornish Auction." The auctioneer lights a candle and pushes a pin into the candle about an inch below the flame. As long as the pin remained in place, the bidding would proceed as in an English auction, but when the pin fell out, the object would go to the last (and current highest) bidder. This method of auction was common in England in the 17th century and is occasionally still used there. Samuel Pepys brags in his diary of his success in a candle auction.

Real-world Background of Experimental Auctions

The English auction is the most commonly used method for conducting oral auctions in English-speaking countries. Commodities that are frequently sold by English auction include antiques, artworks, cattle, horses, wholesale fruits and vegetables, old books, real estate, and used farm and industrial equipment.

The Dutch auction takes its name from the fact that it is used in the wholesale produce and cut-flower markets in the Netherlands. In some Dutch flower markets, the procedure is automated by a clock mechanism visible to all bidders. An indicator hand moves counterclockwise through a series of descending prices. Any buyer can stop the clock by pressing a button near his seat. Pressing the button indicates that the buyer accepts the lot being sold at the price on which the indicator hand stopped. The Dutch auction is also used in fish markets in England and in Israel, and in tobacco markets in Canada. You may be familiar with a variant of this procedure that is sometimes used to mark down clothing in retail stores.

Sealed-bid, first-price auctions are commonly used in the awarding of construction contracts, which go to the *lowest* bidder. The bidders in this case are of course suppliers, not demanders. First-price, sealed-bid auctions are also sometimes used for selling real estate and art treasures.

Sealed-bid, second-price auctions do not seem to be widely used. This method of auction is used in stamp collectors' auctions and a multiple unit version of this method has been used by the U.S. Treasury to sell long-term bonds.[2]

A very readable account of the economic theory of auctions is found in *Games, Strategies, and Managers* by John McMillan, [8]. McMillan describes many important applications of auctions in the modern economy. Some examples are the sale of oil leases, the sale of insolvent banks and savings-and-loan institutions by the Federal Deposit Insurance Corporation (FDIC) after the savings-and-loan crisis in 1988, bidding for major construction projects, wine auctions, auctions to allocate airport gate space and takeoff and landing slots, auctions to allocate tasks among computers, auctions for defense procurement, and auctions for the television broadcasting rights for the Olympics.

Private Values in Auctions

Information Environments

The objects sold in our experimental antique auction are worth different amounts to different people. Each potential buyer is perfectly aware of his own willingness to pay for the object, but does not know what others are willing to pay. When this is the case, we say that the object is being sold in an information environment of **private values**. In some auctions, however, the object that is being sold actually has the same value to anyone who buys it, but at the time it is sold, potential buyers are not sure about its value, and different people have different estimates of this value. When this is the case, we say that the good is being sold in an information environment of **common values**.[3]

---

[2]This information comes from Vernon Smith's discussion of auctions in *The New Palgrave: A Dictionary of Economics.*

[3]It is common to speak of "private-values auctions" or "common-values auctions." Readers should be aware that these terms refer to the *information environment* in which the auction is conducted and *not* to the *institutional rules* of the auction. In either

English Auctions with Private Values

In an English auction with a private-values information environment, it is never profitable to bid more for an object than your willingness to pay for it. If you bid more than your Buyer Value, and if nobody else outbids you, you will lose money. It would also be a mistake to drop out of the bidding at prices lower than your willingness to pay. In fact, it is quite easy to see that in a private-values information environment, the optimal strategy is to participate in the bidding until the price reaches your Buyer Value and then to drop out of the bidding. That is, whenever the price is below your Buyer Value and you do not currently have the high bid, you should raise the bid.

This simple bit of reasoning allows us to predict the outcome of an English auction with private values. Here we will make a slight simplification to avoid inessential complications: We will assume that if a bidder has a choice between not getting the object and getting the object for a price equal to his Buyer Value, he will choose to bid his Buyer Value. In this case, if everyone bids rationally, the object will always be sold to the bidder with the highest Buyer Value at a price that is either equal to the second-highest Buyer Value or one minimum bidding increment above the second-highest Buyer Value.[4]

Sealed-bid, Second-price Auctions

In a sealed-bid, second-price auction, the object is sold to the highest bidder at a price equal to the second-highest bid. As we will see, in this type of auction, it is optimal for each participant to bid his or her actual Buyer Value. The highest bidder will therefore be the person with the highest Buyer Value and the price that she will pay is the second-highest bid, which is equal to the second-highest Buyer Value.

We claim that in the sealed-bid, second-price auction, the most profitable thing to do is to always bid exactly your Buyer Value. The reason for this is that if you bid an amount B, you are guaranteed that if the object sells for

---

information environment, the institutional rules could specify an English auction, a Dutch auction, or a sealed-bid auction.

[4]If the bidding increment is $1, then in the course of bidding, the exact outcome depends on who holds the bid when it is exactly equal to the second-highest Buyer Value. If the bidder with the highest Buyer Value holds this bid, then he wins the object at that price since the bidder with the second-highest Buyer Value will go no higher. If the person with the second-highest Buyer Value holds this bid, then the bidder with the highest Buyer Value will raise the bid by $1, and get the object for $1 more than the second-highest Buyer Value.

any price below B, you will get it. Moreover, if the good sells for a higher price than B, you will *not* get the good. Given this situation, the best thing for you to do is to make a bid that is equal to your Buyer Value. In the exercise below, we ask you to work through this argument in detail.

Exercise: How to Bid in a Sealed-bid, Second-price Auction[5]

Let V be your Buyer Value, let B be your bid, and let X be the highest bid made by anybody else in the auction. Suppose that you bid more than your Buyer Value, so that $B > V$.

If $B > V$, then ignoring ties[6] there are three possibilities, depending on X. These possibilities are:

- (a) The highest bid made by anybody else is greater than your bid $(X > B > V)$.

- (b) The highest bid made by anybody else is greater than your Buyer Value, but smaller than your bid $(B > X > V)$.

- (c) The highest bid made by anyone else is smaller than your Buyer Value and smaller than your bid $(B > V > X)$.

Exercise 13.1 In Case (a), your profits from bidding B would be

(greater than? smaller than? equal to?) _____
your profits from bidding your Buyer Value V. In Case (b), your profits from bidding B would be (greater than? smaller than? equal

to?) _____ your profits from bidding your Buyer Value V. In Case (c), your profits from bidding B would be (greater

than? smaller than? equal to?) _____ your profits from bidding your Buyer Value V.

Exercise 13.2 Explain why it follows from these answers that it never

pays to bid *more than* your Buyer Value. _____

_____

---

[5]Answers to this exercise are found on page 367.

[6]For the time being we will ignore the possibilities that $X = B$ or $X = V$. With a little more work, this result extends to these cases.

Suppose that you bid less than your Buyer Value, so that $B < V$. When $B < V$, there are again three possibilities, depending on X. These possibilities are:

- (d) the highest bid made by anybody else is smaller than your bid ($X < B < V$).
- (e) the highest bid made by anybody else is greater than your bid but smaller than your Buyer Value ($B < X < V$).
- (f) the highest bid made by anyone else is greater than your Buyer Value ($B < V < X$).

Exercise 13.3 In Case (d), your profits from bidding B would be

(greater than? smaller than? equal to?) _____
your profits from bidding your Buyer Value V. In Case (e), your profits from bidding B would be (greater than? smaller than? equal

to?) _____ your profits from bidding your Buyer Value V. In Case (f), your profits from bidding B would be (greater

than? smaller than? equal to?) _____ your profits from bidding your Buyer Value V.

Exercise 13.4 Explain why it follows from these answers that it never

pays to bid *less than* your Buyer Value.   _____

_____

Exercise 13.5 If in a sealed-bid, second-price auction it never pays to bid more than your Buyer Value and it never pays to bid less than your Buyer Value, how should you bid in this type of auction?

_____

Exercise 13.6 If you know the Buyer Values of all participants in a sealed-bid, second-price auction, and if everybody is bidding rationally, can you predict the high bid? Can you predict the price paid by the

high bidder? _____

Equivalence of Auctions

In a private-value information environment, if all players behave optimally, an *English auction* and a *sealed-bid, second-price auction* have essentially the same outcome. In each case, the object is sold to the person with the highest Buyer Value at a price that is equal to (or nearly equal to) the second-highest Buyer Value.

In a private-value information environment, it also turns out that a *Dutch auction* is equivalent to a *sealed-bid, first-price auction*. In both auctions, the object goes to the highest bidder at the price that he bid, and in both auctions, the bidder must choose a bid without knowing the bids of any other bidders. The price at which a bidder would choose to say "Mine!" in a Dutch auction should be the same as the bid price that he would submit in a sealed-bid, first-price auction.

Each bidder in a sealed-bid, first-price auction or in a Dutch Auction will want to bid some amount that is smaller than his Buyer Value. A bidder who bids more than his Buyer Value would lose money if he gets the object. A bidder who bids exactly his Buyer Value would make zero profit whether or not he gets the object. A bidder who bids less than his Buyer Value will make a profit if his bid happens to be the high bid, and will make zero profit if his bid is not the high bid. Any bidder must decide how much below his Buyer Value his bid should be. The lower his bid, the less likely he is to win the object, but the more profit he makes if he does win the object.[7]

Reserve Prices

Regardless of the type of auction, it is possible (and frequently happens) that a seller will announce a **reserve price** for the article that she is selling. The seller declares that she will only accept bids that are at least as high as her reserve price. If she doesn't get any bids that meet her reserve price, she will keep the article. In many circumstances, a reserve price will enable the seller to get a higher price for the object being sold, but sometimes it may happen that the reserve price is set too high and the seller cannot sell the object at all. In the following exercise, we explore how this works.

Exercise: Icing the Deal[8]

While cleaning her attic, a homeowner finds a commemorative photo of Wayne Gretsky that she decides to sell by means of an English auction. The photo is worthless to the seller, but she hopes that others will want

----

[7]You will find details about optimal strategies for these types of auctions in an optional section that starts on page 368.

[8]Answers are found on page 367.

to buy it. There are only two bidders. The seller doesn't know either of their Buyer Values, but she believes that with probability 1/4 both of them value the photo at $20, with probability 1/2 one of them values it at $20 and the other values it at $100, and with probability 1/4 both value it at $100. The photo is to be sold by means of an English auction. Bidding proceeds in increments of $1.

To make calculations easier, let us assume that in an English auction, the object will be sold for a price exactly equal to the second-highest Buyer Value.

Exercise 13.7 If the seller sells the photo without a reserve price, then:

If both of them value the photo at $20, the photo will sell for _____
If one of them values the photo at $20 and the other values it at $100,

the photo will sell for   _____

If both of them value it at $100, the photo will sell for   _____

Exercise 13.8 If the seller sells the photo without a reserve price,

her expected revenue from the sale is   _____
Hint: The expected revenue is a probability-weighted sum of possible revenues. In this case it is 1/4 times what she will get if both value the photo at $20, plus 1/2 times what she will get if one values it at $20 and the other values it at $100, plus 1/4 times what she will get if both value the photo at $100.

Exercise 13.9 If the seller sets a reserve price, then if at least one of the buyers is willing to pay the reserve price, she will be able to sell it for that price. If neither is willing to pay her reserve price, she will destroy the photo and get nothing for it. If the seller sets a reserve price of $100:
Part c) What is the probability that she will be able to sell the object

for $100?   _____
Part d) What is the probability that she not be able to sell the ob-

ject?   _____

Part e) What is her expected revenue from the sale?   _____
Part f) Does the seller increase her expected revenue by setting a re-

serve price of $100 rather than no reserve price?   _____

Exercise 13.10   Could the seller get a higher expected revenue by setting a reserve price that is:

higher than \$100?   ———————

lower than \$100?   ———————

Common Values in Auctions

We have shown that in a private-value information environment, with either an English or a sealed-bid, second-price auction, the object is sold to the person with the highest Buyer Value at a price that is close to the second-highest Buyer Value. Those who have watched actual English auctions may suspect that outcomes are not always the same as in the more sedate sealed-bid, second-price auction process. Auctioneers work hard to create an atmosphere of excitement and competition among bidders. Sometimes, bidders seem to be "swept away" by the enthusiasm of the moment and bid more than they had initially planned to bid. Sometimes, bidders think that they can "scare off" the competition by increasing the bid suddenly by a large amount. A bidder may make a dramatically larger bid than previous bids in the hopes that other bidders do not have time to reconsider their valuations before the object is sold. These things may happen in real auctions because the information environment is not a private-values environment, but is more like a common-values environment. People are not entirely confident of their own judgment of the value of the object that is for sale. Seeing that someone else is eager to buy may make a bidder raise his own estimate of the object's value.

An important practical example of an auction in a common-values information environment is the auctioning of oil leases. When oil companies bid for leases, each company asks its geologists to estimate the value of the oil deposit that lies beneath the tract that is being offered. The companies may do some preliminary drilling on or near this tract to learn more about the amount of oil that is available. Each company realizes that it is working with partial information, and each realizes that its information may be wrong. Moreover, each company realizes that the other companies have gathered valuable information which they are unlikely to share with competitors. This is a common-values environment because if they knew the actual amount of oil with certainty, the value of the lease would be approximately the same to all companies.

On the basis of its own information, each company can estimate the expected value of the oil deposit. If in a sealed-bid auction, each company were to bid its expected value, then the company that had the highest estimate of the value of the oil deposit would win the contract and would pay its expected value. If several companies each make an estimate and a bid, it is very likely that at least one of them *overestimated* the value of the oil. The company that most badly overestimated the value would "win" the bidding. But this victory would be a hollow one, since winning the bidding with a higher bid than the object is worth means that you will lose money. This effect has acquired the colorful name of the **winner's curse**, since with naive bidding, those who win the auction are likely to be "cursed" by paying more than the object is worth.

Two Common-Values Experiments

Counting Pennies

The following simple experiment illustrates the notion of a common-values information environment. (Your instructor may do this in class with you. It only takes a few minutes.) The instructor brings a jar of pennies to class and passes it around for everyone to inspect. The instructor knows the number of pennies in the jar, but he will not tell you. You are not allowed to open the jar and count the pennies, but you can look at the jar and feel its weight. After you have had a look, you can submit a bid for the object on a piece of paper. After everyone has submitted a bid, the instructor will "sell the jar" to the highest bidder. The highest bidder will receive a payment equal to the total value of the pennies in the jar. After the experiment is over and the buyer counts the pennies that he bought, the jar of pennies will be worth the same amount to every possible buyer. At the time of bidding, however, none of the bidders knows exactly how many pennies are in the jar. All they have are guesses. Everyone is aware that the other bidders are also making guesses about the number of pennies in the jar.

The Unreliable Accountants

Another quick experiment can be used to illustrate the winners' curse. A carload of merchandise is being auctioned off. It has been evaluated by several different accountants. Each accountant has written his evaluation on a slip of paper and dropped it into an envelope. The average of the accountants' estimates is the true market value of the merchandise. Some of the accountants have overestimated the true market value and some have underestimated it. The highest of the overestimates is $50 higher than the true value. The lowest of the underestimates is $50 below the true value. Each of you will be able to draw one slip of paper from the envelope, giving the evaluation of one accountant. You must not show your slip of paper to anyone or look at anyone else's slip of paper. The merchandise will be sold by means of a sealed-bid, first-price auction.

An Escalation Auction

(Your instructor may have conducted this experiment in an earlier class meeting.)

The instructor offers to sell an ordinary dollar bill by means of a rather strange auction. In this auction, the dollar bill will go to the highest bidder, but *both* of the two highest bidders have to pay their bids. In this auction, the bidding probably got well above $1, in which case both bidders lost money (and the "house" made money). Yet there was no time during the auction where one person was doing an obviously stupid thing. For example, suppose you are the second-highest bidder with a bid of $1.10 and the highest bidder has a bid of $1.20. If you quit bidding, you will lose $1.10 and get nothing in return. If you bid $1.30, the other bidder may quit, and if so, you will have to pay $1.30, but since you are now the high bidder, you will get the dollar bill. Thus you will lose only $.30 instead of $1.10.

You might think this auction is bizarre, but it turns out that in the real world, contests that are similar to this auction occur quite frequently. An auction of this type is known as an **escalation auction** or sometimes as an **all-pay auction**.

- Two opposing lobbyists try to win a congressman's favor by bribing him. The congressman will vote on the side of the lobbyist who pays him the most money, but collects bribes from both.

- Two firms are in a race to invent and patent the same product. Each hires a research staff to work on the invention. The firm that finds the invention first gets the patent and all the profits from the invention. But both firms in the patent race have to pay the costs of their research staffs.

- One person sues another over ownership of a piece of property. Each party hires a lawyer. The more one spends on legal fees, the more likely one is to win the lawsuit. Both sides have to pay their legal fees, but only one side gets the piece of property. (An interesting twist on this story is the case where the losing party has to pay the winning side's legal fees as well as its own.)

- Two countries dispute ownership of an area of land that lies between them. Each raises an army to buttress its claim to the land. The country that raises the largest army gets to invade the disputed area, but both countries have to pay the cost of raising the army. (As in the case of the lawsuit, the winning side may sometimes also be able to force the losing side to pay "reparations.")

Answers to Warm-up Exercises

W 13.1: about $60; **W 13.2**: No; **W 13.3**: No; **W 13.4**: If you wait you'll get it cheaper if you get it at all, but you might not get it; **W 13.5**: No, No; **W 13.6**: $0, $2, $2, $2, $2; **W 13.7**: $0, $0, $0, $ − .50, $ − .50.

Answers to Exercises

Ex. 13.1: equal to, smaller than, equal to; **Ex. 13.2**: Bidding more than your BV cannot increase your profit, but may decrease it; **Ex. 13.3**: equal to, smaller than, equal to; **Ex. 13.4**: Bidding less than your BV cannot increase your profit, but may decrease it; **Ex. 13.5**: Bid your Buyer Value; **Ex. 13.6**: It will be the second-highest Buyer Value; **Ex. 13.7**: $20, $20, $100; **Ex. 13.8**: ($20 × (3/4)) + ($100 × (1/4)) = $40; **Ex. 13.9**: 3/4, 1/4, $75, yes; **Ex. 13.10**: No, No.

Optimal Bidding Strategies (Optional)

This section is more advanced than much of the material in this book. If you are terrified by probability and simple algebra, you will want to skip it. But if you like to see striking results emerge from simple mathematics, read on.

In general, working out an optimal strategy for a bidder in a sealed-bid auction is very difficult. But for the case of our in-class experiment, this calculation can be worked out with a bit of elementary mathematics. Recall that your Buyer Value was determined by two digits from your social security number. The Buyer Value of a randomly chosen individual is equally likely to be any integer from 0 to 99. Therefore, the Buyer Values are said to be **uniformly distributed** on the integers from 0 to 99. Knowing the Buyer Value of one class member gives no additional information about the probability distribution of Buyer Values of other class members. When this is the case, we say that Buyer Values are **statistically independent**. We can now prove the following theoretical result.

Proposition 13.1 *(Optimal bidding strategies) In a sealed-bid, first-price auction in an information environment of private values with n bidders, if private values are uniformly distributed over the integers from 0 to 99, then there is an equilibrium in which each individual bids the fraction $\frac{n-1}{n}$ of his or her Buyer Value. The object is sold to the person with the highest Buyer Value at a price equal to the fraction $\frac{n-1}{n}$ of that Buyer Value.*

According to this proposition, the larger the number of bidders, the more each bidder should bid. For example, if only 2 people are bidding, each will bid half of his Buyer Value, while if 10 people are bidding, each will bid 90% of his Buyer Value.

The proof of this proposition is outlined below.

For starters, consider the case where there are only two bidders. Suppose that your Buyer Value is V and you make a bid of B. If you win the bidding, then your profits will be your Buyer Value minus your bid, or $V - B$. If you want to maximize your expected profits, then you will try to maximize the probability that you have the high bid times your winnings, $V - B$.

The probability that you win the object with a bid of B depends on the strategy of the other bidder. Suppose that the other bidder has Buyer Value X and bids the amount αX, where α is some fraction between 0 and 1. Then the probability that you will win the object is the probability that $\alpha X < B$, or equivalently, the probability that $X < \frac{B}{\alpha}$, where X is the other bidder's Buyer Value. Since Buyer Values are uniformly distributed over the integers from 0 to 99, the probability that $X < \frac{B}{\alpha}$ is just $\frac{1}{100}\frac{B}{\alpha}$.[9] The expected profits that you will make from bidding B are therefore

$$\frac{1}{100}\frac{B}{\alpha}(V - B) = \frac{1}{100\alpha}B(V - B).$$

Since $1/100\alpha$ is a positive constant independent of your bid, B, you can maximize your expected profit by choosing B to maximize $B(V - B) = BV - B^2$. If you don't know any calculus at all, you might at this point have to solve the problem by trial and error. But just the tiniest bit of calculus allows you to maximize this expression by setting the derivative of $BV - B^2$ with respect to B equal to zero. When you do this, you find that $V - 2B = 0$, or equivalently, $B = V/2$. This shows that when there are two bidders, your optimal strategy is to bid one-half of your Buyer Value.

If there are 3 bidders, then in order to win the auction, you have to outbid *both* of the other bidders. If each of the others bids the fraction α of his Buyer Value, then the probability that you outbid one specific competitor is $\frac{1}{100}\frac{B}{\alpha}$ and the probability that you outbid both of them is $\left(\frac{1}{100}\frac{B}{\alpha}\right)^2$. More generally, if there are n bidders, each of whom bids the fraction α of his Buyer Value, the probability that you win the auction with a bid of B is $\left(\frac{1}{100}\frac{B}{\alpha}\right)^{n-1}$. With a bit of algebra and a bit of calculus, you can show that when there are n bidders, you will maximize your profits by setting $B = \frac{n-1}{n}V$, that is, by bidding the fraction $\frac{n-1}{n}$ of your Buyer Value.

We have shown that if all other bidders bid a fixed fraction of their Buyer Values, the best thing for you to do is to bid the fraction $\frac{n-1}{n}$ of your Buyer Value. It follows that if everyone bids the fraction $\frac{n-1}{n}$ of their Buyer Values, then everyone will be using an optimal bidding strategy. Since everyone bids the same fraction of their Buyer Values, the winning bidder will be the person with the highest Buyer Value.

---

[9]This is not exactly right, since $\frac{B}{\alpha}$ may not be an integer. For simplicity we work the rest of this example as if Buyer Values were randomly chosen real numbers between 0 and 100. With a little more work, one can show that the answers are also correct when Buyer Values are required to be integers.

Lab Notes for Experiment 13

An English Auction

In Tables 13.1–13.3, record the requested information for each auction group in each Session.

Table 13.1: Outcome of English Auctions

	Group A	Group B	Group C	Group D
Highest Bid				
High Bidder's Buyer Value				
High Bidder's Profits				
Highest Buyer Value in Group				
Second-Highest Buyer Value				

Table 13.2: Outcome of Dutch Auction

	Group A	Group B	Group C	Group D
Winning Bid				
Winning Bidder's Buyer Value				
Winning Bidder's Profits				
Highest Buyer Value in Group				
Second-Highest Buyer Value				

Table 13.3: Outcome of Sealed-bid, First-price Auction

	Group A	Group B	Group C	Group D
Highest Bid				
High Bidder's Buyer Value				
High Bidder's Profits				
Highest Buyer Value in Group				
Second-Highest Buyer Value				

Table 13.4: Outcome of Sealed-bid, Second-price Auction

	Group A	Group B	Group C	Group D
Highest Bid				
Second Highest Bid				
High Bidder's Buyer Value				
High Bidder's Profits				
Highest Buyer Value				
Second-Highest Buyer Value				

NAME _____ SECTION_____

Homework for Experiment 13

For these homework exercises, assume that if a bidder's only choice is to bid his Buyer Value for the object or not get the object at all, he will bid his Buyer Value. Assume also that in an English auction, the object will be sold for a price exactly equal to the second-highest Buyer Value.

Problem 13.1 For the English auction experiment that was conducted in your classroom,

Part a) if everyone had bid rationally, the sales price would have been as follows in:

Group A _____ Group B _____ Group C _____ Group D _____
Hint: Use the information about Buyer Values found in Table 13.1.
Part b) the actual sales prices in the experiment were as follows in:

Group A _____ Group B _____ Group C _____ Group D _____
Part c) in which groups was the chest of drawers sold to the person in the

group with the highest Buyer Value? _____

Problem 13.2 In the English auction in your classroom:

Part a) The seller's total revenue from all groups was _____
Part b) How much would the seller's total revenue have been if she had set a reserve price of :

$75? _____ $80? _____ $90? _____ $95? _____ $99? _____
Hint: If no demanders are willing to pay as much as the reserve price, the seller gets $0. If at least two demanders are willing to pay the reserve price or higher, then the price gets bid up in the same way that it would with no reserve price. If only one demander is willing to pay the reserve price or higher, the object is sold to that demander at the reserve price.

Problem 13.3 In a Dutch auction, if everyone bids wisely, will the object necessarily be sold to the person with the highest Buyer Value? Explain why or why not.

_____

_____

Problem 13.4 In the Dutch auction experiment in your classroom,
Part a) in which groups, if any, was the portrait sold to a bidder who did

not have the highest Buyer Value in that group?   _____
Part b) in which groups, if any, would the seller have gotten a higher price
if the portrait had been sold in an English auction rather than a Dutch
auction? (Assume that everyone would bid rationally in the English

auction.)   _____

Problem 13.5 In a sealed-bid, first-price auction, if everyone bids wisely,
will the object necessarily be sold to the person with the highest Buyer
Value? Explain why or why not.

_____

_____

Problem 13.6   In the sealed-bid, first-price auction experiment in your
classroom,
Part a) in which groups, if any, was the bedstead sold to a bidder who did

not have the highest Buyer Value in that group?   _____
Part b) in which groups, if any, would the seller have gotten a higher price
if the bedstead had been sold in an English auction rather than a sealed-
bid, first-price auction? (Assume rational bidding in the English auction.)

_____

Problem 13.7 In a sealed-bid, _second-price_ auction, if everyone bids rationally, will the object necessarily be sold to the person with the highest
Buyer Value? Explain why or why not.

_____

_____

Problem 13.8 In the sealed-bid, second-price auction in your classroom, **Part a)** in which groups, if any, was the chamberpot sold to a bidder who

did not have the highest Buyer Value in that group? _____
Part b) in which groups, if any, would the seller have gotten a higher price if the chamberpot had been sold in an English auction rather than a sealed-bid, second-price auction? (Assume rational bidding in the English auction.)

_____

Experiment 14

Bargaining

Deals for Wheels

The term is over and the dormitory is almost empty. You, however, plan to stay on campus to take summer courses. Now that the weather is warm, you would like to have a bicycle. You have checked the prices of used bicycles at the local shops and know that a bicycle of the kind you want costs $100. You have heard that a departing senior is about to get rid of her bicycle. You are not personally acquainted with the bike owner and will not see her again after she leaves campus. If she doesn't sell the bike to you, she plans to abandon it. The senior knows that you would be willing to pay $100 for her bicycle, and you know that it is worth nothing to her if she doesn't sell it to you. You are eager to get the bicycle sooner rather than later, since you are planning a big cycling expedition this weekend.

Instructions

In this experiment, half of the people in class will be designated as buyers and half will be designated as sellers.[1]

A Single Ultimatum

In Session 1 each buyer sends a message to a seller, making an offer for the bicycle. The seller can either accept or reject the buyer's offer, but does

---

[1]In some sessions, the instructor may choose to run a second round, in which those who were sellers in the first round play the role of buyers in the second round, and those who were buyers in the first round play the role of sellers in the second round.

not have an opportunity to make a counteroffer. If the buyer offers a price of P, and the seller accepts the offer, the buyer gets profits of $(100 - P)$ and the seller gets profits of P. If the seller rejects the offer, the bike is abandoned and buyer and seller both get profits of $0.

In each round, activity proceeds as follows:

- Each buyer writes his identification number and a bid for the bicycle on a sheet of paper.

- The market manager collects all of the bid sheets and mixes them so that buyers and sellers are not aware of their trading partners' identities.

- The manager distributes one of the bid sheets to each of the sellers. The sellers then decide whether to accept or reject their bids. Each seller writes her identification number and marks "accept" or "reject" on the bid sheet that she received.

- The market manager collects the sheets, and announces the outcomes and the resulting profits for each player (without revealing the identities of trading partners).

A Two-stage Bargaining Process

In Session 2 each buyer again sends an offer to a seller, but this time the seller can either accept the offer or reject it and make a counteroffer. If the seller rejects the buyer's offer and makes a counteroffer, the buyer then must decide whether to accept or reject the counteroffer. If the buyer rejects the counteroffer, then the seller will simply abandon the bicycle.

Making offers and counteroffers takes time. If the buyer's first offer is rejected, then he will not be able to use it for this weekend's expedition, in which case the bicycle will be less valuable to him. If the seller accepts the buyer's first bid, the bicycle will be worth $100 to the buyer. If the seller rejects the buyer's first bid and makes a counteroffer, and if the buyer accepts the counteroffer, then, because of the delay, the bicycle will be worth only $60 to the buyer.

If the seller accepts the buyer's initial bid, then profits of buyer and seller are as in the previous session. If, however, the seller rejects the buyer's initial bid and makes a counteroffer at a price of P, then if the buyer accepts the counteroffer his profits will be $(60 - P)$ and the seller's profits will be P. If the buyer rejects the seller's counteroffer, then the buyer and seller will both get profits of $0.

Bargaining will proceed as follows:

- Each buyer writes his identification number and a bid for the bicycle on a sheet of paper.

- The market manager collects all of the bid sheets and shuffles them.

- The manager distributes one of the bid sheets to each of the sellers. Each seller writes her identification number on this bid sheet and either writes "accept" or writes a counteroffer on the sheet.

- The market manager collects the sheets, records the profits of buyers and sellers for those bids that are accepted, and returns those with counteroffers to the original bidders.

- The original bidders who receive counteroffers mark either "accept" or "reject" and return their sheets to the market manager, who announces the outcomes and the resulting profits.

A Three-stage Bargaining Process

In this session, if the seller rejects the buyer's first offer and makes a counteroffer, the buyer will get a chance to reject the counteroffer and make one more offer before the bargaining is over. As in Session 2, making offers and counteroffers takes time and reduces the value of the bicycle to the buyer. If the buyer's first offer is accepted, the bicycle is worth $100 to him. If his first offer is rejected and the buyer accepts the seller's counteroffer, the bicycle is worth $60 to him. If, instead, the buyer rejects the seller's counteroffer and makes another offer that is accepted by the seller, then the bicycle is worth $36 to the buyer.

Bargaining will proceed as follows:

- Each buyer writes his identification number and a bid for the bicycle on a sheet of paper.

- The market manager collects all of the bids and shuffles them.

- The manager distributes one of the bid sheets to each of the sellers. On her bid sheet, each seller writes her identification number and either writes "accept" or writes her counteroffer.

- The market manager collects the sheets, records the profits of buyers and sellers for the accepted bids, and returns those bids that are sent back with a counteroffer to the original bidders.

- The original bidders either write "accept" or they write a second offer on the paper.

- The market manager collects the sheets, records profits of buyers and sellers for the accepted bids, and returns those on which buyers have made a second offer to the sellers.

- Sellers who have received second offers now write either "accept" or "reject" on the bidding sheets.

- The market manager collects the remaining sheets and calculates profits.

Warm-up Exercise

Please work these exercises before coming to class.[2]

W 14.1 You are a seller in Session 1. The buyer offered you a price of $1, although you know that the bicycle is worth $100 to him. What are your profits if you accept the offer? $ _____ What are your profits if you reject the offer? $ _____ If you are trying to maximize your profits, should you accept or reject this offer? _____

W 14.2 If you are a buyer in Session 1, what would be the advantage to you of offering more than $1 for the bicycle?

_____

W 14.3 In Session 2, the value of the bicycle to the buyer if the seller accepts his initial offer is $ _____. The value of the bicycle to the buyer if the seller rejects his first offer and the buyer accepts the seller's counteroffer is $ _____

W 14.4 You are a seller in Session 2. The buyer offers you $10 for your bicycle. If you refuse the offer and make a counteroffer of $50, what will the buyer's profit be if he accepts the counteroffer?$ _____ What will the

---

[2]Answers to these questions are found on page 391.

buyer's profit be if he rejects the counteroffer? $ _____ If the buyer is a

profit-maximizer, should he accept or reject the counteroffer? _____

W 14.5 You are a seller in Session 2 and you refuse the buyer's first offer. If the buyer is a profit-maximizer, what is the highest price that you could

counteroffer and expect him to accept? $ _____

W 14.6 You are a buyer in Session 2. You and the seller both know that if the seller rejects your first offer and makes a counteroffer, you will accept any counteroffer that is less than $60 and you will reject any counteroffer that is $60 or higher. If you offer the seller $50 for her bicycle, what is the

most profitable thing for her to do? _____ If this is what

she does, how much profit will you make? $ _____ How much profit will

the seller make? $ _____

W 14.7 You are a buyer in Session 2. What is the lowest initial offer that you can make so that it is definitely not in the seller's interest to refuse your

initial offer and make a counteroffer? $ _____

W 14.8 In Session 3, the value of the bicycle to the buyer if the seller

accepts his initial offer is $ _____. The value of the bicycle to the buyer if the seller rejects his first offer and the buyer accepts the seller's counteroffer

is $ _____ . The value of the bicycle to the buyer is $ _____ if the seller rejects his first offer, the buyer rejects the seller's counteroffer, and finally the buyer makes a second offer that the seller accepts.

W 14.9 You are a seller in Session 3. You have refused the buyer's first offer. If you make a counteroffer of $50 and the buyer accepts your counteroffer,

what will his profits be? $ _____ The buyer has the option of rejecting your counteroffer and making one last offer for the bike. If you reject this last offer you will get nothing for your bicycle. If the buyer rejects your counteroffer and offers you $1 for the bicycle and if you accept this offer,

how much will the buyer's profits be? $ _____

Discussion of Experiment 14

Have you heard this fine old joke?

> Two economists have just completed a leisurely restaurant dinner. For dessert, the waiter brings a plate with two pieces of chocolate cake, one of which is much larger than the other. He offers the plate to the first economist, who takes the large piece.
>
> The second economist says irately: "If the waiter had offered me the plate first, I would have taken the smaller piece."
>
> The first replies: "What are you complaining about? You *got* the smaller piece."

Session 1–The Ultimatum Game

The experiment that we ran in Session 1 is known as the "ultimatum game." The buyer in this experiment gets to make a single offer, an "ultimatum," that the seller must either accept or reject. If the seller rejects the ultimatum, buyer and seller both get zero profits from the transaction. If the seller is a profit-maximizer, then the buyer knows that the seller will accept any positive price rather than giving the bike away. Therefore the buyer would maximize his own profits by offering the seller a price of $1. In this case, the buyer makes a profit of $99 from the deal and the seller gets a profit of $1.

Suppose that you are a seller, and a buyer offers you $1 for your bicycle. You know that the bicycle is worth $100 to him, but that if you don't sell it to him you will get nothing for it. Would thoughts like this cross your mind? "That rat! He is trying to cheat me. If he were playing fair, he would 'split the difference' and offer me $50. I'll teach him a lesson. I'll reject his lousy offer!" This strategy would be a good idea if you think that you will deal with this buyer again, and that he would remember that you were tough the last time he tried to exploit you. But we have arranged this experiment so that buyers and sellers will never discover each others' identities. "Teaching the buyer a lesson" does not directly increase your future profits, since you will not encounter him again, and since he does not even know who refused his offer. In fact, if there is a second round of this session, you will be a buyer rather than a seller, so you have nothing to gain from making buyers behave more generously.

Suppose that you are a buyer in Session 1. When you think about what offer to make, do you wonder whether an offer of $1 will offend the seller? There are two things that you should notice about offering her only $1. First, the seller may be annoyed by your small offer and may want to punish you, and second, it doesn't cost her very much to inflict a big punishment on you. It costs the seller just $1 in lost profits to reject your offer, and this rejection will inflict a $99 punishment on you. If you offer her, say, $25, she still may be annoyed that you did not offer an equal split, but now it will cost her $25 to punish you and the punishment inflicts only $75 worth of harm on you. If you offer her $50, she will probably think that you are fair and generous, and will most likely accept your offer. The downside of offering $50 is that your profits are smaller than they would be if you could get her to accept a smaller offer.

Many people who participate in this experiment feel a tension between a desire to maximize profits and an impulse to "play fair" and to punish "wrongdoing" by others. In recent years, economists and other social scientists have been engaged in an intense debate about this matter. When people meet each other in anonymous one-time bargaining encounters, do they learn to behave as profit-maximizers, or is their behavior determined by their notion of fairness? And where do notions of fairness come from? How can we predict what people will regard as "fair" in various environments?

Participants in this debate have devised and run a large number of clever experiments in attempts to distinguish between alternative theories. These experiments have typically been conducted under carefully controlled conditions, using paid volunteer subjects. The experiments have revealed some interesting and perhaps surprising regularities. If you want to read more about the controversy and the resulting experiments, we recommend that you look at the survey article on bargaining experiments by Alvin Roth in the *Handbook of Experimental Economics* [6] and the discussion of bargaining games in *Experimental Economics* by Davis and Holt [3].

In the published results of controlled ultimatum game experiments, the most common proposal made by the buyer is to split the total payoff equally. (In our experiment, this means that the buyer would offer $50 for the bicycle.) In the reported experiments, some of the buyers proposed lower prices, which would give themselves more than half of the profit. When this happened, sellers receiving the offers frequently rejected them, even though they would make more money by accepting.

Researchers have debated whether the buyers in ultimatum games offered equal divisions of profit because they were concerned about fairness, or because they were afraid that an "ungenerous" offer would be rejected by spiteful sellers. In an attempt to answer this question, researchers devised a game called the "dictator game." In the dictator game, one player is allowed to propose a division of a fixed sum of money between himself and another player, and this division will be the outcome whether the second player likes it our not. If we were to run the bicycle market as a dictator game, the buyer could offer the seller any price between $0 and $100, and the seller would have to accept the offer. When the dictator game experiment was run, the most common outcome was for dictators to take about 3/4 of the profits, but about a fifth of all the dictators took the entire profits and another fifth of them divided the profits equally. Later, this experiment was conducted as a "double-blind experiment," in which even the experimenter could not determine how individual dictators behaved. In the double-blind experiment, dictators chose to take the entire profits in 2/3 of the cases, and only a very small percentage of the dictators made offers as generous as an equal split. These results suggest that many of those who propose equal division in the ultimatum game do so because they fear that a small offer will be rejected.

We are left with the question of why, in so many cases, the player receiving the offer is willing to give up profits to punish an ungenerous offer. Perhaps the answer is that subjects do not solve for the action that gives them the highest payoff, but instead base their actions on previous experience. The ultimatum game experiment has been carefully designed so that a seller will always make greater profits by accepting rather than rejecting a low offer. This experiment is quite different from our usual experience in bargaining with others, because in the experiment your actions are anonymous. There is no chance for further bargaining after a first offer is rejected, and there is no way to build a reputation as either a hard bargainer or as a pushover. Many experimental subjects may not fully realize that this is the case. Instead of figuring out the action that is most profitable in this particular environment, they may simply take actions that "feel right" because similar actions have been found to be successful in similar situations in the past. Everyone has had to deal with bullies and exploiters, and most people have learned that it is worthwhile to stand up for their own interests. In normal life, if you habitually accept insulting offers, you are likely to become known as an easy mark and to be exploited in the future. It is valuable to earn a reputation for firmness in bargaining situations. An experimental subject who applies behavior that works well in everyday bargaining situations to the laboratory is therefore quite likely to reject low offers.

A second explanation is that people are willing to pay at least something to punish "injustice," even if they realize that punishing the wrongdoer will not influence their future profits. We suspect that many of us harbor such feelings and that we are likely to impose such punishment if it is relatively cheap to do so. If you are a seller in Session 1 and you are annoyed at a greedy buyer who offers only $1 for your bicycle, it will only cost you $1 to reject the offer and reduce that swine's profits by $99.

Session 2–Two-stage Bargaining

The experiment that we conducted in Session 2 is known as a two-stage, sequential bargaining game. This experiment, like the ultimatum game, has been run many times by experimental economists. As in the ultimatum game, experimental behavior does not fully correspond to the predicted behavior of two selfish, profit-maximizing players, each of whom knows that the other is a selfish, profit-maximizer.

In the two-stage bargaining experiment, there is a fixed sum of money to be divided between Players 1 and 2. Player 1 proposes a division to Player 2. Player 2 can either accept or reject the proposed division. If she accepts the division, the money is divided as proposed by Player 1. If she rejects the division, she can make a counteroffer, but less money is left to be divided than if the first offer had been accepted. If Player 1's offer has been rejected and Player 2 has made a counteroffer, then Player 1 can either accept the counteroffer, in which case the division is as proposed by Player 2, or reject the counteroffer, in which case both players get zero.

In the ultimatum game, in order to determine his own action, Player 1 must first figure out which offers Player 2 would accept and which she would reject, and then choose to make the offer that is best for him, given Player 2's response. The procedure of solving for best strategies by working backward through the course of play from the end of the game to the beginning is known as **backward induction**, and it can be extended to games where each player has several turns in which to take actions. The solution that is found by solving in this way is known as the **subgame perfect** outcome.

Let us apply the method of backward induction to the two-stage bargaining experiment in Session 2. We first think about the last possible move in the game. We get to the last stage of the game if the seller rejects the buyer's initial offer and makes a counteroffer. In this case, the last possible move occurs when the buyer decides to accept or reject the seller's counteroffer. At this stage of the game, the value of the bicycle to the buyer is $60. So a profit-maximizing buyer will accept the counteroffer if it is $59 or smaller, and will otherwise reject it. This means that if the seller rejects the buyer's initial offer, she can expect to get $59 by making a counteroffer. The buyer therefore knows that his initial offer will be rejected if it is smaller than $59, and will be accepted if it is $60 or greater. Knowing this, the buyer will make the lowest offer that the seller will not refuse, which is $60. When he does this, the buyer makes a profit of $40. If he offers less than $59, the seller will refuse the offer and make him a counteroffer that leaves him with only $1 in profit. If he offers more than $60, the seller will accept the offer, but the buyer's profit will be less than $40. So the best the buyer can do is to initially offer $60. The subgame perfect outcome is for the buyer to make an initial offer of $60, and for the seller to accept this initial offer.

Notice that in the subgame perfect outcome, although the buyer's first offer is accepted, the buyer's offer is determined by what *would have* happened if the bargaining had continued. The buyer realizes that if his initial offer is too low, the seller will exercise the option to reject and make a counteroffer. In the bicycle example, we see that for this reason the buyer must offer the seller *more than half* of the total profit from the transaction. This is true because if the seller rejects the buyer's initial offer, she will be able to play an ultimatum game with the buyer, in which she would offer the buyer a profit of only $1 and take the remaining profits of $59 for herself.

In two-stage sequential bargaining experiments that have been conducted under laboratory conditions, researchers have found that most initial offers lie between equal division and the subgame perfect solution. For Session 2 of the bicycle experiment, this would mean that most offers would be greater than $50, but less than $60. Researchers have found that in two-stage sequential bargaining experiments, about fifteen percent of the first offers are rejected, and in more than two-thirds of the cases where the seller rejected the initial offer and made a counteroffer, she ultimately received a lower profit than she would have made if she had accepted the initial offer.

Session 3–Three-stage Bargaining

The experiment in Session 3 is known as a three-stage sequential bargaining game. This experiment is similar to that of Session 2, except that if the buyer's first offer is rejected and the seller makes a counteroffer, the buyer can reject the counteroffer and make a second offer. If bargaining reaches the stage where the buyer makes a second offer, the value of the bicycle to the buyer will have fallen to $36.[3] The seller must then either accept the second offer or there will be no sale.

To find the subgame perfect outcome, we again work backward from the end of the game. If bargaining continues as far as the last round where the buyer makes a second offer, then in the last round, the seller would accept any offer of $1 or more. At this stage the bicycle would only be worth $36 to the buyer, so if the buyer's second offer is $1, the buyer would make a profit of $35 and the seller would make a profit of only $1. Therefore in the previous stage of bargaining, the seller knows that the buyer will accept any counteroffer that leaves him with a profit of more than $35. Since the bicycle will be worth $60 to the buyer at this stage, the seller should offer the bike at a price of $24. At this price the buyer would make a profit of $60 − $24 = $36, and would therefore accept the counteroffer. We have found that the highest price that the seller can guarantee herself by refusing the buyer's first offer and making a counteroffer is $24. Working forward one more stage, when the buyer makes his initial offer he knows that the seller will accept any offer greater than $24. So the subgame perfect outcome for our three-stage sequential bargaining game is that the buyer offers $25 for the bicycle and the seller accepts this offer.

In three-stage sequential bargaining experiments conducted under laboratory conditions, researchers have found that most first offers are between equal division and the subgame perfect outcome, but closer to equal division.

Conclusion

There are at least two interesting lessons to be learned from this experiment. It is instructive to see how you should behave if you are trying to maximize your profits *and* if you are bargaining with a clever and selfish profit-maximizer. It is also important to think about how to behave if you, or some of the individuals you deal with, are motivated not only by profit-maximization, but also by some notion of fairness.

In the ultimatum game and sequential bargaining games (as in many interpersonal relationships), the best way to figure out your own most-profitable action is to "put yourself in the other person's shoes" in order to determine how that person will react to what you do. For example, in the ultimatum game in Session 1, the buyer needs to ask himself, "If I were the seller, which offers would I accept and which would I reject?" In the

---

[3]In each successive round of bargaining, the total profit of buyer and seller is 60% of that in the previous round.

sequential bargaining games, the same kind of reasoning has to be carried out, but with more steps. The way to solve these things is to work backward. That is, to think about what will happen in the last turn of bargaining and then, having decided this, to think about what will happen on the next-to-last turn, third-to-last turn, and so on.

In the subgame perfect outcome for the ultimatum game, the buyer got almost all of the profit, but in the two-stage sequential bargaining game, where the seller gets to make the last offer, the seller gets more than half of the profit. In the three-stage sequential bargaining game, the buyer again gets to make the final offer, but the subgame perfect outcome is less extreme than in the ultimatum game. If you solve for the subgame perfect outcome in the four- and five-stage sequential bargaining games, you will find that as more stages are added, it remains the case that the buyer's initial offer is always accepted, and as the number of stages gets larger, this offer gets ever closer to an equal division of profits. This is a special case of a remarkable result that was discovered by Ariel Rubinstein. A rather informal statement of Rubinstein's theorem is the following:

Proposition 14.1 *Rubinstein's theorem (informal version). If the exchange of offers and counteroffers is fast enough so that the value of the object being sold decreases only slightly between each offer and counteroffer, and if the buyer and seller are approximately equally impatient to finish the bargaining, then the outcome of multistage bargaining, where many rounds of offers and counteroffers are permitted, is that the buyer makes an initial offer that divides buyer's and seller's profits approximately equally and this initial offer is accepted.*

It is likely that most of the bargaining situations that people experience in everyday life are not of the single take-it-or-leave-it type, but part of a process in which there is time for several offers and counteroffers. It is plausible that in experimental bargaining games, people call upon their experiences in more open-ended situations where the best strategy is to offer approximately an even split of profits and to reject offers that do not give you about half of the total gains. This policy, which is usually sensible, is carried over to experimental situations, even though this happens not to be the best way to play in the ultimatum game or the two-stage bargaining game.

Even if ultimatum games and two-stage bargaining games are simpler than the bargaining situations encountered in ordinary life, they are worth studying, because their simplicity makes it possible for us to work out exact answers to how rational, selfish profit-maximizers would play. The lesson that you learn about the need to put yourself into the other players' shoes in order to imagine their responses to your own actions is an important principle that extends to much more complicated and realistic bargaining environments.

Please be warned that the games in this experiment are artificially concocted in such a way that the pursuit of self-interest leads to actions quite contrary to ordinary notions of politeness and fairness. It would be a great mistake to conclude from these examples that treating other people with kindness, respect, and generosity is not worthwhile, or that the correct response to bullies and tyrants is to knuckle under whenever resistance is costly. The world in which we live is one of repeated encounters, usually not anonymous, in which people develop reputations and affections, and in which rational people often return generosity with generosity. But, you may ask, "doesn't the theory suggest that it is in our interest to take what we can get when we are sure that nobody is looking?" The answer, we think, is "no." It is extremely difficult, if not impossible, to deceive others consistently. Arguably, the best way to convince others that you will play cooperatively in long-term relationships is to develop in yourself a genuine concern for their welfare that will prevent you (at least most of the time) from deceiving them, even when it is possible.

Our experiments have focussed on profits as the only motive for behavior. We are well aware that people may care about the well-being of others, and that they may value fairness and standards of decent behavior for their own sake. Moreover, the tools of economic theory continue to be powerful instruments for understanding behavior of people and markets when their motives are more diverse than the simple pursuit of wealth.

Exercise: Bargaining Against a Robot[4]

Suppose that you are bargaining against a robot that is programmed to choose a strategy that maximizes its own profit against rational opponents. If two alternative options are equally profitable for the robot, it will toss a fair coin to decide what to do. You don't care at all how much money the robot makes, but you do want to maximize your own profit.

You are trying to buy an object from the robot that is worth $0 to the robot. It is worth $100 to you if you get it on your first offer. Each offer

---

[4]Answers to these exercises are found on page 391

or counteroffer that is made uses up one period of time. Each period of time that passes before the object is sold causes the value of the object to you to fall to 80% of its value in the previous period. For example, if your first offer is rejected and the robot makes a counteroffer that you accept, the object will be worth $80 to you when you get it. If your first offer is rejected and you reject the robot's counteroffer, and it accepts your second offer, the object will be worth $64, and so on. Neither you nor the robot can make change for a dollar, so you and the robot have to make offers and counteroffers in dollar units. If at the end of the time allotted for offers and counteroffers, no agreement is reached, then you and the robot both get $0.

Exercise 14.1   If you can make only one offer, and the robot must either accept your offer or reject it, how much should you offer the

robot for the object? $ _____

Exercise 14.2   Suppose that the robot is allowed to make a counteroffer to your first offer, and you must either accept or reject the counteroffer. If the robot rejects your first offer, what price will the

robot ask in its counteroffer? $ _____ What price should you offer

the robot when you make your initial offer? $ _____

Exercise 14.3 Suppose that the robot can make a counteroffer to your first offer, and if you reject the counteroffer, you can make a second offer that the robot must accept or reject. If the bargaining process gets to your second offer, the object will be worth only $64 to you when

you get it. What price would you offer on your second offer? $ _____

and what would your profits be? $ _____ If the robot rejects your first offer and you accept the counteroffer, the object will be worth $80 to you. What price will the robot propose in its counteroffer in

order to prevent you from rejecting the counteroffer? $ _____ What

would the robot's profits be if it made that offer? $ _____ What is the lowest price that you can offer initially and be sure that the robot

will accept your initial offer? $ _____

Exercise 14.4   (Optional) If you want to make your head spin, try working out your best initial offer for the four-stage game, where the robot can make a counteroffer to your second offer, and you either accept it or reject it and the game is over. If you still feel fine, then try the five-stage game where you can reject the robot's counteroffer to your second offer, and make a third offer that he must either accept or reject and the game is over. Masochists may want to go further.

Food for Thought

■   Labor negotiations between unions and firms are in many ways similar to the bargaining problem in this experiment. Explain how it is that the value of a labor contract to the workers and to the firm decreases as time passes without an agreement.

■   Sometimes the bargaining problem posed here is said to be a problem of "how to divide a shrinking cake." Can you think of other real world examples of bargaining over the division of a shrinking cake?

Lab Notes for Experiment 14

Recording Bargaining Outcomes

In Table 14.1, record the offers made by each buyer in Session 1. In the column "A/R," write the letter "A" if the offer is accepted and "R" if it is rejected by the buyer. In the next two columns calculate the seller's profit and the buyer's profit.

Table 14.1: Offers and Outcomes: Session 1

Offer	A/R	Buyer's Profit	Seller's Profit	Offer	A/R	Seller's Profit	Buyer's Profit

Record the results of Session 2 in Table 14.2. In the first column, record the buyer's offer. If the seller accepted the offer, write an "A" in the second column. If the seller rejected the offer and made a counteroffer, then write the price that the seller counteroffered in the second column. If the seller made a counteroffer, then write either an "A" or an "R" in the third column, depending on whether the buyer accepted or rejected the counteroffer. In the last two columns, calculate the seller's and the buyer's profits. Remember that if the first offer is rejected and the counteroffer is accepted, the bicycle is worth only $60 to the buyer.

Table 14.2: Offers and Outcomes: Session 2

First Offer	A/C	A/R	Buyer's Profit	Seller's Profit	First Offer	A/C	A/R	Seller's Profit	Buyer's Profit

In Table 14.3 record the outcomes of all the bargains in Session 3 that *were settled without the buyer making a second offer.* (We will record other outcomes in a separate table.) In the first column, record the buyer's offer. If the seller accepted the buyer's initial offer, write an "A" in the second column. If the seller rejected the offer and made a counteroffer, then write the price that the seller counteroffered in the second column. In the last two columns, write the seller's and buyer's profits. Remember that if the first offer is rejected and the counteroffer is accepted, the bicycle is worth only $60 to the buyer.

Table 14.3: Offers and (Easy) Outcomes: Session 3

First Offer	A/C	Buyer's Profit	Seller's Profit	First Offer	A/C	Seller's Profit	Buyer's Profit

In Table 14.4, record the results of bargaining in those instances in Session 3 where the seller rejected the buyer's initial offer and the buyer rejected the seller's counteroffer. In the first column, record the buyer's first offer. In the second column, write the seller's counteroffer. In the third column, write the buyer's second offer. Write an "A" in the fourth column if the seller accepted the second offer or an "R" if the seller rejected the second offer. In the last two columns, record the buyer's and seller's profits.

Table 14.4: Hard Bargaining: Session 3

First Offer	Counter-offer	Second Offer	A/R	Buyer's Profit	Seller's Profit

Homework for Experiment 14

Problem 14.1 Use the information in Table 14.1 to complete Table 14.5. For each range of initial offers, find the number of such offers, the percent of these offers that were rejected, and the average profit for demanders who made initial offers in this range (including those whose offers were rejected and who therefore made $0).

Table 14.5: Initial Offers and Outcomes: Session 1

Initial Offer Range	Number of Such Offers	Percent Rejected	Average Profit of Buyers*
$0-9			
$10-24			
$25-39			
$40-49			
$50			
More than $50			

*Include $0 profits for those whose offers were rejected.

Problem 14.2 In Session 1:

Part a) the total profits of buyers and sellers were $ _____ .

Part b) if no offer had been rejected, total profits of all buyers and sellers

would have been $ _____ .

Part c) Recall that the market efficiency of an outcome is the ratio of the total profits made by buyers and sellers to the maximum possible total

profits. What was the market efficiency of the outcome in Session 1? _____

Problem 14.3   Use the information from Table 14.2 to complete Table 14.6. For each range of initial offers, the third column records the percent of these *initial offers* that were rejected. The fourth column records the average profit ultimately made by buyers whose initial offer was in each range.

Table 14.6: Initial Offer Range and Outcomes: Session 2

Initial Offer Range	Number of Such Offers	Percent Rejected	Average Profit of Buyers
$0-9			
$10-24			
$25-39			
$40-49			
$50			
more than $50			

Problem 14.4   In Session 2:

Part a) what fraction of all initial offers were rejected?   _____
Of those sellers who rejected the buyers' initial offer, what fraction ultimately got a *higher* price for their bicycles than they would have received if

they had accepted the buyer's initial offer?   _____

Problem 14.5   In Session 2:

Part a) the total profits of buyers and sellers were $ _____ .
Part b) if no offer had been rejected, total profits of all buyers and sellers

would have been $ _____ .
Part c) What was the market efficiency of the outcome of

Session 2?   _____

Problem 14.6   Use the information from Tables 14.3 and 14.4 to complete Table 14.7. For each range of initial offers, the third column records the percent of these initial offers that were rejected. The fourth column records the average profit ultimately made by buyers whose initial offer was in each range.

Table 14.7: Initial Offer Range and Outcomes: Session 3

Initial Offer Range	Number of Such Offers	Percent Rejected	Average Profit of Buyers
$0-9			
$10-24			
$25-39			
$40-49			
$50			
More than $50			

Problem 14.7 In Session 3:

Part a) the total profits of buyers and sellers were $ _____ .

Part b) if no offer had been rejected, total profits of all buyers and sellers

would have been $ _____ .

Part c) What was the market efficiency of the outcome of

Session 3?   _____

Appendix A

Further Economic Principles

A.1 Smooth Supply and Demand Curves

In our experiments, the supply and demand curves look like stairways. For a demand curve, the vertical rise in a step of the stairway represents the difference between one Buyer Value and the next. In a large population, the gaps between one demander's Buyer Value and the next higher and lower Buyer Values are likely to be very small, and the demand curve will consist of many small steps. We can therefore "smooth out" the small steps and approximate the demand curve by a smooth curve. Likewise, if the gaps between adjacent Seller Costs are small, we can draw a smooth supply curve.

Algebra of Linear Supply and Demand Curves

Smooth supply and demand curves do not have to be straight lines, but straight lines are nice to use as examples because they are easy to draw and easy to describe algebraically.

  If the supply curve is an upward-sloping line, it can be described by an equation $p = cq + d$, where p is the price and q is the quantity. We see from this equation that the supply curve has slope c and intercepts the vertical axis at d. If the demand curve is a downward-sloping line, then its equation can be written as $p = a - bq$, where the slope is $-b$ and the intercept is a.[1]

  A competitive equilibrium occurs where the supply curve crosses the demand curve. If the supply curve crosses the demand curve at quantity q^*

---

[1]These equations for the supply and demand curves can be rearranged to make q appear as the "dependent variable" and p as the "independent variable." Thus these supply and demand equations are equivalent to $q = \frac{p}{c} - \frac{d}{c}$ and $q = \frac{a}{b} - \frac{p}{b}$.

and price p^*, then it must be that $p^* = cq^* + d$ and $p^* = a - bq^*$. If both of these equations hold, then $cq^* + d = a - bq^*$. We can solve this last equation to find the quantity q^* at which supply equals demand. Once we have found the equilibrium quantity, we can find the equilibrium price by substituting the equilibrium quantity into either the supply or the demand equation.

Exercise: Linear Supply and Demand[2]

Exercise 1.1 Suppose that the supply curve is given by $p = 10 + .1q$ and the demand curve by $p = 45 - .15q$. On Figure A.1, draw the supply and demand curves that correspond to these equations and mark the equilibrium price and quantity.

Figure A.1: Linear Supply and Demand Curves

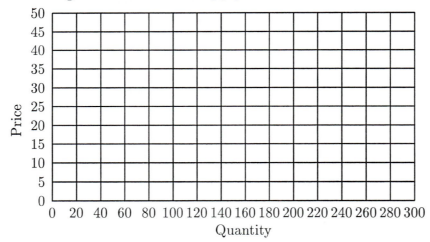

Exercise 1.2 The supply curve meets the demand where $10 + .1q^* = 45 - .15q^*$. Solve this equation to find the competitive equilibrium

quantity, $q^* = \$$ _____. Then substitute the equilibrium quantity into the equation for the *supply* curve to find the equilbrium price,

which is $_____. Would you have found a different price if you had substituted the competitive equilibrium quantity into the equation for

the *demand* curve? _____

---

[2]Answers to this exercise are found on page 419.

A.2 Comparative Statics of Market Changes

Economists have a simple and powerful method for studying the impact of changes in economic variables on prices, quantities, and profits. This method is known as **comparative statics**. To carry out a comparative statics analysis of a change in market fundamentals, follow these steps:

- Draw the supply and demand curves that applied before the market change, and determine the original competitive equilibrium price and quantity.

- Determine whether the change has altered the demand curve, the supply curve, or both.

- Draw the new supply curve and/or the new demand curve.

- Find the new competitive equilibrium price and quantity, and compare them to the initial equilibrium price and quantity.

Comparative statics analysis of shifting supply and demand curves can take us a long way toward understanding the economics of the world around us. We illustrate this with the following example.

A Market for Motel Rooms

Let us consider the economics of the motel business in a resort community. We will visit a town that has 20 small motels, each of which has 10 rental units. Motel-keepers have learned that renting a room for a night costs them $20 more than leaving it unoccupied.[3]

The market supply curve is drawn in Figure A.2. At prices lower than $20 per night, none of the motel-keepers will want to rent out their rooms, so the supply curve has a vertical segment that runs from the origin $(0,0)$ up to the point $(0,20)$. At a price of $20, all 20 suppliers will be just indifferent between renting or not renting their rooms. Therefore the supply curve includes a horizontal line segment where the price is $20 and the quantity runs from 0 to 200 units. At any price above $20, each of the 20 suppliers will want to supply all 10 of their units. No matter how high the price goes, only 200 units are available, so the supply curve must have a vertical

---

[3]This $20 cost includes the cost of cleaning the room, washing the sheets, replacing stolen towels, and any other costs that would be avoided if the room were left empty. It does not include the construction cost of the motel, or any other fixed costs that would have to be paid whether the rooms were rented out or not.

segment that extends upward from the point where the price is $20 and the quantity is 200 units.

Figure A.2 shows the demand curves for the months of August through November. The demand curve labeled August Demand Curve shows demand in a peak summer month. In September, as the days get shorter and cooler, everybody's Buyer Value decreases by $20. In October and November, as the weather worsens, Buyer Values continue to decline. In each month, every demander's Buyer Value is $20 lower than it was in the previous month.

Figure A.2: Supply and Demand: August–November

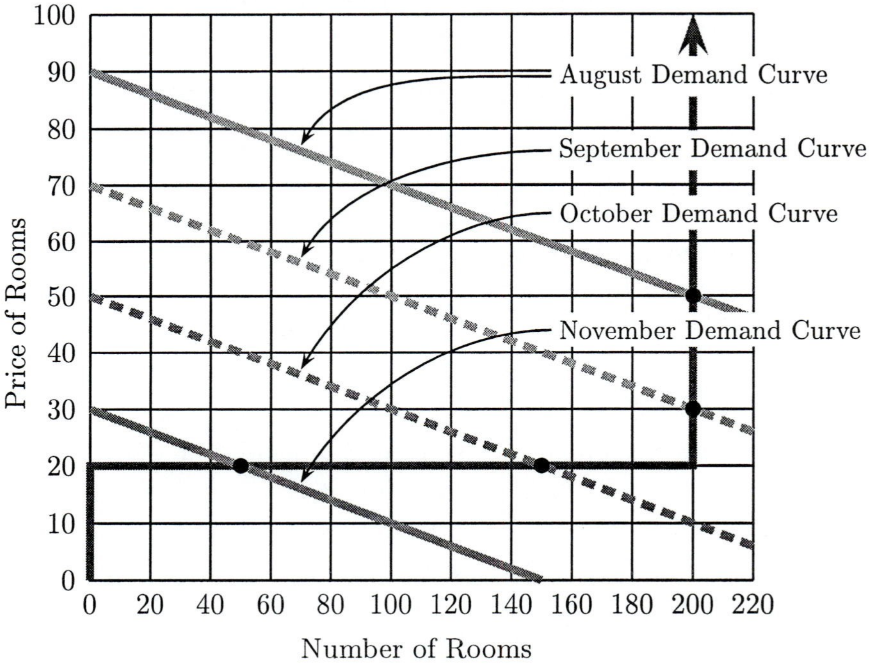

The August demand curve crosses the supply curve at the point where 200 rooms are rented at $50 per night. The September equilibrium price falls to $30 per night and all 200 rooms continue to be occupied. Thus, the $20 downward shift in demand from August to September reduces room prices by $20, and does not change occupancy rates. At the October equilibrium, 150 rooms are rented for $20 per night, and 50 rooms remain empty. In November, the demand curve again shifts downward by $20, but during this month, the *price* does not fall, it remains at $20 per night. The only effect of the demand shift is to reduce the number of rooms rented from 150 to 50.

The contrast between the results of the demand shift from August to

September and the shift from October to November reveals that a downward shift in demand can have strikingly different effects, depending on the shape of the supply curve over the relevant range. The supply curve is vertical between the equilibrium points for the months of August and September, and the downward shift in the demand curve from August to September causes prices to fall by the full amount of the shift, while the number of rooms rented does not change. Between the equilibrium points for October and November, the supply curve is horizontal, and the downward shift in demand does not change the equilibrium price at all, but does reduce the number of rooms rented.

The downward shift in demand from September to October lowers *both the price and quantity* of rooms rented. Figure A.2 shows that in September, all rooms were rented at a price of $30. In October, after the demand curve shifted down by $20, the price fell by $10 and the number of rooms rented fell from 200 to 150.

Exercise: Shifting the Supply Curve[4]

We return to the supply and demand curves that you drew in Figure A.1, where the demand curve is given by $q = 45 - .15q$ and the supply curve by $p = 10 + .1q$. If you drew your curves correctly, they will look like those in Figure A.3. Suppose that Seller Costs increase by $10 per unit for all sellers, so that the equation for the new supply curve is $p = 20 + .1q$.

Exercise 1.3 On Figure A.3, use a dashed line to draw a new supply curve, with equation $p = 20 + .1q$. This new curve is parallel to the

old supply curve, but it is shifted upward by $ _____.

Exercise 1.4 The new dashed supply curve crosses the old demand

curve at a quantity of _____ and a price of $ _____. Check that the answer you find graphically is the same as the answer you find algebraically.

Exercise 1.5 When the supply curve shifted up by $10, the equilib-

rium quantity went (up, down) by _____ and the equilibrium price

went (up, down) by $ _____.

------

[4]Answers to this exercise are found on page 419.

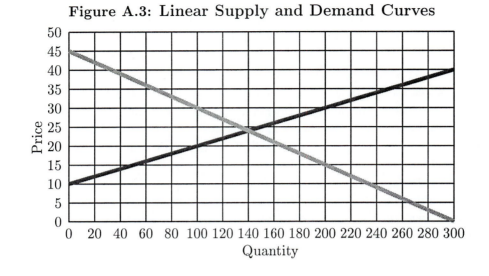

Figure A.3: Linear Supply and Demand Curves

Exercise 1.6 Suppose that the supply curve is given by the equation $p = a + .1q$ and the demand curve by the equation $p = 45 - .15q$. Write formulas for the competitive equilibrium quantity and price as a function of the variable a, where $0 \leq a \leq 45$.

Two Riddles about Supply and Demand

Here are two riddles, each of which seems puzzling at first, but both of which have very satisfactory explanations. The key to solving these riddles, and many others like them, is to ask: "Which curve shifted, supply or demand?"

- The price of a lift ticket at Michigan's Mt. Brighton ski resort is $20 on weekends and holidays, and $16 on ordinary weekdays. Yet the ski slopes are far busier on weekends and holidays than they are during the week. Does this mean that high prices make people demand more lift tickets?

- In June, supermarkets stock oodles of fresh strawberries, and sell them at low prices. In December, strawberries are rare, and extremely expensive. Does this mean that high prices make strawberry growers supply fewer berries?

For a ski resort, the costs of providing rides on the lifts or space on the slopes is about the same on weekdays as it is on weekends. Therefore, the supply curve does not change by much throughout the week. What shifts is the demand curve. Since Saturday is not a work day or a school day, if the price were the same on both days, more people would want to buy tickets on Saturday than on Tuesday. Figure A.4 shows supply and demand curves that are consistent with a ski resort having 400 customers on Saturday when it charges $20, and only 200 customers on Tuesday when it charges $16. As we see in the figure, even though demand curves for any given day slope down, it is possible for both the *quantity* of tickets sold and the *price* of tickets to be lower on Tuesday than on Saturday, because the Tuesday demand curve is different from the Saturday demand curve. The supply curve is the same on both days, and so the price-quantity combinations found on Saturday and on Tuesday both lie on the same supply curve.

Figure A.4: Supply and Demand for Lift Tickets

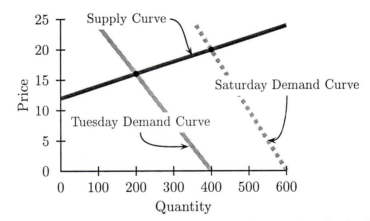

Unlike skiers' desires for lift tickets, consumers' appetites for fresh fruit do not change significantly from day to day, nor from season to season. What does change in the berry market, and dramatically so, is the *supply* of strawberries. In peak season, local farmers can produce strawberries inexpensively. During other seasons, fruit must be grown in indoor hothouses, or imported from distant sources with high spoilage and shipping costs. As a result, the supply curve for strawberries during peak season is different from the supply curve at other times of the year.

Suppose that in June, when strawberries sell for $1 a carton, the number of strawberries sold is 200 boxes a day, and in December, when strawberries sell for $15 a carton, the number sold is only 10 boxes a day. The graph in

Figure A.5 shows a possible explanation for what happens. Higher costs in December result in an upward shift of the supply curve, while the demand curve remains unchanged.

Figure A.5: Supply and Demand for Strawberries

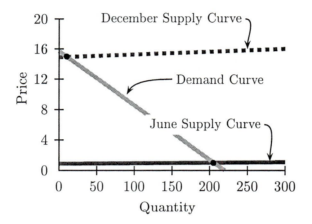

A.3   Elasticity of Demand and Supply

Supply and demand curves show the way that quantities supplied and demanded depend on price. Typically we expect that as the price rises, the quantity demanded will fall and the quantity supplied will increase. For many applications it is crucial to know more. We would like to know by *how much* quantity will change when the price changes.

For example, suppose that we want to measure the *responsiveness* of demand to price. Probably the first thing that you would think of is to look at the *steepness* of the demand curve. If the demand curve is relatively flat, then a change in the price will be associated with a large change in the quantity demanded. If the demand curve is relatively steep, a change in the price will be associated with a small change in the quantity demanded.

In Figure A.6 we have drawn two different demand curves. Suppose that initially the price is 5 and thus the quantity demanded is 200 in both markets. This point is marked as A on each curve. Now consider what happens when the price falls from 5 to 4. The new price-quantity combination is labeled B on each curve. With the relatively flat demand curve on the left,

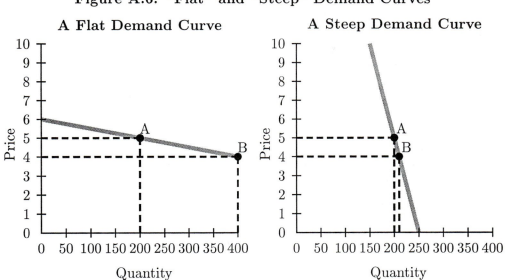

Figure A.6: "Flat" and "Steep" Demand Curves

the quantity increases to 400 units, while with the steeper demand curve on the right, the quantity increases only to 210 units. We see that the flatter is the demand curve, the more responsive is the quantity demanded to price changes.

There is, however, a problem with measuring responsiveness by the slope of the demand curve. The problem is that the slope of the demand curve depends on the units in which we measure price and quantity. For example, if initially the price on the vertical axis is measured in cents and we now measure it in dollars, the resulting demand curve will be only 1/100th as steep as before. Similarly, suppose that initially the quantity is measured in gallons. Since four quarts are equal to one gallon, if we measured quantity in gallons, the demand curve would be four times as steep.

Since it is convenient to measure responsiveness in a way that doesn't depend on the choice of units, economists usually measure the responsiveness of one variable to another by estimating the *percentage* change in the first variable that would be caused by a one percent increase in the amount of the second variable. We define the **price elasticity of demand** to be the percentage change in quantity that results from a one percent increase in the price of that good as one moves along the *demand* curve. Similarly, the **price elasticity of supply** is defined to be the percentage change in quantity resulting from a one percent change in price as one moves along the *supply* curve.

The Price Elasticity of Demand

For any change in price, the elasticity of demand can be calculated by dividing the percentage change in quantity that results as one moves along the demand curve by the percentage change in price. Writing this definition as a formula, we have

$$\text{Price Elasticity of Demand} = \frac{\text{Percent Change in Quantity Demanded}}{\text{Percent Change in Price}}.$$

(A.1)

Consider the examples in Figure A.6. In the demand curve on the left, when the price decreases from \$5 to \$4, the quantity demanded increases from 200 units to 400 units. Thus a 20% decrease in the price results in a 100% increase in quantity. The price elasticity of demand, which is the ratio of the percentage change in quantity to the percentage change in price, is therefore $\frac{100}{-20} = -5$. In the demand curve on the right, when the price decreases by 20% from \$5 to \$4, the quantity increases by only 5%, from 200 to 210. The price elasticity of demand in this case is therefore $\frac{5}{-20} = -\frac{1}{4}$.[5]

Let us introduce a bit of notation so that we can manipulate the definition of price elasticity. Consider two points on the demand curve, where the first point is given by an initial price and quantity, p and q, and the second by a new price and quantity, p' and q'. We define the change in prices to be $\Delta p = p' - p$ and the change in quantities to be $\Delta q = q' - q$. Then the percentage change in prices is equal to $100\frac{\Delta p}{p}$ and the percentage change in quantities is $100\frac{\Delta q}{q}$. Let us define E_d to be the price elasticity of demand. Then we can write the definition of the price elasticity of demand as[6]

$$E_d = \left(100\frac{\Delta q}{q}\right) \div \left(100\frac{\Delta p}{p}\right).$$

(A.2)

By manipulating Equation A.2, we can find another useful way to express price elasticity:

$$E_d = \frac{p}{q}\frac{\Delta q}{\Delta p}.$$

(A.3)

---

[5]Notice that a 20% decrease in price remains a 20% decrease, whether we measure money in cents, dollars, Deutschmarks, or Euros. Likewise, a 100% increase in quantity remains a 100% increase, whether quantity is measured in quarts, gallons, ounces or tons. Since rescaling prices and/or quantities does not change either the numerator or the denominator, we see that the price elasticity is independent of the units of measurement.

[6]In general the elasticity of demand as defined here will depend on both the initial price p and the final price p'. When we want to stress this dependence, we can write E_d as a function, $E_d(p, p')$.

Since prices are recorded on the vertical axis and quantities on the horizontal axis, the slope of the demand curve is given by $\Delta p/\Delta q$. Thus Equation A.3 can be expressed in the following way:

$$E_d = \frac{p}{q}\left(\frac{1}{\text{Slope of the Demand Curve}}\right). \qquad (A.4)$$

If the demand curve is a straight line, then its slope will be constant at all price-quantity combinations. From Equation A.4, we see that if the price is high (and hence the quantity low), p/q will be large and therefore E_d will be a negative number with a large absolute value, and if the price is low (and hence the quantity high), p/q will be small, and therefore E_d will be a negative number close to zero. Thus demand becomes more inelastic as you move downward and to the right along a linear demand curve.

Exercise: Elasticity with a Linear Demand Curve[7]

Suppose that the demand curve is a straight line described by the equation $p = 50 - .25q$.

Exercise 1.7 Draw the Demand Curve on Figure A.7.

Figure A.7: Elasticity on a Linear Demand Curve

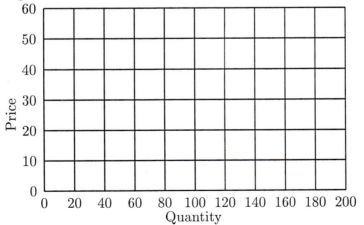

Exercise 1.8 The slope of this demand curve is _____. What is the

---

[7]Answers to these questions are found on page 419.

price elasticity of demand when $p = 20$? _____. What is the price

elasticity when $p = 40$?_____ **Hint:** Use Equation A.4.

Exercise 1.9 At what price is the price elasticity of demand equal to

-1? _____ **Hint:** You know the slope of the demand curve. You can substitute this slope into the right side of Equation A.4 and set the left side equal to -1. This will determine the ratio p/q. You also know that $p = 50 - .25q$, and hence you can solve for p.

Elastic and Inelastic Demand

The demand for a good is defined to be **price elastic** (at the price p) if the price elasticity of demand at p is between $-\infty$ and -1, and to be **price inelastic** if the price elasticity of demand is between -1 and 0. For example, if the elasticity of demand is -2, then demand is elastic, and if the elasticity is $-.25$, demand is inelastic.[8]

There are two extreme cases of linear demand curves. At one extreme the demand curve is vertical, and at the other extreme it is horizontal. If the demand curve is vertical over a range of prices, then the quantity demanded will be the same at all prices in the range. In this case, as can be seen from the definition in Equation A.1, the price elasticity must be zero. Demand is said to be **perfectly inelastic** when the elasticity of demand is zero. At the other extreme, as the demand curve becomes more nearly horizontal, demand becomes more elastic. In the limiting case, as the demand curve approaches a horizontal line, the price elasticity approaches minus infinity. When the demand curve is horizontal, demand is said to be **perfectly elastic** and we define the elasticity of demand to be minus infinity.[9]

The Price Elasticity of Supply

The price elasticity of supply for any good is defined to be the ratio of the percent change in quantity divided by the percent change in price as one

---

[8]Notice that since the price elasticity of demand is a negative number, the more responsive (elastic) quantity is to price, the more negative is the demand elasticity.

[9]Do you like silly mnemonics? A vertical demand curve is perfectly **I**nelastic because it is shaped like the letter I. A horizontal demand curve is perfectly **E**lastic because it is shaped like one of the shelves on the letter E.

moves along the *supply* curve for that good. Typically, the supply curve is upward sloping, so the price elasticity of supply is a positive number. Supply is said to be *price elastic* if the price elasticity of supply is greater than 1, and price inelastic if the price elasticity of supply is between 0 and 1. In the extreme case of a vertical supply curve, the elasticity of supply is zero, and supply is said to be perfectly *inelastic*, and in the extreme case of a horizontal supply curve, the elasticity of supply is infinity, and supply is said to be perfectly *elastic*.

A.4 Demand Elasticity and Total Revenue

In the winter of 1999, an unexpected hard frost in the central valley of California destroyed about half of that region's navel orange crop. The central valley's navel oranges constitute about 70 percent of the United States' eating oranges (as opposed to juicing oranges).

Wasn't this a disaster for California orange growers? Before you start sending your old clothes to Bakersfield, take notice of what happened to orange prices. In a few days after the frost, the wholesale price of oranges rose from $10 to $20 a box. So what happened to the total revenue of orange growers, which is *quantity times price*? Since the central valley produces 70% of the navel oranges in the United States, and since half of its crop was destroyed, the total output of navel oranges in the U.S. decreased by about 35%. The percentage increase in price (100%) was greater than the percentage decrease in quantity (35%), and so total *revenue* of orange growers *increased* because of the frost. Looking just at California's central valley, orange growers in that area lost half of their crop, but the price doubled. So total revenue of California growers remained approximately unchanged. For orange growers in Florida, the frost in California was a bonanza. The frost had no effect on the size of their own harvest and it caused the price to double.[10]

Supply and demand analysis can give us a clear understanding of the effects of the frost in California. The frost had no effect on the amount that consumers are willing to pay to eat an orange and thus the demand curve remained unchanged. The frost shifted the supply curve. Before the frost, the supply curve for oranges to be consumed in 1999 was a nearly vertical

---

[10]Since a killing frost in California does not, on average, harm California growers, and is good for Florida growers, does this mean that *everyone* should be praying for crop damage? Of course not. When crops fail and food prices go up, the losers are consumers of food products, who must pay more per unit and consume less.

curve in which the quantity that was expected to be supplied was roughly the number of healthy oranges on the trees in California and Florida. After the frost, the supply curve shifted to the left, as the number of available oranges decreased by 35%. Figure A.8 illustrates this situation.

Figure A.8: Frozen O's in Fresno

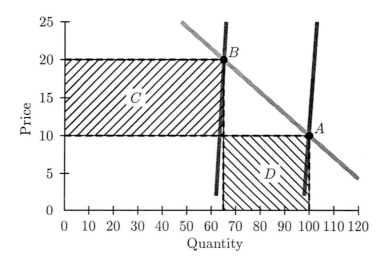

The initial equilibrium, before the frost, is shown at the price-quantity combination A, where 100 units of oranges are sold at a price of \$10. After the frost, the supply curve shifted to the left, and the equilibrium moved to the point B, where 65 units of oranges are sold at a price of \$20. Total revenue at point A is $100 \times \$10 = \$1000$, and total revenue at point B is $65 \times \$20 = \$1300$. On the diagram, the area marked D represents the loss of revenue to the growers because they could sell only 65 rather than 100 units. This loss is more than offset by the gain in revenue that resulted as the price rose from \$10 to \$20. The gain in revenue is represented by the area marked C. As we see from the diagram, the area gained, C, is larger than the area lost, D, and so total revenue is increased.

In general, if the supply curve shifts and the demand curve remains unchanged, the price and quantity move from one point on the original demand curve to another. Since the demand curve is downward sloping, it must be that quantity and price move in opposite directions. Therefore we cannot be sure whether total revenue will move in the same or opposite direction as the quantity sold, unless we know whether the percentage change in price is greater than or smaller than the percentage change in quantity.

Here is where elasticity enters the picture. The price elasticity of demand tells us how responsive the quantity demanded is to a change in price. If we know the elasticity of demand, we will be able to predict the effect of movements along the demand curve on total revenue. For example, if demand is price elastic $(-\infty < E_d < -1)$, then if the price decreases, the quantity will increase more than proportionately, and hence total revenue will rise. If demand is price inelastic $(-1 < E_d < 0)$, then if the price decreases, the quantity will increase less than proportionately, and total revenue will fall. If the price increases instead of decreases, then similar reasoning shows that with elastic demand, total revenue will fall, while with inelastic demand total revenue will increase.

These observations allow us to state a very useful general principle:

Proposition A.1 *With a downward-sloping demand curve, as you move along the demand curve:*
(i) price and total revenue move in the same direction if demand is price inelastic.
(ii) price and total revenue move in opposite directions if demand is price elastic.

Let us apply this proposition to the case of the frozen oranges. The 35% reduction in quantity caused by the frost resulted in a 100% increase in price. This means that the price elasticity of demand for oranges was about $-35/100 = -.35$. Since $-1 < -.35$, we see that the demand for oranges is inelastic. Thus we can say the following: Since the demand for oranges is price inelastic, weather that is bad for the size of the orange crop will increase the total revenue of orange growers and weather that is good for the size of the orange crop will decrease total revenue of orange growers.

If you look at the financial pages of any newspaper, you will frequently find reports on the response of commodity markets to changes in supply conditions. Stories like this give you a good opportunity to test your newly gained knowledge of comparative statics methods and price elasticities. The following exercise is based on one such news story.

Exercise: Corn Flakes[11]

In the summer of 1996, the *New York Times* reported that the U.S. Department of Agriculture increased its prediction of the size of this year's corn crop by 2 % to about 9 billion bushels. On the day of the announcement, the price of corn futures to be delivered in December 1996 fell by 6.25 cents to $2.84 a bushel, the lowest price since August 1995.

Exercise 1.10   Does this price change correspond to a movement along the demand curve or along the supply curve? _____

Exercise 1.11   Assuming that the increased prediction came as a complete surprise to the buyers of corn futures, what is your estimate of the price elasticity of demand for corn?_____

Exercise 1.12   Did the total money value of the expected corn crop rise or fall as a consequence of this news? _____

Exercise 1.13 It is reasonable to guess that this 2% increase was not a complete surprise. Many commodity traders keep track of the weather in the midwest and get crop reports from farmers before the USDA reports come out. A commodities analyst was quoted as saying "People thought the crop was getting bigger but not this big." Suppose that the day before the announcement, traders thought the USDA would report a 1% increase instead of a 2% increase. Then the predicted crop would only be 1% higher than people expected it to be. If that is the case, what would be your estimate of the price elasticity of demand for corn? _____

A.5   Taking It to the Limit (Optional)

If you have studied even a little bit of calculus, you will be pleased to see that dealing with slopes and elasticities becomes easier, rather than harder, when you can take limits and derivatives instead of puttering around with finite differences.

---

[11] Answers to this exercise are found on page 419.

Elasticity and Slope

Let us define a demand function $Q(\cdot)$ so that $q = Q(p)$ is the quantity demanded at price p, and let $dQ(p)/dp$ be the derivative of $Q(\cdot)$ at price p. If we look at Equation A.3, we see that for a price change from p to p', the elasticity of demand can be written as

$$E_d = \frac{p}{q}\left(\frac{Q(p') - Q(p)}{p' - p}\right). \tag{A.5}$$

Recall from calculus that the slope of the graph[12] of the function $Q(\cdot)$ at a point p is equal to

$$\frac{dQ(p)}{dp} = \lim_{p' \to p} \frac{Q(p') - Q(p)}{p' - p}.$$

Now we can define the limiting value of the demand elasticity as p' is taken arbitrarily close to p. From Equations A.3 and A.5, it follows that

$$E_d(p) = \frac{p}{q}\left(\frac{dQ(p)}{dp}\right). \tag{A.6}$$

Constant Elasticity: A Special Case

In general, the elasticity of demand depends on the initial price. Thus the elasticity can vary as one moves along the demand curve, much as the *slope* can vary as one moves along a curve. There is an interesting class of special cases where the elasticity of demand is constant all along the demand curve. Suppose that the demand function takes the form $Q(p) = Kp^c$, where K is a positive constant and c is a *negative* constant. If this is the case, the elasticity of demand is constant and equal to c. We can prove this by the following bit of calculus. First notice that

$$E_d(p) = \frac{p}{q}\left(\frac{dQ(p)}{dp}\right) = \frac{p}{q}cKp^{c-1}. \tag{A.7}$$

Since $q = Q(p) = Kp^c$, it follows that $p/q = p/Kp^c = 1/Kp^{c-1}$. Substituting this last expression into Equation A.7 and simplifying the result, we have $E_d = c$.

---

[12]In accordance with a longstanding tradition in economics, we draw demand curves with quantity on the horizontal axis and price on the vertical axis. If we graphed $Q(p)$ with price on the horizontal axis and quantity on the vertical axis, then $Q'(p) = dQ/dp$ would be the slope of the graph at point p. Given our convention of labeling the axes, the slope of the demand curve at the point (q, p) is $1/Q'(p)$ which is the derivative of the inverse function of $Q(\cdot)$.

Elasticity and Total Revenue

To see whether revenue is an increasing or a decreasing function of price as we move along the demand curve, we define total revenue as $R(p) = pQ(p)$ and take the derivative of $R(p)$. We find that

$$\frac{dR(p)}{dp} = Q(p) + p\frac{dQ(p)}{dp} = Q(p)\left(1 + \frac{p}{Q(p)}\frac{dQ(p)}{dp}\right). \tag{A.8}$$

Recalling the definition of price elasticity in Equation A.3, and noticing that $Q(p) = q$, we see that the expression on the far right of Equation A.8 simplifies so that

$$\frac{dR(p)}{dp} = Q(p)\left(1 + E_d(p)\right). \tag{A.9}$$

Therefore revenue is an increasing or decreasing function of p depending on whether $(1 + E_d(p))$ is positive or negative. Thus revenue is an increasing function of p if $E_d > -1$ (demand is inelastic) and a decreasing function of p if $E_d < -1$ (demand is elastic).

Elasticity, Price, and Marginal Revenue

A downward-sloping demand curve can be described as the graph of a function from prices to quantities, or alternatively, as the graph of a function from quantities to price. Thus we have defined $Q(p)$ to be the quantity that would be demanded at price p. We also could define $P(q)$ to be the highest price at which the quantity q would be demanded.[13] The slope of the demand curve where quantity is q is then equal to $dP(q)/dq$.[14]

In the previous paragraph, we expressed total revenue as a function of *price* by defining $R(p) = pQ(p)$. We can equally well express total revenue as a function of *quantity*, by defining a function $\mathcal{R}(q) = qP(q)$. Let us write $MR(q)$ to denote *marginal revenue* when the quantity is q. Marginal revenue is defined to be the limiting value of the extra revenue received by suppliers per extra unit sold as the units get small. Thus marginal revenue is

---

[13] If $q = Q(p)$, then it must also be true that $p = P(q)$. Two functions that are related in this way are said to be *inverse functions*.

[14] A standard calculus result is that the derivative of a function is just the inverse of the derivative of its inverse function. That is, if $p = P(q)$, then

$$\frac{dP(q)}{dq} = 1 \div \frac{dQ(p)}{dp}.$$

simply the derivative of $\mathcal{R}(q)$ with respect to q, so that $MR(q) = d\mathcal{R}(q)/dq$. Applying the rule for the derivative of a product of two functions, we have

$$MR(q) = \frac{d\mathcal{R}(q)}{dq} = P(q) + q\frac{dP(q)}{dq}. \qquad (A.10)$$

If we set $p = P(q)$, we can rearrange the right side of A.10 to get

$$MR(q) = p\left(1 + \frac{q}{p}\frac{dP(q)}{dq}\right). \qquad (A.11)$$

Since $dP(q)/dq$ is equal to the slope of the demand curve, we see from Equation A.4 that $(q/p)dP(q)/dq$ is equal to $1/E_d(p)$, where $E_d(p)$ is the price elasticity when $p = P(q)$. Therefore we can rearrange Equation A.11 as follows:

$$MR(q) = p\left(1 + \frac{1}{E_d(p)}\right). \qquad (A.12)$$

From Equation A.12 you can see that as demand becomes more elastic, so that E_d is closer to $-\infty$, $1/E_d$ becomes an increasingly small negative number and marginal revenue becomes closer to price. We can also see from this equation that if demand is inelastic ($-1 < E_d < 0$), marginal revenue is negative.

Answers to Exercises

Ex. 1.1: You will find these lines drawn in Figure A.3 on page 406; **Ex. 1.2**: 140, $24, No; **Ex. 1.3**: $10; **Ex. 1.4**: 100, $30; **Ex. 1.5**: Down by 40, up by $6; **Ex. 1.6**: $q = 180 - 4a$, $p = 18 + .6a$; **Ex. 1.8**: $-1/4$, $-2/3$, -4; **Ex. 1.9**: 25; **Ex. 1.10**: Along the demand curve; **Ex. 1.11**: Pct change in quantity is 2%. Pct change in price is $(-6.25 \div 290.25)100 = -2.15\%$. Elasticity is therefore about $2 \div -2.15 = -.93$; **Ex. 1.12**: It rose slightly; **Ex. 1.13**: About $-1/2$.

A.6   Real-world Investigative Projects

This assignment will be made at your instructor's discretion. Even if your instructor does not ask you to turn in an investigative report, we recommend that you think about what you would do if it were assigned.

We hope that by now you are getting into the spirit of hands-on economics–observing and analyzing laboratory markets in action. We would like you to apply a similar approach to the real-world "experiments" that go on in everyday commerce. This assignment will allow you to engage your curiosity and investigative skills in looking at the workings of some of the markets that you will find going on around you. Working in groups of two or three is likely to make the project more fun and will allow you to share tasks. We will suggest a few markets that make for interesting investigations, but feel free to make up a project of your own, particularly if you have a good source of information or a special interest in some particular market.

As part of your research, you may decide to talk to some people directly involved in a particular business enterprise. If so, remember that these people are not *required* to talk to you. Many will enjoy helping you if you are friendly and interested, but keep in mind that they are doing you a favor.

- **The Ski-Resort Industry.**   Below are some suggestions for researching this project:

    - Research the prices that ski resorts charge for lift tickets during the week and on weekends and holidays. You may find this information in ads in ski magazines or in resort brochures from travel agencies and ski shops. For resorts with lodges, also look into the way that room-rental prices vary by month of the year and between weekends and holidays.

    - Compare patterns of pricing for ski resorts, like those in Michigan and Vermont, that attract primarily locals, with patterns of pricing for resorts, like those in Montana and Utah, that attract a clientele from around the world. (Before gathering the data, would you guess that there is more variation between weekend and weekday rates in the East or in the Rockies?) Information about ski resort pricing in Europe would be an interesting addition to your data.

    - Try to find out how the number of lift tickets sold varies between weekdays and weekends and from month to month throughout the year. You may find some of this information in trade magazines, but your best source will probably be ski resort employees or managers.

  – Look for evidence of shifts in supply of and/or demand for lift tickets and lodging at ski resorts from year to year.

  – Give a possible explanation for your observations involving shifts in supply curves or in demand curves.

• **Seasonal Demand for Motel Rooms.** You may want to look for information on this topic in motel registers and travel guides like the AAA travel guide, the Michelin travel guide, and the Mobil travel guide. Choose any region, in the U.S. or abroad, for your study. Below are some questions you might try to answer:

  – For your region, how do room rates vary from season to season?

  – How do occupancy rates vary by season? (To answer this question, you may have to look at a trade journal or interview a sample of motel operators.)

  – Do you find greater seasonal variation in prices and/or in occupancy rates for hotels and motels that are in resort areas or for those in urban areas?

  – Try to explain your observations in terms of supply and demand curves.

• **Markets for Fruits, Vegetables, and Seasonal Fish.** Choose a perishable food product like sweet corn, strawberries, or fresh peaches that has a relatively short local growing season.

  – Find as much specific information as you can about the seasonal variation of prices for the product(s) that you study. You may find this in newspaper ads or by interviewing someone in the grocery trade or the produce business.

  – Look into the variation of the amount of the product sold throughout the year.

  – If you find information about both prices and sales of your product throughout the year, draw a graph with price on the vertical axis and quantity on the horizontal axis. Plot points representing the price-quantity combinations that you observe for different times of the year.

- Whether or not you have enough information to draw a graph relating price and quantity, explain how you would interpret a graph that is drawn in this way. Could the curve that you constructed by plotting price-quantity combinations be a demand curve? Could it be a supply curve?

- **Local Labor Markets for Low-wage Jobs.** Investigate the low-wage job market in the area around your university or in some other city or town where you have good access to information.

  - Compile as large a list as you can of low-wage jobs and the wages being paid for them. Find out what people are earning in the local fast-food restaurants, convenience stores, and coffee shops. You can expand your list as you search. You may find information by looking in help-wanted ads from newspapers, or by asking low-wage workers[15] or employers of low-wage workers.

  - If you find variation among the wages for different low-paying jobs, provide a possible explanation for it. Are the wages higher for nastier or more dangerous jobs?

  - Are some employers having trouble attracting as many workers as they would like? Are these the employers who are paying the lowest wages?

  - Are the wages for the jobs that you investigated greater than the federally mandated minimum wage?

- **Professional Sports.** Try to document changes in recent years in the earnings of professional athletes in various professional sports. Can you find shifts in supply or demand that might account for these changes?

---

[15] Be discreet about how you ask these questions, if you don't want a greasy cheeseburger flipped in your face.

Index